BACK OF THE YARDS

BACK of the YARDS

The Making of a Local Democracy

ROBERT A. SLAYTON

The University of Chicago Press
Chicago and London

Robert A. Slayton is assistant professor of history
at Chapman College.

The University of Chicago Press, Chicago 60637
The University of Chicago Press, Ltd., London
© 1986 by The University of Chicago
All rights reserved. Published 1986
Paperback edition 1988
Printed in the United States of America

97 96 95 94 93 92 91 90 89 88   76543

Library of Congress Cataloging in Publication Data

Slayton, Robert A.
  Back of the yards.

  Includes index.
  1. Community organization—Illinois—Chicago—
Case studies.   2. Packing-house workers—Illinois—
Chicago—Case studies.   3. Neighborhood—Illinois—
Chicago-Case studies.   I. Title.
HN80.C5S56   1986   307'.14'0977311   85-16518
ISBN 0-226-76198-3 (cloth)
ISBN 0-226-76199-1 (paper)

In memory of
Abraham David Slayton
and to
Sylvia Slayton Fuhrman

Contents

Contents

Illustrations

List of Illustrations

Acknowledgments

This is a community study in more ways than one; dozens of individuals, and even more interviewees, took the time and trouble to lend assistance. They did not know the author and had no personal interest in furthering his work, yet they responded. For this I am grateful. They include, among the local clergy and religious: Monsignor Frances Bracken; Sisters Mary Hugoline Czaplinski and Mary Dosithea Ruz of the Guardian Angel Day Care Center and Home for Girls; Sister Mary Fulgenta, principal of the St. John of God School; the Reverend Armand Gress, pastor of St. Michael; the Reverend Marion Habig of St. Augustine; the Reverend Raymond Jasinski, pastor of St. John of God; the Reverend Charles Kouba, pastor of SS. Cyril and Methodius; the Reverend John Kurty, pastor of St. Mary; the Reverend Cyril Lukashonek, pastor of St. Archangel Michael; Sister Mary Maynard, principal of the St. Joseph School; Sister Dolores Munoz, principal of the St. Michael School; the Reverend Vito Mikolaitis of Nativity Blessed Virgin Mary; Sister Mary Anne Omastiak, assistant principal of the St. Michael School; the Reverend Joseph Peplansky, pastor of Immaculate Heart of Mary Vicariate; and the Reverend Edward Slattery, pastor of St. Rose of Lima.

The entire staff of the Back of the Yards Neighborhood Council was most gracious, including Patrick Salmon, Theodora Barskis, Helen Dinucce, Herlinda Gamboa, Wanda Senn, La Verne Tawech, and Ruth Zoch. Others who helped were William Gleeson, Valerie Skuta, and the staff of the *Back of the Yards Journal;* Henry Winkler, president of the Back of the Yards Senior Citizens Club;

Wendell and Edward Tylka of Tylka Brothers Press; Enid Sigunick of Tilden High School; Phillip O'Connor; and Daniel Houlihan.

Over one hundred interviewees participated in this study. We talked in living rooms and kitchens, business offices, and churches. All permitted me to enter part of their life, all are now a part of mine. To each one, I thank you. I also wish to express my appreciation to those who searched for and lent family photographs for use in this book.

Certain individuals deserve special mention. Joseph and Helen Meegan shared their time, their love, and their stories. All these gifts are cherished; the emotion is reciprocated. Margaret Starr Crema, head librarian of the Back of the Yards Branch of the Chicago Public Library, was a friend, counselor, and guide. Sister Eleanor Soroka proved a gem in an unusual setting. Sanford Horwitt provided valuable information, advice, and camaraderie. Edward Burke of the Fourteenth Ward provided access to valuable documents.

Others helped with the manuscript in many different ways. At Northwestern University, Josef Barton was part of this work before it started. His training, guidance, advice, and suggestions have shaped this book in more ways than I could ever acknowledge. Over the years our relationship has changed, from teacher to mentor to friend. All of these roles he handled beautifully, although I must admit that I enjoy the last the best, as I suspect he does as well. Robert Wiebe also taught me, not only about history, but about compassion and humanity and teaching. Albert Hunter assisted in many ways, and Henry Binford has been both counselor and friend. Daniel Lewis first sent me to Back of the Yards, an assignment for which I remain grateful. In addition, Olivier Zunz offered encouragement and discerning comments, and Perry Duis was a helpful reader. Leland Senn was a model typist whose meticulous eye and unending patience eased the production of this manuscript.

Rita LaVerde Slayton, my wife, has been part of this book long before its inception. At every stage of my life and my career, she has offered sage advice, unyielding faith, and frequent spells of tolerance. For many reasons, including these, I love her.

My debt to my parents is acknowledged in the dedication and revealed on every page of this manuscript.

Robert A. Slayton

BACK OF THE YARDS

We the People Will Work Out Our Own Destiny
Official motto of the Back of the Yards Neighborhood Council

Introduction:
The Making of a Community

Aerial View of the Stockyards, 1904
Chicago Historical Society ICHi-04090

Forty-one years after its founding, the community to the west of the Chicago stockyards—known as Back of the Yards—exploded onto the national scene in sensational fashion. The occasion was the publication in February 1906 of Upton Sinclair's novel *The Jungle*, a graphic description of an immigrant's exploitation by the Chicago meat-packing industry that quickly became a best seller. It stayed at the top of the lists in the United States and Great Britain for six months and publishers translated it into seventeen languages. Jack London proclaimed it the *Uncle Tom's Cabin* of wage slavery and Eugene Debs declared, "It marks an epoch."[1]

The purpose of the book was not to tell about a Chicago immigrant community but to proselytize for a political belief. The young writer was a socialist, author of several political novels, and a contributor to left-wing magazines who had written a series of articles for the *Appeal to Reason*, a Kansas socialist paper with a circulation of several hundred thousand. Among the pieces was a front-page challenge to the packinghouse workers after their failed strike in 1904, an article whose headline read:

YOU HAVE LOST THE STRIKE!
And Now What Are You Going To Do About It?[2]

That same year, 1904, Sinclair's *Manassas*, a novel describing the evils of chattel slavery, appeared, and Fred Warren, the *Appeal's* editor, asked him to write a similar exposé of wage slavery, offering a $500 advance in exchange for serial rights.[3]

The young author started immediately. In October 1904, he journeyed to Chicago and the stockyards district, where he spent seven weeks. Sinclair's vivid novel about life Back of the Yards stemmed from his skill as a social investigator. He interviewed laborers, doctors, social workers, and saloonkeepers. Other socialists helped the author to find his way around. He took the official tours of the packing plants, then returned poorly dressed, finding that "by the simple device of carrying a dinner pail I could go anywhere." Wandering alone one Sunday afternoon, he saw a wedding party go into the hall behind a saloon. Entering quietly, he stood against the wall and watched the goings-on. After dinner he returned, then "stayed until late at night . . . just watching . . . and engraving the details on my mind." From this came the wedding scene he used to introduce the book, a superb piece of narrative that one biographer called "the best Sinclair ever wrote."[4]

Returning home to Princeton, New Jersey, Sinclair wrote for

three months, composing the major part of the manuscript. But he stuck at the ending, wishing to conclude with a call to socialism but not knowing how to incorporate it into the narrative. He turned to other pursuits, and late in 1905 ended his novel with a clumsy description of the redemptive powers of socialism. Critics decried this sloppy finish, including Sinclair himself, who wrote in his *Autobiography*, "I ran wild at the end."[5]

His major audience, however, was not socialists but the urban middle class. Since the 1880s, this group had been subjected to new forms of mass corporate distribution and advertising, and it had responded with increased consumption of name-brand items. Now they faced the possibility that their trust was misplaced, that company labels meant unsanitary conditions and noxious ingredients rather than quality control and a better product. Particularly appalling were the book's descriptions of the terrible undisclosed additions to their dinner menus, such as rat dung in the sausage and human remains in the lard. These disclosures were enough to create gastric discomfort and moral outrage in the group that formed the primary market for such merchandise. The same readers, familiar with the revelations of muckrakers and prepared to accept as fact the corruption of big business, also responded to Sinclair's critique of the industry's oligopolist practices.

The hubbub created by *The Jungle* resulted in the passage of the Pure Food and Drug Act and the Meat Inspection Act that very year, 1906. Readers ignored Sinclair's appeal to socialism however, a fact commemorated by the author's much-quoted lament, "I aimed at the public's heart and by accident I hit it in the stomach." They also overlooked his description of an immigrant community in one of the emerging working-class neighborhoods of Chicago. No crusade developed to improve these sections and the standard of living of their residents, even though their plight formed the bulk of the narrative. Sinclair's rich and vivid depiction of this environment, like his awkward call to socialism, remained unnoticed.[6]

One group, however, did understand what an important neighborhood Back of the Yards was, and returned often. Social workers remained fascinated with the neighborhood for many years. In 1911, Sophonisba Breckenridge and Grace Abbott studied the community's housing, and their work was followed up by Alice Miller in 1923 and by Edith Abbott in 1936. Clifford Shaw's 1930 work *The Jack-Roller* was an examination of juvenile delinquency in the area. The presence of the University of Chicago Settlement House as a sponsor and guide to graduate students guaranteed a long series of theses and dissertations on the neighborhood west of the Union Stock-Yards.[7]

The impetus for these investigations came from the Sociology Department of the University of Chicago. Even before the turn of the century, these academics had focused on the urban environment as the proper subject for examination and analysis. Part of this interest stemmed from the pervasive social changes taking place in the United States at that time. The country was being transformed into an urban, industrialized, immigrant nation. All manner of citizens, from Progressive Party politicians to middle-class housewives, were aware of the problems the transition was creating, and thought about solutions. Many of the resulting conclusions were racist, xenophobic, and concerned with mass expulsions. The University of Chicago sociologists, for their part, tried to use their training to shed light on the changes and to cut through a rhetoric of ignorance and fear.

The second major influence on the academics was the metropolis in which they lived. Chicago was the great heartland city, home to the United States' heaviest industries and a seemingly endless series of social dilemmas. Never before had people placed a gold coast next to a slum, but in Chicago this was standard procedure. No one could figure out why such novel situations occurred, so the sociologists turned the lakefront city into their own private laboratory for investigating the ills of their society.

The sociologists perceived a world constantly in danger of dissolving into chaos. They sought to understand the bonds that tied people together so that they could save the city and themselves; in doing so, they laid the basis for all future investigations of community.

The first success of the sociologists, and their most complete, was a victory for tolerance and objectivity. At the turn of the century, the standard explanation for urban disorder was a racist type of eugenics, a theory that stressed the inferior biological quality of the recent immigrants. Madison Grant, author of *The Passing of the Great Race*, and other promoters of this concept argued that the newcomers came from inferior racial backgrounds. It was only natural, therefore, for their presence to lead to crime, poverty, and disease.[8]

The sociologists' response was the theory of human ecology. They argued that immigrants, like other people, and like plants and animals, responded to their environment. It was the conditions imposed on them, and not their genetic structure, that guided people's behavior, both individually and in groups. To prevent revolution and to solve the problem of urban disorganization, therefore, the United States did not need immigration quotas or compulsory purification of its population, but instead campaigns to improve the conditions in which people lived. Using this progressive doctrine, now an almost unchallenged formula for social recovery, investigators compiled statistics and worked to improve housing, sanitation, and diet.

The sociologists, however, did not let this theory remain static. Instead, they expanded it, often with negative results for the industrial immigrant sections they continually studied. As time passed, the scholars found within the city a segregation into districts, a "systematic sorting of populations and functions." This occurred because of a combination of forces, such as competition for valuable land and the flow of population. These forces worked, over time, to differentiate the sections of the city on the basis of the functions they served and who lived there. Direct, conscious human intervention was not involved in this sorting out. And once the zones were formed, they grew, attracting the people and jobs that fit best into their makeup. Robert Park called these "natural areas," since they resulted from seemingly haphazard, impersonal forces rather than from deliberate human actions.[9]

The most interesting of these areas were the slums in which the immigrants lived, and here the sociologists' prejudices overcame their training. In order to analyze the urban, immigrant, residential district, scholars compared it to a single, positive model, the small town or village community of their youth. This was the ideal, and in time idealized, situation—a community that bound its residents to each other by links of mutual interest, common heritage, and shared institutions.

When the scholars, themselves the product of these idealized and distant homes, examined the urban communities, they were blind to similar bonds of community among immigrant workers. Instead, they found a terrible disorganization where, according to Robert Park, " the intimate relationships of the primary group are weakened and the moral order which rested upon them is gradually dissolved." Harvey Zorbaugh, in *The Gold Coast and the Slum*, echoed this sentiment, claiming that the local areas of the city were "vastly different from the town or village community." Within them, there was "no common body of experience and tradition"; therefore, "Local life breaks down."[10]

Men like Park, Zorbaugh, and Ernest Burgess also viewed the

urban immigrant slum as a temporary institution. Park argued that communities, both human and botanical, had fixed life spans. They grew, flourished, and eventually declined. Armed with this ecological knowledge, the Chicago researchers viewed slum areas as temporary domiciles where immigrants learned to cope with U.S. society and out of which they moved, as quickly as possible, into middle-class, stable communities. The original neighborhood was left either in a state of decay or subject to the same abuses by a new wave of disorganized immigrants.[11]

The residents' transience caused other problems. Scholars found the greatest problem of these urban deserts to be the lack of those bonds that kept people together and an abundance of those that kept them apart. There was no common history, no physical symbols to mark the people's identity. Zorbaugh anguished over the lack of the churches, graveyards, homes, and factories around which formed the traditions and rituals that "are the core of . . . self-consciousness and solidarity." In the city, he found that "local groups . . . have no such symbols" and therefore no such heritage. To make matters worse, there were no institutions around which sentiments could form. The most important of these, religion, had disappeared because, "the church has ceased to bear any vital relationship to local life."[12]

The view of the city as a heartless, homeless place, early advanced by Chicago social theorists, has recently been labeled by Barry Wellman and Barry Leighton the concept of "community lost." It focused on the impact of large-scale social changes on community structures and contrasted the result with the perfect town of an idealized past. Urban residential areas were hopeless, transient sections with few bonds to hold families, a maelstrom of uninhibited activity, places to be experienced and left as soon as possible.[13]

Ironically, the most provocative Chicago study of recent years, a Marxist critique by Charles Bowden and Lew Kreinberg called *Street Signs Chicago*, supports this interpretation. They argue that the dominant feature in the history of Chicago was its usefulness as a place to do business. Communities were a distant priority, "so far down this list that they are off the page." According to this view, there are no communities, no neighborhoods; it is, in fact, nothing more than an ameliorative tactic of power brokers to state that there are or ever were such creatures: "Nobody ever came to Chicago to found a neighborhood or to save the lake shore . . . Nobody came for the weather." People came for money, and to get that mon-

ey they amassed power. None of this took place in the local communities, which became places for people to hang their hats till they
could get out and get closer to power and wealth. Industrial immigrant districts were "temporary places for temporary people," and
all "share one characteristic: people will do anything to get out of
them." Thus, Bowden and Kreinberg, in the 1980s, echoed Park's
and Burgess's views of the 1910s and 1920s.[14]

The theories on which this book rests are often in contrast to
those of the sociologists and the Marxists, sometimes in agreement,
and occasionally represent a difference in emphasis. The basic thesis
is that communities did exist in urban industrial immigrant districts, that bonds between people did form, and that institutions did
persevere. It is closest to what Wellman and Leighton refer to as
the "community saved" argument—that urban communities have
persisted as sources of stability and support, indeed that these are
the critical environments of urbanism in the United States. Back of
the Yards is, therefore, not just an example, but the primary arena
where immigrant workers lived their lives.[15]

This work also draws on a long series of studies by social historians who have changed our entire view of the past. For example,
E. P. Thompson's *The Making of the English Working Class* laid
the groundwork for later investigations, teaching us that "we cannot understand class unless we see it as a social and cultural function." Academics in the United States have pursued that declaration, expanding our knowledge and understanding in all fields of
social history. John Bodnar, Roger Simon, and Michael Weber summed up this approach when they wrote, "Beyond the somewhat narrow models of ethnic succession and mobility, real people were
attempting to create lives for themselves in the midst of numerous,
countervailing forces."[16]

This book, therefore, is an attempt to advance our knowledge of
those models, forces, and efforts. It stands squarely in the tradition
of the works cited above, and often confirms their findings. While
we have chosen a single neighborhood as our focus, the goal remains
the same—to describe exactly how people in working-class areas
responded to pressures and shaped their own version of community.

The primary thesis is that residents of these inner city areas did
form *communities*, even by a rustic definition of that term. George
Hillery, in an article in *Rural Sociology* on definitions of community, included three elements in his description: networks of interper-
sonal ties which provide sociability and support, residence in a
common locality, and solidarity of sentiments and activities. All of

these existed in Back of the Yards, and in the other communities across the United States that it so much resembled.[17]

These conditions developed because the residents of these areas had clear, common goals and the means of achieving them. They sought stability and order, a secure environment in which they could carry out their lives. The key to this achievement was a small, dependable group of friends and relatives who could be trusted in all circumstances and relied on for any support. These segmented cliques had slim means, but they managed by loyal service and creative use of resources to nurture several generations of immigrants and their children. In time, the size of these segments grew, and their character, based on an Old-World village or a Chicago street corner, gave way to a new sense of nationalism. The forces that taught and enforced this powerful identification were the very institutions the sociologists missed—particularly the church, the foreign-language press, and local leadership. The ability of these forces to reorganize the entire stockyards community along lines of their own choosing testified to their authority and to their dynamism.

This entire system of small cliques and stability, ethnic enclaves and protection, also succeeded because it slipped within the cracks of the packers' domination. Back of the Yards, like Hamtramack in Detroit or Homestead in Pennsylvania, was controlled by industrial giants. Owners, superintendents, and foremen worried about productivity and any off-the-job activities that might lead to unionism. They ignored, however, the way in which workers went about their daily lives outside the factory or the social structures and institutions they developed. The packers granted, in other words, huge, quiet areas of freedom within which the workers created a stable community, one eventually powerful enough not only to defeat the packers but to survive their passing.

This is another major theme of this work. While residents sought stability, they also created a democratic system based on local control of the social structure. The story of Back of the Yards, and of all similar communities across the United States, is a study of democracy's deep roots and of the dynamic cultural and social shifts that buried or resurrected it. This is of crucial importance because the small group's concept of freedom was at the core of the urban experience in the United States.

Community and democracy, however, were not simple, inflexible structures; they were complex and changing patterns. They did not always appear at such dramatic moments as the Back of the Yards Neighborhood Council's birth in 1939. At times they were quiet,

persistent influences, at other times passive structures responding
to the social environment and to its leaders. Their appearance and
their strength, therefore, ebbed and flowed, mirroring the reality of
Back of the Yards' history, with its dimming and recrudescence of
democracy and of community forms and traditions.

It should also be noted that this is a story of working-class adaptation. The stockyards residents lived their lives in many overlapping worlds. The factory, the family, the church, the social club, the
tavern, and the grocery store all served as different arenas in which
to fight the battle for peace and stability, and we cannot always
make clear exactly how or to what degree intersections occurred.
As James Borchert put it in his study of alley life in Washington,
D.C., "these divisions are extremely artificial and arbitrary . . . at
virtually every level it is difficult to determine where one ends and
the other begins." Instead, we must try to understand the components and then explain the patterns that developed from them.[18]

It is also true that these communities, in Back of the Yards and in
steel, auto, and railroad complexes, were not eternal entities. Park
and Burgess, Bowden and Kreinberg were right when they claimed
that communities had limited existences and that they were temporary places. What these authors missed was the duration of their
life span and just how complete and powerful a community could
grow within this period of time.

Back of the Yards was, in this sense, a typical case. From its
creation in 1865 to the present, there have been three communities
in this location. The first, from 1865 to 1900, consisted of skilled
Irish and German workers and their families, people who laid down
the roots of a new community. The second, from 1900 to 1970, was
initially composed of unskilled Slavic workers who slowly built upon
a basis of solidarity, support, and protection and who eventually
created a thriving and closely knit residential district. The third
community, begun in 1970, marked the beginning of the rise to dominance of the Mexican group in Back of the Yards, a movement that
at this writing is yet to be fulfilled, although the pattern of future
development is clear.

The question, therefore, is one of scale. If the scholar chooses to
define Back of the Yards, or any other industrial community, as a
transient zone where immigrants came and were eventually replaced by new groups, considerable supporting evidence is available. Back of the Yards has experienced different waves of immigrants, and the area's demography is still changing. In this work,
however, we argue that such an analysis uses too wide a screen and

that there is much to learn from a finer mesh and a closer examination. Our focus is on a single example—the middle, Slavic community—albeit with forays into both older and newer groups. Our point is that, while there was large-scale movement in and out, within the established boundaries important communities did grow and reach fruition—communities we must study and get to know if we are to understand the history of the immigrant working class in the United States.

This book, therefore, is in many ways a case study. Like Bodnar, Simon, and Weber's *Lives of Their Own*, this investigation stemmed from the "belief that a more accurate understanding of the urbanization of migrants could result from a microscopic analysis of individuals in the process of fabricating life strategies in response to specific urban and industrial conditions." The small scale enables us to watch and analyze, in close detail, how workers lived and the kinds of societies they formed. It is also, of course, a limited base upon which to frame generalizations, creating the need for discretion in drawing conclusions.[19]

Given these qualifications, Back of the Yards is a singularly fruitful place to carry out an investigation. The same factors that made it so interesting to social workers fifty years ago make it of equal interest to present-day historians. Its larger context was and is Chicago, the most dynamic new city of the United States' industrial age. Between 1870 and 1900, Chicago grew from a city with 298,877 people living on 35 square miles to a metropolis of 1,698,575 people on 190 square miles. Immigrants and their native-born children made up over three-fourths of the total population at the latter date. Within thirty years, the population was to double again.[20]

Everything about Chicago was big and sprawling, at once both typical of the experience of all U.S. cities of the time and an exaggerated version of them. This urban giant housed some of the nation's largest and most basic industries, specializing in enormous production units such as those in steelmaking and meat-packing. Chicago's meat-packing industry alone manufactured over $256 million worth of products in 1900. This was 32.7 percent of the industry's national total, only slightly less than the output of the next six meat-packing centers combined. Other industries in Chicago produced goods of all kinds, both for industry and consumers. Sales networks and department stores were developed to market these goods, and mail-order houses shipped Chicago's merchandise from coast to coast, making the city synonymous with industrial bounty.[21]

Chicago's problems also seemed to dwarf those of other cities.

Corporations like United States Steel and Swift & Company were ruthless giants, ruling with little concern for social consequences. A pervasive desire to make money tainted the city's culture and philosophy. One clergyman declared that "Chicago people are money and pleasure mad." Extremes of wealth and poverty coexisted: Marshall Field spent $75,000 on his son's birthday party while a laborer earned $350 a year. The vastness of Chicago's problems evoked different responses. Great struggles for industrial democracy erupted in the factories and union halls, producing vast and violent strikes like the Pullman strike of 1894. Five years earlier, Jane Addams had opened the door of Hull House in an attempt to improve relations between the middle and working classes. It became the foremost institution of its kind in the country, nurturing a generation of reformers.[22]

If Chicago deserved study because it typified the modern city, then Back of the Yards was the model industrial neighborhood. Though the stockyards dominated the community, it remained part of the larger municipality. It was thus subject to the entire range of urban social and governmental forces, stemming from powerful sources outside the neighborhood, but which could impose conditions on the local scene. Thus, Back of the Yards differed from the isolated company town, but was similar to such metropolitan communities as Hamtramack. The situation in Back of the Yards, therefore, represented the most common circumstances of industry domination of the urban worker's life in the twentieth century.

Within the community, the packer's role was all-encompassing. The region sprang into existence in 1865 following the opening of the Union Stock-Yards, and eventually forty-five thousand people came to work in the pens and factories of the yards, a massive complex which affected every facet of the lives of the workers and their families. A family's home, their children's future, the sounds they heard at night all were influenced or determined by company decisions. The most powerful weapon was control of employment and wages, which defined what the worker could do with his or her life. Packers also used the workplace to manipulate the social structure, fostering national and occupational segregation and blocking attempts at unity which might be turned against them. Most of all, they shaped the physical environment, forming a landscape dominated by the most pervasive stench in the industrial United States.

Despite all this, workers survived and even prospered. They formed social networks that supplied necessary goods and information which became enormous resources for mutual support and resulted in broad areas of stability and control. Such experiences in freedom formed the basis for collective action to improve their lives. Some of these projects, such as unions, were aimed directly at the packers. Most of them were used to expand the workers' areas of self-regulation from tavern groups and shopping societies at the corner store, through the social-athletic club, and eventually to the formal structure of church and political party.

This autonomy had its drawbacks as well. Based on ethnicity, it balkanized the neighborhood into a series of exclusive, self-supporting social clusters. The neighborhood's greatest triumph, therefore, was its founding of the Back of the Yards Neighborhood Council, the oldest community group in the United States still in existence, which managed to overcome nationalist barriers and achieve community-wide goals. Its effectiveness, however, rested on the concepts of stability and democracy that workers, their families, and their leaders had been forging for so many years.

The reasons Upton Sinclair selected Back of the Yards as his subject are still valid. It was a characteristic product of the major social forces transforming the United States in the first half of the twentieth century. By examining how community arose there, we can understand how workers responded to these forces and found a way to deal with them. They did more than blindly react, however. In searching for a way to make Back of the Yards a stable and secure place to live, they helped shape the social environment of the urban United States and laid the basis for the life patterns of future generations of workers and their families.

1

The World the Meat-Packers Made

The Stockyards and Its Smokestacks seen from Ashland Avenue
Chicago Historical Society

The first thing anyone noticed about the neighborhood was the stench. As visitors traveled south on the Ashland Avenue streetcars, "once they hit 39th or 43rd [Streets] you'd see them . . . have a handerchief around their noses because the smell was real bad," according to Stanley K. Sister Mary D. recalled her arrival at the Guardian Angel Day Care Center and Home for Young Ladies in 1932. She had been sent up to the nursery and "was taking care of the children. I thought they all had their pants full, excuse the expression. I was looking around. I said, 'Oh my goodness, who made in their pants?' . . . that smelled terrible. I didn't know, nobody told me about it."[1]

This odor was the combined product of enormous slaughterhouses, miles of penned hogs, sheep, and cattle, fertilizer plants, rendering vats, city garbage dumps, a fetid sewer known as Bubbly Creek, accumulated alley trash, and a few tanneries. Residents' comments included, "Oh man, it stunk," and "horrible, just horrible." At the same time, however, there was also the remarkable human capacity for adjustment, many respondents claiming that the locals never noticed it, that "we got so accustomed to it, after we moved . . . we missed it." To foster this adaptation, which really was just a matter of time, parents told their children that the smell was "healthy" for them. It reached the point that Paul J. could proudly state, "Oh yes, we are famous for our smell."[2]

This unique characteristic and the reactions to it were typical of life in Back of the Yards. It was a place dominated by a single industrial complex, formed for a unique purpose, with all decisions aimed at furthering that cause. The needs of business shaped the landscape in every possible way, including sights and sounds and smells. It did more than that to workers, however, for they had to deal constantly with this power. Decisions on every aspect of living came in response to what went on in the factories. Where one lived, what one ate, what one smelled were all determined, or at least influenced, by the meatpackers.

Workers responded by creating quiet worlds of their own, where they pursued their goals of security and freedom. This den of factory smoke, therefore, was the arena of struggle between industrial giants and immigrant workers—one seeking control of profits; the other, peace and stability.

The neighborhood bounded by Pershing Road (39th Street) on the north, Garfield Boulevard (55th Street) on the south, Racine Avenue on the east, and Western Avenue on the west was not always an industrial center. The area began as a section of the Township of Lake, so-called because of the low level of its marshy land, only a few feet above Lake Michigan. Pools of varying depths dotted the area, and in the 1880s young parishioners "went frog, crab and even snake hunting in dozens of miniature lakes around St. Augustine's; they caught fish in the big ditch on Western Avenue." It was recorded in an account of St. Augustine's parish in the late nineteenth century that "Time and again, wedding carriages got stuck in the mud . . . the bridal couple had no alternative but to walk or wade to church." Some of the ditches bordering the street reached depths of ten feet, and children built rafts to travel on the south branch of the Chicago River before it became the waste bin of the packers.[3]

For years the area was sparsely settled. Pioneers included S. S. Crocker and John Caffrey, who arrived in the early 1850s, when the first sections were under development. Crocker earned the title "Father of the Town of Lake" and built the first road. By February 1865, when the area was incorporated as a village, there were still fewer than seven hundred residents. The post office was a private affair with one postmaster. Up until 1868 the police force consisted of two horses and four men. The first newspaper, the *Weekly Sun,* appeared 29 November 1869, and at election time, seventy-five voters went to the polls.[4]

What changed all of this, of course, was the introduction of meatpacking to the Town of Lake. As J. C. Kennedy wrote in 1914, "No other neighborhood in this, or perhaps in any other city, is dominated by a single industry to the extent this one was." By the early 1860s, the packing industry, though still centered in Cincinnati (the original "Porkopolis"), began to move westward to Chicago. As early as 1848, the Bull's Head Stock Yards began operations at Madison Street and Ogden Avenue on the West Side. For several decades thereafter, across the city's length and breadth, stockyards were opened to house the animals that poured out of boxcars. By 1864, numerous yards dotted the city.[5]

That year, a group of investors headed by John Sherman sought a site for a large, unified stockyards operation. They needed space, not only for pens and rail sidings, but enough for a meat-packing industry to develop on adjacent land. The entire complex had to be fairly remote from the city, as befit a malodorous business. The chosen site consisted of 320 acres, from Pershing Road to 47th Street, and from Halsted Avenue to Ashland Avenue. The owner was "Long John" Wentworth, an early mayor of Chicago and a real-estate speculator who sold it for $100,000. Later additions included a block of twenty-five acres adjacent to the northwest sector and a right of way south from the City of Chicago for a rail line.[6]

Work began quickly. By 1 June 1864 and through a wet summer, nearly a thousand men labored to build a stockyards center out of the marshes. Often dressed in their leftover army uniforms, workmen planked the ground, dug wells and drainage ditches, and erected wooden sheds and permanent brick buildings as well as the pens. On Christmas Day 1865, the Union Stock-Yards opened at the Halsted entrance.[7]

The consolidated yards grew rapidly. In 1867, Phillip Armour built his first plant in Chicago, and Gustavus Swift arrived in 1875. The original wooden entrance was replaced in 1879 by a limestone gate, designed by the architectural firm of Burnham and Root, which featured a sculptured bull's head in the center of the arch. What gave the Chicago packing industry its greatest spur, however, was technology, particularly four developments: the refrigerated railroad car, the canning process, the introduction of assembly-line methods, and the discovery of by-products that could be made from hitherto waste material.[8]

The yards grew from tracks of iron and steel than ran from Texas to Chicago, then across the country and, via ship, around the globe. In the last third of the nineteenth century, as the urban population boomed, vast markets for foodstuffs developed in areas where no plants could grow or livestock survive. Patents for the refrigerated railcar appeared in 1868, and in 1869 fresh beef traveled from Chicago to Boston under Nelson Morris's supervision. Gustavus Swift, in 1879, introduced the first fully reliable refrigerator car by putting ice at the top of the car. This cooled the air and made it heavier so that it dropped to the floor and forced warm air out through the ventilators. The refrigerated railcar permitted the shipment of dressed beef, thus slashing costs, since only the useful meat, not the entire animal, was shipped. More than any other, this invention was responsible for the growth of the yards, because it centralized slaughtering. This created the need for a vast industrial complex strategically located between the Texan and Midwestern cattle and hog fields and the markets in the Eastern cities. Refrigerated railcars guaranteed the rise of the Chicago yards.[9]

Canning, like refrigeration, opened up vast markets to Chicago's processed meats. Again, by 1879 (a fortunate year for meat-packers), engineers perfected an economical and reliable method of seal-

Map 1
Back of the Yards
Map by Keith Schlesinger

Roman Catholic Churches

1
Immaculate Heart of
Mary Vicariate
Mexican

2
Holy Cross
Lithuanian

3
Sacred Heart
Polish

4
St. Augustine
German

5
SS. Cyril and Methodius
Bohemian

6
St. John of God
Polish

7
St. Joseph
Polish

8
St. Michael
Slovak

9
St. Rose of Lima
Irish

ing tins hermetically, following years of experimentation. Food products could be packaged so as to prevent later spoilage, regardless of climate or the passage of time.[10]

The third development was the introduction of assembly-line or, more accurately, disassembly-line methods to butchering. Early on, the idea of hanging a carcass on an overhead moving chain came into use in the larger shops. The biggest obstacle to rapid production was the removal of the pig's hide but, between 1876 and 1888, increasingly efficient machines smoothed this rough spot in the work process. The constantly moving line of meat also led to many practices associated with industrialization, such as the elimination of many skilled positions, minute divisions of labor, and the infusion of women into the work force.[11]

Finally, the packers learned to process all possible parts of the animal, prompting the comment that they "used every part of the hog but the squeal." In 1860, few by-products existed, among them hides, sausage, and lard. Half of the animal was waste. In 1886, Nelson Morris hired Dr. Herman Schmidt, the first full-time chemist in the packing industry. At first viewed with distrust, scientists quickly gained respect and eventually became the saviors of the industry. By 1900 there were over forty by-products, including glue, medicine, bristles, and soap.[12]

The industrial empires of the meat packers were soon among the nation's greatest. By 1910 the complex of yards, industries, banks, and other structures—known collectively as "the Yards"—covered 500 acres, had 13,000 pens, 300 miles of railroad tracks, 25 miles of streets, 50 miles of sewers, 90 miles of pipes, and 10,000 hydrants. On a hot day, 7 million gallons of water fed the needs of cattle, machines, and humans. The site also produced its own electricity and had stations creating other forms of power as well. In 1919, a boom year, the plants processed 14,903,487 animals, including 7,936,634 hogs and 2,331,233 cattle. On one day in 1920 alone, 122,748 pigs came to the yards. In 1919 the federal census reported employment in the meat-processing plants of Chicago as 45,696 persons, 60 percent of the neighborhood's *entire* population. One Swift & Company factory had more than 11,000 employees. That year, the total value of meat and meat products in Illinois, an industry dominated by the area between Halsted Street and Ashland Avenue, reached $1.284 billion.[13]

To run these factories, the packers needed workers. About 1870, Phillip Armour permitted twenty of his old hands to build cottages on company land at 43rd Street and Packers Avenue. Two years later the Hutchison Packing Company erected seven houses for foremen one block north. The first of these settlements became known as Armour's Patch; the second, New Patch.

Thus the packers began a pattern of influencing the workers' choice of residence, at times directly by building projects, but more often by paying such low wages that families chose to live nearby rather than pay carfare. This was a typical urban pattern, with workers' colonies arising on the fringes of industrial or downtown employment centers. In Back of the Yards, a warehouse eventually took over Armour's Patch. It became known as Castle Garden because it symbolized the first job or point of entry for newcomers. Local wags commented that their kinfolk went right from Castle Garden in New York to Castle Garden in Packingtown. A settlement at 47th Street and Ashland Avenue was Arnoldsville, and the area south of 51st Street became New City. Years later, Ernest Burgess and other sociologists at the University of Chicago used the latter term for Community Area 61, the community now known as Back of the Yards.[14]

The residents of these early communities were Irish and German, roughly 60 percent Celtic and 30 percent Teuton. By 1881, for example, there were at least sixty families from the Emerald Isle west of the stockyards, and St. Rose of Lima Church opened at 48th Street and Justine Avenue, one block east of Ashland Avenue, to tend to their needs. Two years later, on 8 July 1883, the church moved to Ashland Avenue at 48th Street and dedicated a new building. Shortly after, a parish school was opened, and by 1885 the Sisters of Mercy had undertaken the teaching, the church's most essential function next to the holding of religious services.[15]

The Germans, who came from Prussia and the Rhineland and were skilled butchers and sausage makers, developed independent institutions of religion and community at the same time. St. Augustine, a Catholic church at 50th Street and Laflin Avenue, lists 1879 as its founding date; it was then that Father Peter Fischer built a small frame church and opened a parish school, under the direction of a lay minister, for eleven families. Nearby, German Protestants were active. In 1884, sixteen charter members signed the constitution that founded St. Martini Evangelical Lutheran Church. Their church was at 49th Street and Loomis Avenue and they chose Reverend F. Leeb as their pastor. Seven years later, the congregation moved to 51st Street and Marshfield Avenue. This put

German Lutherans three short blocks from German Catholics, separated only by Ashland Avenue and centuries of religious conflict. Few bridged the gap.[16]

The next national group to enter Town of Lake was Bohemian. The first of the Slavs, like the Germans who proceded them, were sausage makers and artisans who moved, in the 1880s, from the Pilsen area to a less crowded neighborhood.

By 1891 there were enough Bohemians to require a parish, and Father Thomas Bobal, born in the small village of Zuzkovice in Moravia, came and started celebrating Mass. In August 1892, the Bohemians opened a new frame church and its school held classes that summer. Father Bobal remained pastor at SS. Cyril and Methodius for the next sixty-three years, till 1953. Other Bohemians created the Community Methodist Church in 1882, and Mary McDowell of the University of Chicago Settlement House occasionally attended services there. Bohemians also started the first nonreligious social facility in the area, Columbia Hall at 48th Street and Honore Street, later known as School Hall because Bohemian national societies used it for teaching children their parents' language and their national heritage. August Loula built it, aided by the Building and Loan Association of Nove Mesto ("New City" in Bohemian).[17]

In 1877, there arrived in Town of Lake the first members of the group that came, more than any other, to be identified with the Slavic generations of the community. The Zulawski family was the first of several Polish clans who moved there in the late 1870s and early 1880s from the Polish settlement on the north side of the city, particularly from the area around Noble and Blackhawk streets and Milwaukee Avenue. Large numbers began to arrive during the strike of 1886, when packers imported them as scab labor. Most stayed and more followed. By 1910, various estimates listed the Poles as anywhere from 36 to 49 percent of the community's population.[18]

Like every ethnic group in Back of the Yards, the Poles created a community network all their own. St. Joseph, the first Roman Catholic church for Poles in the neighborhood, was dedicated on 19 December 1886 at 48th Street and Hermitage Avenue. For twenty-five years a series of pastors reigned, till Father Stanislaus Cholewinski took over on 5 July 1910. A native of Poznan, in Prussian Poland, he became the stabilizing influence at St. Joseph's, building it into one of the major Polish churches in the city. He served for fifty-five years, following the pattern of pastors who stayed in one parish their whole life. Such long tenures were typical in the neighborhood's churches, and these pastors and priests became important local leaders. Father Cholewinski retired in 1965 at the age of ninety, eight months before he died.[19]

Two other Roman Catholic churches served the local Polish community. St. John of God, south and east of St. Joseph's, at 52nd and Throop streets, opened its doors in 1906. Homes in this area were more expensive, and St. John of God had the highest status of the Polish religious triumverate. As the Town of Lake community expanded and the area around the church filled in, membership rose dramatically. In 1908, there were 300 families and 360 children in the school; according to a census taken on 22 October 1922, 2,400 families belonged to the church and 2,508 children attended the school run by the Felician Sisters for St. John of God.[20]

At the other end of the social scale, Father Frances Karabasz began to organize the third Polish Catholic church, Sacred Heart, in July 1910. It was located at 46th Street and Wolcott Avenue, in the poorest of the Polish sections. The membership, originally 660 families, was drawn from the Polish group with the least social status—the *goral*, or "mountaineers," who came from the rolling heights of the Tatra Mountain range. Other Poles regarded them as the equivalent of hillbillies. They had their own distinctive accent, dress, customs, and societies, and they clung together in a tight clannish fashion. Their first religious building was both church and school, demonstrating again the overwhelming importance of religious instruction. A thousand parishioners could attend services and there were ten classrooms. Father Karabasz stayed on as pastor for forty-four years, until 1954, then lived in the rectory until his death in 1972 at the age of 91.[21]

Poles were, however, only one of a succession of Slavic immigrants to enter the community. In the 1890s and on into the 1900s, Slovaks, Lithuanians, Russians, Rusins, and Ukranians moved into separate sections of the neighborhood west of the yards. Each immediately set out to create a community—building churches, opening stores so that the women could question prices in their own language, and trying to provide for all the needs of their people. In 1898, the Slovaks built St. Michael's Church at 48th Street and Damen Avenue, the first Roman Catholic church for Slovaks in Chicago and soon the largest in the United States. Another group of Slovaks began a Lutheran congregation in 1913 and built a church in 1918. The Lithuanians arrived in 1887. Fearful of being dominated by their archenemies the Poles, they also sought an anchor for their community. In 1902, officials of their charitable organization, St. Vincent Ferrer, went to Archbishop James Quigley and requested their own parish for the Town of Lake. Quigley agreed, if they could find sixty families, thus guaranteeing a minimum of support. A committee started canvassing the area and in 1904 the parish was founded; Father Alexander Skrypko, a native of Subaciai, Lithuania, was pastor. In 1905, the church, Holy Cross, arose at 46th Street and Hermitage Avenue. That year the church census showed 525 families, 2,700 people; by 1916 there were 1,100 families, 6,850 people. Russian immigrants also built a church, St. Archangel Michael Greek Orthodox, at 43rd and Honore streets in 1910. Even earlier, in 1903, an assembly of Rusin families from Ruthenia, now part of the Southwestern Soviet Union, joined to form a community. The first requirement, of course, was a church, and St. Mary (Byzantine Rite) opened at 50th Street and Seeley Avenue. The Ukranians formed their own Nativity of the Blessed Virgin Mary parish (Ukranian) in 1911 at 50th Street and Paulina Avenue.[22]

Thus, each group of immigrants in turn declared and maintained its ethnicity and its native language, erecting nationally oriented churches as quickly as possible to symbolize their separate identity. They shared, however, one common experience, whether they were Irish, German, Polish, or Russian: all, or their parents, were immigrants who had struggled to make the transition to the world of the meat-packers. Life in Europe had never been good. Mary M. remembered of her childhood in Slovakia that there was "not much food and not much variety." There was no medicine and no cloth, so she and her mother learned how to spin flax to make linen. Monsignor Edward Plawinski observed that "some of the Poles . . . they came with practically nothing . . . the only thing the parents had in Poland was a farm." That farm, moreover, meant considerably less and less as landholdings decreased in size. Catherine I. explained that "the farm wasn't too rich to live and the family grows." As a result, "people was looking for a little better living."[23]

To find this, they came to the United States where "there was work and jobs," according to Joseph G.; more simply, as Catherine I. put it, they came "for money." One member of the family, usually the oldest son, arrived first. Sometimes it was the father; as in the case of Sister Mary V., whose father later sent for his wife and two daughters, one of them the future Benedictine nun. Often there were long separations. Anthony W.'s father, for example, left their home in Poland to go to the United States but instead stayed in Liverpool for four years, working in a magnesium plant and a sugar refinery. Finally, in 1888, he made the ocean voyage, but winds blew the ship off course and it landed in Newport News, Virginia, instead of New York. From there he hopped a freight train to Chicago, where a member of a Jewish assistance group, probably the Hebrew Immigrant Aid Society, placed him in the Polish community in Brighton Park, just west of Back of the Yards. There he worked in a lumber yard and earned extra money on weekends playing the violin at weddings. He moved to Back of the Yards when he got a better job as a janitor for one of the packers. Finally, he was able to send for his family.[24]

To mitigate the problem of both passage and adjustments, the immigrants set up networks to provide advice and material aid. They sent home letters filled with information and money. The homes of earlier arrivals became way stations for the friends and relatives who followed from the old country. Joseph T. and Joseph G. both lived with relatives when their families came to Chicago, and these people helped each of them find an apartment of their own. William B. claimed that newcomers knew the precise location of their own ethnic churches, that "they knew it before they even got here, where to go." Nevertheless, it remained a question of making the best of a tough situation, hard on everyone. Joseph G. arrived in Chicago at the age of four. It was night and he was crying because his mother, the only parent on the trip, kept pulling him by the hand as she balanced the pillows and feather comforter strapped to her back, simultaneously clutching various parcels and bags. He was tired and wanted her to carry him, but she could not because her hands were full.[25]

The world Joseph entered and in turn helped create was not a pretty one. It was crowded and it was strange. In 1920, the Bureau of the Census counted 75,920 people in the neighborhood, an area barely exceeding two-and-one-half square miles. Although this was the largest number of residents ever reported by the Bureau, the true count had to be much higher, given the language barriers and the fear of government officials. In 1919, the Chicago meat-packing and slaughtering industry, concentrated on the South Side, was the largest employer in the city, and the neighborhood revolved around the pens and the packers. A study of six selected blocks in 1923 showed that 54 percent of all heads of households were employed in the yards.[26]

Making matters worse amidst this crowding, people could talk only to a small number of their neighbors. The fact that they were largely foreign born or the children of immigrants did not mean that this was a homogenous population. Residents came from all over the map and did not necessarily speak each other's language or even care to have contact with one another. Of the 75,920 inhabitants counted in the 1920 Census, 32,345, or 42.6 percent, were foreign-born: of these, 44.6 percent were Polish; 15.9 percent were Czecho-slovakian (including Slovaks and Bohemians, the former pre-dominating); 12.4 percent were Russian (including Rusins and Ukranians); 7.3 percent were German (probably including some Poles, as did the Russian figure, since Poland had only recently re-gained independence); 6.7 percent were Lithuanians; and 2.5 per-cent, or 812, were foreign-born Irish. Similarly, the best available data showed that by 1909, 46.4 percent of all workers in the stock-yards were of Slavic background, up from 14.0 percent in 1896. While they were clearly becoming the major force in the area, the Slavs had little unity or power because they included so many differ-ent ethnic groups.[27]

The setting was grim and foul, as well as crowded. "This world," a Lithuanian-American author exclaimed, "would not have been un-usual to Dante." A cloud of smoke produced by the factories and coal stoves hung over everything. The neighborhood was drab, a dull grey. The two-story houses looked identical and there were few parks or open spaces. One visitor wrote that "anyone who spends even a few brief hours in . . . 'back of the yards' is impressed by the want of color. Grey streets, grey houses and smoke-laden air com-bine to give a background of unrelieved monotony."[28]

The area did, however, have its own special sights and sounds and odors, all of which reaffirmed the dominance of the packers. Anthony W. remembered the workmen walking down Gross Ave-nue, now McDowell Avenue, to the main entrance to the packing complex. Genevieve N. recalled rats "like cats" running across 43rd Street, going from their nightly feast in the meat warehouses to the relative peace of homes during the day. Cattle were a frequent sight; cowboys on horseback drove them from one plant to another on the local streets of the yards complex and occasionally a steer got loose and ran into the residential section, creating consternation, excitement, and a long retold story. There were also bugs. Because of poor garbage collection, "the alleys . . . were terrible . . . the swarms of flies were uncountable," in the words of Father Vito Mikolaitis. Other swarms came from the fertilizer plants. Trucks from these companies made regular trips to the local butcher shops. Ted P., son of the owner of one such store, affirmed that they bought up "all [the] spoiled and rotten meat," including those in-fested with "maggots and stink and bugs." The fertilizer trucks were wide open, with only a canvas top to cover "a million flies." Factories ground all this into nutrients for the soil, producing one of the worst stenches in the yards.[29]

The neighborhood also lived among its own special set of noises. In a remarkable document composed for the author, Anthony W., a Pole, wrote about and captured the sounds of a typical day. At 5 A.M. he heard the sounds of locomotives, "the pulsating chugs and . . . from time to time the whistles of various pitches." About 6 A.M. the churchbells rang the Angelus, signalling a brief period of silent prayer and, at 7 and 8, the Mass, echoed by factory whistles announcing the start of the workday. About 7:30, there was the sound of children going to school, "talking and voices out loud greeting and calling one another." At 8:00, the school bell at St. Joseph's clanged, heralding the start of classes. During the day there were the noises of people talking, the creaking of wagons, the crunch of locomotives, and especially the assorted noises of the streetcar. These included the constant ringing of bells (one for a stop, two for starting up, and three for an emergency stop), the winding sound of the motor and the grinding of gears during start up, and the click of the iron wheels on the tracks. Sometimes the car stopped short and the friction flattened a wheel on one side. The result was a distinctive "plop plop" that could be heard for a block when the car moved at any speed, and that made the ride "annoying," in Mr. W.'s polite word. At noon, churches rang the Angelus again, the yards' whistles signaled lunchtime, and children came home from school. After lunch, they congregated in the schoolyard around 12:30, throwing and bouncing balls and skipping rope. At 12:45, the bell ringer walked from one end of the yard to the other, clanking his bell as children formed into lines of girls and boys. At 3:00, the school bell rang again, and at 6 P.M. the Angelus sounded. At night, one heard the streetcars and especially the puffing of locomotives "and the screech of the wheels . . . going around the bends." This did not bother the residents, however; Mr. W. concluded his reminiscences with the comment: "But after a hard day's work we would sleep through it all. One got used to it and thought nothing of it, realizing it was a form of survival, living and an existence."[30]

The neighborhood also had its landmarks, evidence of industrialization and the packers' handiwork. The city dumps, on Damen Avenue between 47th and 43rd streets, were four great holes where clay had been removed for nearby brickyards owned by Alderman Thomas Carey of the Twenty-ninth Ward. After the clay companies had excavated them, the city's garbage wagons refilled them. The city used one for solid waste, private carting companies filled two others, and the packers dumped their waste into the last. The meat men burned their wastes, however, so a "smouldering fire" was always going; a moat surrounded it to prevent it from spreading. Alderman Carey profited every which way from this operation. He sold the clay from the holes, charged the city for the privilege of dumping there, violated the city's sanitation regulations with impunity, and charged professional scavengers as much as $15 a week to go through the garbage. After they finished, the women and children would pick over the remains, retrieving stove wood, old mattresses, pieces of food, worn garments, furnishings and, rarely, a previously overlooked item of value such as a silver utensil. For the children, especially, it was a grand bazaar. Amidst the filth and decaying matter, all kinds of treasures could be found, including an occasional broken toy.[31]

The dump symbolized many of the rules of existence in Back of the Yards. It typified the domination of the neighborhood by powerful forces: residents had no say about what went into or out of the pits or about how the refuse was handled. On the other hand, the piles were used as a resource by local people determined to survive.

A similar manifestation of industrial dominance was one of the best-known waterways in the urban United States. Bubbly Creek was one of the south branches of the Chicago River, and the packers who used it as their communal sewer failed to enlarge it to carry their enormous wastes. Despite dredgings by the federal government, the City of Chicago, the Sanitary District of Chicago, and private corporations that removed several hundred thousand cubic yards of material, the river-bed rose at the rate of almost half a foot a year between 1900 and 1921. In 1929, a report to the Sanitary District claimed that this was "a very sluggish stream, utterly inadequate to receive the wastes of even a young industry." At this time the daily output of "suspended matter" from the factories to the sewers of Chicago was a staggering 131,500 pounds, Swift & Company alone accounting for 52,170 pounds. All this "putrefying organic matter" released "gaseous ebullition," or bubbles, giving rise to its infamous name.[32]

Stories about Bubbly Creek were legion. It caught fire once, and in 1915 a reporter tried to row across but turned back when a six-foot bubble enveloped his boat. Many people supposedly fell in and never came back, and even those who did were hardly welcome. One woman told how, "My uncle fell into Bubbly Creek one night and grandma wouldn't let him in the house till the next day." Residents said it looked like a "street that had been freshly tarred," "like pudding," or "a crusty old thing." If the best comment is the most succinct, however, it came from Ted P., who simply explained, "It was a filthy piece of water."[33]

As the neighborhood and city grew, transportation changed, but there was always a link between the neighborhood and the larger metropolitan area. At first the only way to get to downtown Chicago was the Grand Trunk Railroad, which ran six trains daily for a five-cent fare and had a station at 49th Street and Justine Avenue. In 1888, Ashland Avenue got a streetcar line, but it took a half-day to get to the Loop and back. If too many passengers got on and the horses could not pull the weight, some riders disembarked and even pushed if necessary. In cold weather, trainmen threw a thick layer of straw on the floor for insulation. Later improvements included coal stoves (considered a luxury at the time), blowers to distribute the hot air beneath the seats, and curtains to roll down in a summer rain. In 1908, an elevated streetcar line began to offer service from the Loop to the yards, easing the problem of transportation considerably. Not until the 1930s and especially the 1940s, did automobiles become a popular form of conveyance in the neighborhood.[34]

City services, another result of urban connections, also underwent changes as the neighborhood grew. Back of the Yards was not a rural town with intimate local controls, but part of a major city and thus subject to a host of government strictures. Various city departments established their presence in the area, imposing order and minimal standards of living. The first regular police force, for example, consisted of four men; the town supervisor was chief. In 1897, the city built the New City Station at 47th Street and Paulina Avenue, a police station with a front of "pressed brick with stone trimming and copper cornices" and an oak interior. There were also call boxes around the precinct, the key to which rested in a nearby drugstore or other public place. Inside was a dial with ten spaces, each labeled with a possible disaster, such as "accident," "drunkard," "fire," "burglar," "murder," or "riot." The victim turned the dial to the appropriate spot, where it stayed, while an alarm at the station summoned assistance.[35]

The performance of these officials was highly idiosyncratic. Stanley K. observed that " you never, never said anything to a policeman." He was "the boss on the street. When he told you to go, you went, or you maybe got a shoe or a hit with the club." On the other hand, this off-handed use of authority could also work in a citizen's favor. One time a foreman called Joseph G. dirty names, so Joseph "hauled off and punched him in the jaw and he was out like a light on the floor." Swift's company police took the worker to the station, where the desk sergeant asked what had happened. Joseph described the epithets used; the officer, deciding that the punishment fit the crime, told him "go on home."[36]

The city also provided for personal sanitation. At the turn of the century and for years after, residents considered the possession of a bathtub or shower a tremendous accomplishment; or as one mother told a social worker, "we have a much nicer place now, we have our own bathtub and everything." The usual way to bathe was to take the big galvanized tub used for washing clothes and fill it with hot water. The eldest child went in first, washed up, stepped out, and the mother added a new bucket of hot water. The next oldest went then, and so on down the line. On each, the mother used the harsh brown Fels Naptha soap. Sue N. remembered that "we would cry because she would scrub and scrub and scrub." Sometimes a sheet was held around the tub for privacy, and occasional disasters oc-cured, such as the time Anthony W.'s brother backed into the hot stove while toweling himself dry.[37]

This procedure was totally unacceptable to a worker coming home from the yards. In 1900, the city built the William Mavor Bath House on Gross Avenue (under the prodding of the University of Chicago Settlement House). It had a small waiting room where cus-tomers stayed until the operator called their names. When the cubi-cles lining the wall were all occupied, a bell rang and the water came on, cold at first, then warming up. After a while, another bell rang and the water went suddenly cold, producing loud yells. The cus-tomers had a clear choice—leave with the soap still on or freeze. It cost a nickel, and residents like Richard P. felt "that was my lux-ury." People stood in line for these showers as they did for the sim-ilar facilities at the parks. Father Vito Mikolaitis remembered rows of waiting citizens at Davis Square Park: "that was constant; you'd see the whole procession of men," each clutching a small package of a towel and a change of clothing. The Settlement House also had showers open to the public. At each of these facilities there were separate hours for men and women.[38]

The most investigated aspect of the neighborhood was its hous-ing. Reformers came again and again, counting rooms, making up separate categories of conditions, and collecting data. The area's housing improved over time, but never enough to satisfy these outsiders.

To residents, however, their housing was one of the most impor-tant aspects of life. In 1913, a researcher noted, "The ambition of the immigrant to own property in America is one of his most strik-ing characteristics. For it he will make almost unbelievable sacri-fices both of his own comfort and that of his wife and children." She added that to these people, "The possession of a house . . . is the highest form of prosperity." The study showed that 37 of 125 women with no husbands, 138 of 297 men who earned less than $2 a day, and

95 percent of the remaining heads of households were property owners.[39]

This passion stemmed from the traditional peasant's attachment to the land. Many of the immigrants in Back of the Yards, as in other cities, had strong ties to the soil. The term *polanie*, for example, by which the Poles described themselves, means "dwellers of the fields." Property represented home and hearth, the bounty of nature, and the satisfaction of a good day's work with the crops. Typical was the old Polish proverb that "a man without land is like a man without legs. He crawls about a lot but gets nowhere." In the New World, ownership of property was translated into ownership of one's home. Acquiring title to a house was a reestablishment of a familiar social pattern, a link to the Old World. It also represented financial security against the caprices of the packers. In time the mortgage would be paid off and never again need the family pay rent; there would always be a roof over the family's head, even in bad times. It was also a way of providing an inheritance for the next generation. Ted P., a stockyards worker, always kept up the house; he would fix something in the home before he would buy shoes for his children. Mr. P. loved his children dearly; he felt, however, that it was important to preserve this for them. As he put it, "If I fix the house up, its going to be a good house; if I die I'm going to leave something good for the kids."[40]

No sacrifice was too great. It was a common practice to purchase a home "even if they have to starve their families to get the money." Women did extra laundry, took in boarders, and children went to work at early ages. Time and again, researchers found that buildings they considered overcrowded and unsanitary were owner-occupied. In multiple unit housing, proprietors commonly took the worst apartment, letting out the others to gain income to pay back the mortgage.[41]

Home buying was astonishingly widespread. A banker from the yards area told U.S. Labor Commissioner Carroll Wright in 1904 that Poles were buying homes "to a most remarkable and unprecedented extent," and that this was almost as true of the Lithuanians. By 1920 residents owned 57 percent of the homes in the area; of these owners, 90 percent were foreign-born. One study showed that it took eighteen years of residence in Chicago for a Pole to buy his first home. The father of a Slovak interviewee, for example, saved enough as a laborer to build a tavern with a hall in the back and three flats upstairs.[42]

Buying a new home followed parochial patterns geared to intimate contacts. Someone might put up a For Sale sign. Usually, one found out by word of mouth: sometimes through the local savings and loan association, sometimes from someone in church, sometimes from neighbors. Anna K. described this as, "one would tell one another," or as Ann P. put it, "they knew from neighbors."[43]

To buy the house "you had as much down as possible." People followed this practice, even when it meant borrowing from relatives or neighbors. Joseph K., Anna's husband, described the procedure: "borrow money as much as you could get, accumulate, to put down to the contractor." With the down payment secure, prospective home owners went to one of the building and loan associations dotting the neighborhood. These operated out of bars, corner stores, and churches and were usually linked to a particular village or national cluster. After that, one scrimped and saved to pay the mortgage. James T. explained that "foreign people, they believe in savings. If they make one hundred dollars they'll save out of it. If they make ten dollars they'll still save out of it." The local parable ran than the final ceremony of baptism was hitting the baby's rump with a building and loan book.[44]

The lots these houses sat on were of average Chicago size, 25 × 125 feet. A house occupied only a portion of this space, so many lots contained two or even three structures. Conditions in the rear dwellings were a mix of rotten stench and airy freedom. On the one hand, they sat closer to the alleys, where the odor of garbage and the swarms of flies were greater. Most of the houses however, occupied the front of the lot, leaving the back clear. Rear buildings, therefore, had space around them: they were, as housing crusaders Sophonisba Breckenridge and Edith Abbott reported, "light and sunny."[45]

What concerned researchers most about housing was the threat of overcrowding and the possible absence of proper light and ventilation. Breckenridge and Abbott found, in 1911, that 25.5 percent of the houses in their sample had only one apartment and 28.3 percent had two. Houses with four apartments accounted for 20.9 percent. More than half the apartments, in both the 1911 investigation and a follow-up report by Alice Miller in 1923, had four rooms. The remainder had, in about equal shares, two, three, or five rooms. Typically, one or two rooms were for common use; all the rest were sleeping rooms. Light and ventilation in most rooms were below acceptable standards because they opened uniformly onto a narrow passage between homes, known in Chicago as a "gangway." Houses were usually built close to the lot lines, so "although only a small proportion of the dark rooms could be explained by lack of window area, 75 percent were clearly due to the fact that the windows opened on a court which was only a narrow passage between two buildings." Almost one-third of the rooms were occupied by two adults, and almost one-quarter were used by a single adult. The usual size of a room for two adults was between 400 and 800 cubic feet; since the room's height was typically 6 feet, floor space varied from 6 × 11 to 10 × 13. Exceptions were found: One man slept in a room only 18 feet square, another in a space 24 feet square and only 4 feet high. One sleeping room for four was only 37 square feet; another, for five, was 59. Researchers even found four apartments whose floor space was less than 100 square feet. All this was the result of the packers' handiwork, the low wages they paid workers. As Thomas Philpott pointed out, "As long as people stayed poor, they could not afford houses fit to live in."[46]

One other important type of living arrangement was boarding. Charles H. claimed that boarders were the lifeblood of the neighborhood; this was, of course, true in all communities of immigrants. Breckenridge and Abbott found that 27.3 percent of all the residents in the Back of the Yards were boarders; more than half the families they studied housed boarders. There were several reasons for this. Vast numbers of immigrants came over as single men, seeking only the jobs the packers offered. They worked long hours and saved money for a home or to send back to the old country, and they needed to procure lodging and food as cheaply as possible. Boarding provided that. It also served as a means for the community to watch over and take care of its strays, what Carl Degler referred to as a form of "social control." As Josephine K. commented about boarders, "You kept track of one another and you knew who was living alone." It permitted widows to make a living and it allowed a wife to augment the family's income with the work she knew and performed best. Mary M.'s mother, for example, had fourteen boarders and made more money than her husband. This gave the family a more flexible income, since one could add or drop boarders as financial need increased or dwindled. Sometimes the practice meant survival, since "in order to exist you had to have an added source of income." Boarding, then, was another social ramification of industrial conditions. Earlier reformers thought that it signaled the end of the family unit, but in fact it meant exactly the opposite, a way of using the family's resources to the fullest and providing, as well, badly needed facilities for immigrants. The authors of the leading scholarly article on the subject pointed out that "the family was not fragile but malleable," that boarding "not only

was a sensible response to industrialization but, in cushioning the
shock of urban life for newcomers, was decidedly humane."[47]

Part of the reason the system worked so well was the method of
placing boarders. They were never total strangers, but always had
some tie to the family or to the father's work; and there was always
some form of social obligation, a need to take care of local strays.
Sometimes they were close relatives from the old country. Louis
P.'s family took in only one boarder, an unmarried uncle. More often
they were distant relatives who came with recommendations, or
even people from the same village who used the immigrant's network of communications. James T.'s father had a good reputation in
Europe, so Slovak newcomers were advised, "You go see (T.) over
there, he'll take care of you." Or a boarder might be someone who
had heard of the family after arriving in Chicago or someone the
father worked with. Some sort of recommendation was essential,
thus ensuring that boarding maintained the social order. And boarders stayed with their own ethnic group, if for no other reason than
to ensure that everyone spoke the same language. This correspon-
dence of background also meant that boarders accepted the household's customs, values, and tastes, and that, in general, a positive
atmosphere prevailed, children addressing boarders as "uncle."
Residents valued them because they carried news from the old
country, and even the local village, in a way quicker and more en-
joyable than letters.[48]

Standard accommodations for lodgers were a bed, food, and laundry at a cost of $3 to $6 a week. Most boarders had their own small
sleeping area, but others used a mattress or folding cot, one of several in a room, and used their trunks as closets. These arrangements led to severe overcrowding: in one interviewee's home, ten
boarders and the family squeezed into a four-room house. The same
mattress might even be used by two or three men, each on a different shift in the yards. Each boarder had his own account at the
corner store and paid it at the end of the week. When the housewife
shopped, she got several packages, one for the family, one for each
of the other residents. At home she tied up each piece of meat before putting it in the soup pot to cook, ensuring that nothing fell off
the bone and that she would not be accused of cheating anyone. As
the meal began, the boarder went to his trunk, *kuferek* in Slovak,
took out a large round rye bread and a jar of mustard, and cut the
bread and spread mustard on it. He then "slopped up his soup,"
according to Charles H., and sat muttering in his native tongue,
"Ah, this is so good, but it is so expensive."[49]

Facilities in these houses improved steadily. Running water was common, but not hot water. In 1894, privy vaults or outhouses were banned, but they still existed in 1911, as did a number of yard water closets, similar to privies, which were prohibited in new housing. One problem with such toilets was cleaning them. Most outhouses were hinged to flip back and expose the pits. This was done at night, and occasionally an exhausted worker fell asleep inside and would be rudely awakened when someone uprooted his perch. The most common arrangement, however, was flush toilets, one outside each house or even one for a cluster of several homes. These were in communal use, like the hall toilet in tenements. This early plumbing was not ceramic, but cast iron, in the shape of a funnel with a water connection built into one side. Given the poor heating in those days and metal's quick response to changes in temperature, using it in the winter must have required either grim determination or a rare sense of balance.[50]

The main room was the kitchen. This reflected, in part, the European peasant's cottage, where the kitchen meant the hearth and its heat, and symbolized domesticity. In the United States the kitchen became the social center: there, eating, cooking, cleaning, talking, advice giving, and all entertaining save the most formal took place.[51]

There was more to the house than its internal facilities, however. Location was also important: residents created an intricate set of status boundaries. The neighborhood was divided into four zones or quadrants, circling counterclockwise around Ashland Avenue and 47th Street as shown on map 2. Each of these areas had special qualities and differing status. Quadrant I had the lowest status; Quadrant IV, the highest. Quadrant I was where the newcomers, the latest immigrants lived. It was crowded, but it lay within walking distance of the yards and jobs; for the same reason, its stench was worse. Because the residents were the country's newcomers and unfamiliar with its ways, the area gained a reputation for being wide-open and generally rougher. Quadrant II, still north of 47th Street, was a bit better. Its residents lived a little further away from the stench and there was a little more space; nevertheless, it was still a home for greenhorns. Quadrants I and II made up the zone of transition, to which the immigrants came and where they spent their early years. In 1920, while the neighborhood as a whole was 42.6 percent foreign-born, 53.4 percent of the residents of Quadrant I were foreign-born and, in the zone as a whole, 52.1 percent were. The section north of 47th Street also had less than half as many homeowners, and far more delinquents and truants, than its southern neighbor.[52]

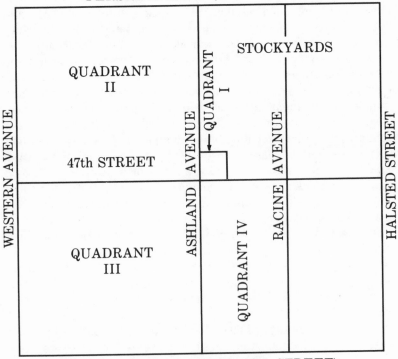

PERSHING ROAD (39th STREET)

STOCKYARDS

QUADRANT II

QUADRANT I

47th STREET

WESTERN AVENUE

ASHLAND AVENUE

RACINE AVENUE

HALSTED STREET

QUADRANT III

QUADRANT IV

GARFIELD BOULEVARD (55th STREET)

Map 2
Residential Quadrants in Back of the Yards
Map by Eugene Senn

Moving south meant a better life style or, as Evelyn Ostrowski put it, "the further you went up to 55th Street . . . was a rise in status." The odor was less, there was more room, and the houses were larger—more expensive and more frequently made of brick rather than wood, another sign of affluence. Quadrant IV was better than Quadrant III because it was closer to Halsted Street—that is, closer to the fancier neighborhoods of the "front of the yards," Bridgeport and Canaryville. It was also closer to Visitation parish on Garfield Boulevard, east of Halsted and the most prestigious parish in the whole area. Thus, St. John of God, the most affluent of the three local Roman Catholic churches for Poles was in Quadrant IV; St. Joseph church, which catered to the average Pole, was in Quadrant III; and Sacred Heart, created for the poor *goral*, was in Quadrant II.[53]

It was possible, therefore, to stay in the neighborhood and advance in status by moving counterclockwise around the axis of 47th Street and Ashland Avenue, and families and ethnic groups did just that. But the transition took long periods of time. In the 1870s and 1880s, Quadrant I held Irish workers. By 1910, they had either moved away or lived near Garfield Boulevard, in Quadrants III and IV, and Slavs had taken their place near the plants. Thirty years later, Quadrant I was becoming Mexican and the Eastern Europeans were moving south and west. At this writing, 1986, the zone of transition is almost totally occupied by people from south of the Rio Grande, Quadrant I more so than Quadrant II. The pattern endures.

There were two major exceptions to this pattern. Any location on Garfield Boulevard was choice, housing only the "elite," a term always used for Boulevarders. A residence fronting this road in Quadrant III was preferable to one on any other street in Quadrant IV. The other qualification, far more common, was that members of any particular ethnic group clustered around their church. The church was the center of local society, so individuals chose to live near where they spent so much of their time. One study, for example, showed that Wood Street, between 47th and 48th streets, a block away from St. Joseph, was 61.6 percent Polish.[54]

This housing pattern, developed by residents, was typical of their response to corporate control. It permitted precise social distinctions that enabled them to cope with their environment. The world of the meat-packers, though pervasive, was not all-encompassing. Workers here, as elsewhere, developed areas of control and democracy where they could establish order and make their own rules. In this way they began the long task of turning an industrial worksite into a thriving community.

A neighborhood as distinctive as this began to acquire a name and a reputation as well. Town of Lake was its common name until 1939, although it was also frequently called New City. Occasionally its original name misled people, as it did poor Sister Mary D., who came to the neighborhood and to Guardian Angel seeking rest and recuperation after an illness. When she heard the name of the district that she would soon make her lifelong home, she reported thinking, "Gee, there must be a big harbor there, boats and ships, that's the way I imagined, because it was Lake [Town of Lake]." Upon her arrival she found that "there's no lake around here. The lake's all the way down there [Lake Michigan, four miles east of Ashland Avenue]." Another name for the neighborhood was Packingtown, but locally this meant only the plants and pens, and even then was used rarely. Upton Sinclair made this label famous in *The Jungle*, but residents like Charles H. felt that it was "a term given to the neighborhood by the newspapers and things like that." Once in a while they called it Back of the Yards, a geographically descriptive term. The formal entrance to the yards was the gate at Halsted Street, and the neighborhood itself was centered on Ashland Avenue, behind the packing complex. In 1939, Joseph Meegan and Saul Alinsky used Back of the Yards for the name of their community organization, and the community has been so designated ever since.[55]

The hind end of a dirty business, Back of the Yards acquired an appropriate reputation. Charles H. described its "reputation for being a poor, rough, tough neighborhood." Residency meant "you automatically, being from Back of the Yards, were able to handle yourself." The area, in essence, was the wrong side of the tracks.[56]

Reformers particularly agreed with this assessment. Back of the Yards was violent, foreign, ignorant, drab and, above all, ugly. Middle-class, the reformers never realized the true color of the area, its people, and their riches of ritual, celebration, and friendship. At one University of Chicago Settlement House session for working women, a professor of English literature read the "well-known" passage from James Russell Lowell, "What is so rare as a day in June?" There was little response, despite the hopes that the "latent aesthetic interests of people in these dreary, cramped circumstances will respond to the appeals of a simple, fine and truly great art." It never occurred to such visitors that it was the question that was wrong. Ignored were the weddings, the dances in halls behind saloons, the children's games, the community patterns and the democracy that the workers and their families created. In these, they would indeed have found their "truly great art."[57]

2

Stages on Life's Way: Youth

Children Playing in the City Dumps at 47th Street
and Damen Avenue
Chicago Historical Society ICHi-18555

The experiences of the youth of Back of the Yards set the stage for their lives as adults. Every day's adventures taught them how to handle and even profit from their environment, to adapt it to their needs. Even more important, they became familiar with the conflict that would dominate their lives, between external control and personal freedom. The arenas of conflict were different for children, but the problem was the same. The young, like their elders, learned how to live within a power structure and yet maintain a private world of independent action and democratic control. In this way they were like their peers in urban areas around the country.

The child entered this life in a ceremony that stressed the importance of personal ties. It occurred within the private world that the workers created and maintained apart from the packer's influence. The first community event the child participated in was the christening. This included Baptism, the first sacrament, which brought the newborn child into initial harmony with God and church. For this occasion, parents dressed the infant in a special outfit, a long lacy dress with a bonnet, usually a gift from the godparents. There was a small book with a holy picture, in which the mother listed the names of all the participants, the most important of which, next to the infant and the parents, were the godparents—relatives, or sometimes close friends, and almost always a couple. Their ultimate responsibility was to take care of the child if the parents died, a very real threat when life was so short. Their immediate responsibilities were mostly to defray the cost of the clothes and the celebration, and to provide emotional support for the family. Among Mexicans, for example, the godfather acquired two titles. *Padrino* defined his relationship to the child and *compadre* defined his relation to the parents.[1]

After the church ceremony there was some kind of party, rarely in a hall because few could afford it; the group was small, anyway, just close friends and relatives. The female members of the family cooked at home, preparing sausage, beef, and maybe even chicken. Neighbors brought over additional dishes, easing the strain on the mother. At the party there would be drinking, and sometimes music and dancing. The father just stood there, as Genevieve N. recalls, and smiled; the well-wishers, according to Paul J., "they'd all come up to that little package and beam."[2]

After that auspicious start, the youngsters' prospects dimmed considerably. In 1900, the death rate of children under six was 40 per 1,000, according to one study. (In Hyde Park, the area around

the University of Chicago, the rate was only half that.) A study of
infant mortality at St. Augustine parish, a German congregation,
produced more shocking data. From 1884 to 1910, the rate of infant
mortality was 141.95 per 1,000; preschool deaths averaged 87.23 per
1,000; and deaths of school-age children, 13.43 per 1,000. Thus,
more than 1 of every 10 children in the parish died in infancy, actually almost 3 out of every 20. This was even more remarkable because the Germans, having been in the stockyards and the United
States longer, earned higher wages and were more likely to adopt
modern methods of medicine and sanitation. In the following period,
from 1910 to 1935, things improved considerably at St. Augustine's.
The rate of infant mortality dropped to 56.71 per 1,000; preschool
deaths, to 50.60 per 1,000; and school-age deaths to 12.53 per 1,000.
Still, the figures were tragic. In Joseph T.'s family, only 6 of 14
children survived the early years. But in the years from 1928 to
1933, when the rate of infant mortality in the City of Chicago was
56.7 per 1,000, it had risen to 74.3 per 1,000 in Back of the Yards.[3]

Fortunately, the children of Back of the Yards were unaware of
these statistics. They invented games, indulged in fantasies, ex-
plored their world, and in general tried to have a good time, like all
children. Elizabeth Donnellan wrote, in 1940, that "a trip down the
streets . . . during the summer time discloses hundreds and hundreds of boys and girls playing in the streets, alleys, vacant lots,
along the railroad tracks, in the playgrounds. There are innumera-
ble children within the boundaries of a single block."[4]

The most important manifestation of the children's world and
their control over it was their games. An examination of this activity demonstrates the kind of training urban youth received in
their earliest years. Johan Huizinga, in *Homo Ludens*, explains that
play is a rational activity, using powers of the mind. It involves the
manipulation of reality to create a separate world removed from
day-to-day life, and it requires its own accepted rules. To Huizinga,
play, a voluntary activity, represents "freedom." It is also democratic because of the participatory method in which new systems
and rules are created.[5]

Play, therefore, instructed the youth of Back of the Yards in certain basic skills. It taught them to exploit their environment to its
maximum advantage, using both their physical and mental powers.
A fragment removed from the dumps became a glorious plaything
for an imaginative child. Second, play taught even the very young
how to create their own social system and how to devise rules so
that the system worked to the benefit of everyone involved. Fan-

tasy worlds peopled by cowboys or kings required intricate organization, and thus resembled larger social orders. The youth of the Back of the Yards, therefore, received their first training in stability and community while playing on the urban side streets. Third, the games were democratic. All the members of the group joined in making the rules. The lack of adult supervision made the youngsters responsible for learning to work out their own problems and getting everyone to agree. Thus, the children's games taught them the basics of small group democracy.

Children always delight in exploring and so expanding their environment. The larger universe of the adults, though sometimes frightening, was fascinating. The boys and girls who lived back of the yards had a unique province to explore, and their most popular game, hide-and-seek, was a game of exploration and discovery. Variations abounded. Someone kicked a can, and the child who was "it" chased it while everyone hid. Paul J.'s friends called it "oley-oley olsen free," which was the cry uttered when someone reached home base safely. Whatever it was called, the rules were basically the same and the youngsters played it well into their teens. Ted P. even hid on roofs when necessary and continued playing until he was seventeen. His final plaintive lament, "I didn't want to quit that game," captured a generation's entertainment.[6]

In Back of the Yards, as in many other urban areas, recreation sometimes involved the whole family, or even much larger groups, thus reinforcing the social networks that bound and protected. Anne H. preferred to stay home evenings, where her father played the violin and everyone danced. Michael D. recalled that his Slovak countrymen "enjoyed their songs and their dances." Anthony W. remembered that accordions were popular throughout the neighborhood.[7]

Picnics were often sponsored by churches to raise funds. Before the turn of the century, Germans from St. Augustine Parish used Oswald Grove at 52nd Street and Halsted Street. The crowd of revelers marched down the roads led by a brass band and followed by Mr. Hough "with a heavy wagonload of delicatessen." In 1898, however, there was a masquerade party at the Grove, and someone informed Father Symphorian, the stern pastor, about it. At next Sunday's sermon he thundered, "My God, what have we come to?" and forbade such amusements. Not until 1934 did St. Augustine sponsor another picnic, and then two thousand people turned out.[8]

The Lithuanians also celebrated. Holy Cross sponsored regular expeditions to Vytautus Park, behind St. Casimir Cemetary, the

Lithuanian resting place. There again, the fundamental components of the workers' world—family, church, and ethnicity—guided the youth even in recreation. For children there were games, sports, and carnival food. One game was played with Lithuanian candies: the vendor picked up a handful and the child guessed if the number of pieces was even or odd. If correct, the youth received them gratis; if wrong, the parents had to pay.[9]

Another form of entertainment, and part of the cultural scene in immigrant communities across the urban United States, was the local ethnic theatre. New York's Yiddish theatre was the outstanding example and has been the subject of historian's scrutiny, but scholars have relatively ignored the productions of other groups in other cities. In fact, drama was a standard form of recreation in most immigrant neighborhoods. Schumacher's, a movie house at 46th Street and Ashland Avenue, hosted a vaudeville company that performed Polish plays. The troupe played a regular circuit of theatres on both the North and the South sides of Chicago, presenting a new play every week. Konstanty G. remembered this theatre particularly well; he played in one of the productions, possibly as the winner of an amateur contest. On Sunday evenings, the Wormser Troupe, a German company, also performed at Schumacher's. A block north sat the Davis Square Theatre, where for a nickel the patron watched a silent movie and a one or two-act play in Polish.[10]

Theatre was not restricted to professional performances by any means. Ann P., for example, at the age of ten used to assemble her friends and go to empty sheds. There they invented plays, sewed costumes, and built props. For publicity, or sometimes just for fun, they paraded down the street singing songs. When a suitable crowd had gathered, the youngsters collected 2¢ from each person and then performed.[11]

Every church also put on plays and sponsored theatre guilds and clubs. As early as 1894, St. Augustine built a stage in the parish hall and continued to put on shows at least through the 1940s. St. Rose of Lima had a Dramatic Club, which in 1924 produced, among other plays, *The Bells of Shannon*. St. Mary's mounted *The Old Country Spindle* in 1937 and had dancing afterward; Holy Cross had an Actors Guild; Sacred Heart had a dramatic circle; and the St. Michael's Young Men's Club put on regular productions in Slovak and English, including a version of *Uncle Tom's Cabin* with verse and melody that Father Ambrose Ondrak, assistant pastor, described as "a musical monstrosity in five spasms." Little children performed for their parents at Community Methodist Church and at St. Augustine. The Slovak church organized the St. Michael's Actors Guild, consisting exclusively of young people who acted in everything from brief skits to three-act plays.[12]

Another, often overlooked form of recreation was the library. Back of the Yards and other immigrant neighborhoods never acquired a reputation for scholary pursuits, but literacy was far higher than most reformers assumed. The Immigration Commission found that 71 percent of the Russian-born males in the meat-packing plants could read and write, as could 75 percent of the Lithuanians, 80 percent of the Poles, and 88 percent of the Slovaks.[13]

The neighborhood did, in fact, contain a number of collections of books. The first libraries were established privately, to serve ethnic groups. St. Augustine's library opened in 1877: by 1893 it owned several hundred German and twenty-five English books; by 1910 it had one thousand German and four hundred English volumes, and in 1912 Brother Aloysius started a card-catalog system. By 1935, the atheneum had 5,413 books, only 1,141 of which were in German, and 4,272 in English.

Sixteen Polish societies organized the Julius Slowacki Library in 1902 at 48th Street and Paulina Avenue, across the street from St. Joseph. They used the upstairs rooms for choir practice, five groups alternating their use of the space; downstairs they installed the library, only thirty books at first, but eventually three thousand, all in Polish. The books were there for student and worker alike; the *Golden Jubilee* book declared, "With faith that a good book is the best friend, that in reading and study of the beautiful Polish literature, in which we do not take second place to any other nation, we may find joy and satisfaction." Lithuanians formed the Aurora Society in 1912, with a lending library of books and newspapers, a bookstore, and classes five nights a week in a variety of subjects. Public libraries also existed in each of the three parks as early as 1911. The combined total of their books in 1935 was 11,381, and they served 153,318 people annually.[14]

Recreation was only part of a child's life, however. Parents did not allow their children to spend most of their time unsupervised. Since factory work restricted adults' free time, they sought proxy parents in the school, usually the one run by the church. Thus, the school was one of the primary institutions of control of the child's life.

Along with home life, school was the core of the child's upbringing. Social workers believed that education was less important in the immigrants' home than the need for jobs and income, but this opinion was of limited accuracy, in part because school-age children were too young to find work anyway. In most houses, schooling was considered all-important. Stephen S., for example, said of attending school, "that was a must . . . No way you could get out of it." As Timothy Smith explained, "Immigrant familes showed as much or more zeal for education as those in which the parents were native Americans."[15]

The immigrants' belief in schooling stemmed from many sources, but the most basic one was a fundamental idea of how children should be raised. Children were the hope of the future and the pride of a family—as Monsignor Edward Plawinski stated, "They loved the children . . . You couldn't do anything to hurt the children." True, these were not "model" parents. They permitted activities that were detrimental to a healthy upbringing and they ignored threatening situations—in part because of their own hardships and in part because of ignorance, but mostly because they believed that, to grow strong and healthy and righteous, a child needed two things in abundance and little else. One was plenty of hearty, heavy meals, just like those in the old country. The other was a firm training in morality and proper social conduct. In Europe, where the social environment of the family was richly structured, these values were easily taught and absorbed. In the United States, parents turned to the schools to help instill basic rules, ways of life, moral concepts, and proper social patterns in their children. Every child, therefore, attended classes. Failure to do so meant failure in life, the possibility of a future of sin, wrongdoing, or indigence. Thus, as the interviewee asserted, "*everyone* had to go to school."[16]

At the same time, there was economic pressure to keep children out of classes. Wages in the packinghouse were insufficient and child labor could supplement a family's income. The concept of ethical training could not totally supplant this, but did act as a powerful force resisting youthful employment. Most of the children went to school.

One offshoot of the immigrant's concept of schooling as moral training was equality of education for boys and girls. Researchers in the Progressive Era, concerned only with the economics of assimilation, concluded that since girls got married anyway, immigrant parents belittled their need for education. Louise Montgomery wrote that "the fundamental idea that the education of the girl is of much less importance than the education of the boy is accepted without question in all of the . . . families." She was wrong, because parents viewed the school's functions as moral as well as economic. If the teacher's job was to see that every pupil started life on the proper road, both boys and girls needed that kind of basic training, at least in their early years.[17]

Statistics support the reality of this equality. The best local Catholic school records came from the three Polish churches in the neighborhood, where Felician nuns kept meticulous records. Two of these institutions, St. Joseph and St. John of God, permitted access to their archives. Five public grammar schools served the neighborhood as well: Fulton, Hamline, Hedges, Libby, and Seward. The records of all these schools show that males and females attended in roughly equal numbers. (See table 1).

A few observations are in order. First, there was considerably less pressure to finish school than to attend it. Schooling usually ended when the child was confirmed at about twelve to fourteen years, or with the receipt of a grammar-school diploma. Second, though the figures are roughly equivalent, there were usually slightly more females, because boys could earn an adult's income earlier in one of the many jobs that merely required brawn. Girls required advanced training, such as commercial courses, to make a living wage. Genevieve N.'s father, for example, finally accepted the idea of educating females when her sister started writing rent receipts for the tenants of the upstairs flats. Boys also had stronger needs for spending money than girls. Though both sexes prized their independence and their ability to buy themselves treats and nice things, boys of dating age were expected to pay for both themselves and their dates.[18]

A final note on general concepts of schooling has to do with U.S. law and culture. In this country, unlike Europe, schools were not only available, but attendance was judicially enforced. The American ethos, which immigrants quickly accepted, was that school was the road to achievement. Any parent who adopted these values, and most did before they ever saw Ellis Island, could do no less than ensure an education for all their family.

John Powers wrote, in *The Last Catholic in America*, that when he grew up "there were two major religions in the world, Catholic and 'Public.'" In Back of the Yards, however, school was most often a parochial institution. Every church, Catholic or otherwise, had its own school. Usually the building for learning went up at the same time as the religious center, or they were one and the same. When the parish or congregation could not afford a school, religious instruction was conducted after public school hours or on Sunday. One study of 900 families in Back of the Yards in 1913 found that 805, or

Table 1. Proportion of Male and Female Students in Graduating Classes in Grammar Schools in Back of the Yards, 1911–40

	St. Joseph		
Year	No. of Students	% of Males	% of Females
1911–15	108	46.3	53.7
1916–20	207	44.4	55.6
1921–25	253	49.4	50.6
1926–30	550	50.0	50.0
1931–35	789	46.8	53.2
1936–40	836	47.0	53.0

	St. John of God		
Year	No. of Students	% of Males	% of Females
1911–15	113	47.8	52.2
1916–20	100	36.0	64.0
1921–25	221	51.1	48.9
1926–30	209	48.3	51.7
1931–35	385	47.0	53.0
1936–40	785	46.9	53.1

	Public Schools		
Year	No. of Students	% of Males	% of Females
1911–15	919	49.0	51.0
1916–20	836	48.9	51.1
1921–25	1,321	48.4	51.6
1926–30	2,236	47.6	52.4
1931–35	2,442	46.3	53.7
1936–40	1,718	47.6	52.4

Notes: All figures are for eighth-grade classes. September enrollments were used for parochial schools. No figures were available from St. John of God for 1917, 1927, and 1928.

Sources: St. Joseph and St. John of God school records; and list of admissions to the High School Department, *The Proceedings of the Board of Education, City of Chicago.*

89 percent, preferred parochial schools for at least part of a child's training. Monsignor Edward Plawinski's statement that "the public school had no show in a Polish neighborhood," seems accurate.[19]

There were many reasons why the residents of Back of the Yards and other immigrant neighborhoods preferred religious schools. Foremost was the moral criterion: if the primary job of education was to teach righteousness, what better place was there than church? Joseph T. declared, "In Europe they were only taught two things—religion and hard work." The church school, residents felt, imparted these values best. This was especially important in the immigrants' unsettled environment, where there was so much more temptation to immorality and parents exercised far less control than in the close-knit world of the peasant farm. St. Augustine's *Pfarbotte* ("Parish Messenger"), the parish bulletin, for example, described a mother's proper attitude towards education: "because she realizes that only there, in a thoroughly Catholic atmosphere can the child be brought up and educated as a Catholic should be, in the knowledge and love of God, as well as in learning. Because she realizes that in other schools there is danger for the child, danger poisoning the mind and soul." And Phyllis H. observed, "What you put in a child's mind when they're small, it stays there." For that reason it was essential that they "got that Catholic start."[20]

According to this view, church academies also had the finest possible teachers, the nuns. "The Sister is a living example of living for Christ and His Church," according to Holy Cross church. "No sermon can preach what her presence in the classroom teaches, day in and day out, year after year. A Catholic boy and girl may forget the geography or history that Sister taught, but all during their life they will not forget the good sister who taught them."[21]

Parents supported this system because they accepted the moral legitimacy and authority of the church. This reassured the parents and helped them adjust to life in the industrial city. Working parents, for example, could not come to school when the trip meant sacrificing a day's wages, so they relied on the nuns. Always they hoped for the best for their children, but they never forgot the economic realities. Ann P.'s mother told her, "I paid for school and I want you to get the education. Don't bring me troubles"—especially those that resulted in loss of pay at the factory. The rigor of the nuns also ensured "the proper upbringing," which meant knowledge of morality—respect for property, authority, and persons. Finally, both parents and children alike were in the midst of deep adjustments, with many fundamental patterns uprooted. They sought anchors for their lives; in this situation the notion of a basic rule of God, enforced by His handmaidens, had a strong appeal.[22]

Another reason to prefer a church school was the formal religious education it offered. Even if the parents did not want their children immersed in a completely religious environment, youth had to be prepared for rituals like communion and confirmation. Thus, before St. Mary's built its school, the cantor conducted catechism classes. Joseph G. called it "school after school," because he went every day after leaving public school. The parents felt this separation to be improper and inconvenient, and they supported the religious schools.[23]

Religious institutions, run by local parishes and intensely concerned with maintaining their ethnicity, also transmitted the group's heritage. Each school taught the language, history, and particular religious ritual of the immigrant group it served, sometimes to the detriment of the classes taught in English. The staff of the school came from appropriate religious orders. Polish institutions were staffed by nuns from the Sisters of St. Felix, or Felicians, an order founded in Warsaw in 1855. The Sisters of St. Casimir, a Lithuanian order, claimed in their official history that their founding brought "a new era in Lithuanian education; here were religious teachers of their race, women who knew their customs and language." Parents viewed this arrangement as the best way of ensuring children's ties to their background, to the old country, and to the immediate family. It also mitigated the terrible generational conflict that separated immigrant's parents and their native-born children, by tying youngsters to the culture, heritage, and language of their elders. Parents fought any attempt to dilute nationalism. A catechism used at SS. Cyril and Methodius school had pages both in Bohemian and in English; this, the parents decided, made it far too easy for their children to ignore the language of their ancestors, and they asked for a version strictly in Bohemian. Further evidence of the importance of ethnicity came from the paths students took to school. Children who had to attend a Catholic school often passed several others located closer to home, on the way to their own group's building. Evelyn Ostrowski, for example, a Pole, walked right past SS. Cyril and Methodius, a Bohemian church and school, every morning on her way to St. Joseph. A few rebellious parents took their children out of ethnic institutions rather than force them to learn a language besides English. St. Rose of Lima, an Irish parish, reaped the benefits of these protests, but every student had to attend classes in Irish history.[24]

Such ethnic provincialism created many problems. The need for priests and sisters of specific nationalities drained and often exceeded the resources of the religious orders. Classes stayed crowded, however, if the alternative was to permit someone from a different branch of the church to teach in an ethnic school. Coordination of facilities was impossible; when the national origin of the population shifted, old schools were emptied while immigrant children jammed new ones.

Facilities in the parish school were often poor and overcrowding was common. St. Michael's school, for example, began in a basement in 1902 with eighty-two pupils. For the next seven years the organist, Thomas Griglak, and two sisters taught the progeny of a swelling Slovak population in two classrooms. Even after a twelve-room school building opened in 1909, there were still fifty-to-sixty students in a class, and there were years when the students went only half-days. Louis P., a Pole from St. John of God, remembered classes as large as eighty or ninety, and two or three students jammed into one seat. Worst was the catechism class at St. Mary's, taught by the cantor in Old Slavonic. There was only one room, so each year the older students had to listen to newcomers reciting lessons they had been hearing for years.[25]

Life in the classroom was a combination of religion, scholarship, discipline, and ethnicity. A typical list of subjects from the Record Book of St. Joseph School, Fall 1913, follows:

Religion	Spelling
History	History of Poland
Polish Reading	History of the Church
English Reading	Geography
Polish Grammar	Dictation
English Grammar	

Thus, of eleven subjects, two were in religion and three in Polish culture. Grading was via a standard report card, signed by parents. When nuns at St. Michael's school prepared their students' report cards, they marked any grade of 100 in gold ink, 99 to passing in black, and failures in red.[26]

Though religion appeared only briefly on the course sheets, it played an enormous role in the child's school day, since this was considered the core of the child's education in morality. Every morning began with Mass in church. Each class sat as a section, girls in the front pews and boys in the next rows, where the sister seated right behind them could watch them. Boys were considered unruly. After Mass, there were prayers in the classroom, and later in the day, sessions in hymn singing. Every day there was at least one section of catechism, taught by a priest and, in some schools, there was Bible study as well. The sessions drilled the church's beliefs and rules into every youngster's mind—translations of the Baltimore catechism were used—shaping the children's outlook in fundamental ways and affecting the way they observed and dealt with the world. It was many years before some of them questioned any of this teaching. Charles H., for example, was enjoying an omelet in a restaurant one Friday, when he heard a customer order steak, breaking the rule against eating meat that day. Charles was sure God would strike the man dead. He waited for him to keel over, then followed him out the door, dumbfounded that the sinner still walked.[27]

Various methods were used to reinforce religious beliefs. Pressure to follow the religious path was exerted at weekly confession. Ted P. confessed to a zealous priest who "wouldn't let you out of that confessional. He would lecture you and lecture you and lecture you." When you left the booth "your face would be red as a beet and everybody in the church knew you really got it off of him, you were really a sinner." Another way was to emphasize the omnipotence of God and His ministers. Nuns at St. Augustine told Colette D. that the priests in the bell tower could see everything that went on in the neighborhood. John Powers, in *The Last Catholic in America*, quoted one of his teachers: "you may be able to fool your parents . . . and sometimes even the good sisters. But never God. He is everywhere. He sees everything. He hears everything. No matter where you go God is watching you," a situation Powers described as "God's constant surveillance." Another method was fear. Children learned the horrors of sin and that a wayward path led automatically to Lucifer. Sue N. claimed, "we had fear instilled in us," and Stanley K. explained, "they had you dead [ready to go to hell] at eight."[28]

The first instructor in these schools was usually "a poorly trained organist . . . with the pastor giving catechetical instructions." This was true at many parochial schools, including St. Michael, Nativity BVM, and Holy Cross, but in time teaching became the sole domain of the sisters, every nationality represented by a different order. The symbol of parochial education was, and remained, a nun.[29]

The record these women left was a mixed one. Originally, they were untrained, unqualified, and too few for the mammoth job facing them. It was many years before even the majority of nuns received formal certification. In the 1920s, a researcher studying the Polish Roman Catholic schools in Chicago reported that the Felicians were ill-prepared and that the Sisters of the Resurrection did "poor" work. On the other hand, despite immense difficulties and with little power to improve conditions, faced with large classes and underfed children, they provided the majority of their students with an adequate education. Immigrants themselves, the sisters experienced the same traumas and crises of adjustment as their kinspeople. Some cracked under the strain, such as the nun who locked Ted Ostrowski in a darkened cellar as punishment. Others rose to the challenge. Sister Mary V. began work at fourteen, but the nuns at St. Michael's took her in and fed and educated her. She recalled that, "they took such delight to teach me." That was the spirit, the light that every teacher searched for. As in every group of teachers, only some of the religious found it.[30]

Above all, the nuns enforced discipline, an ultimate form of control. Ted P., reliving his days at St. John of God, reported that "if you stepped out of line, if you breathed too hard when a sister was talking . . . she'd come over and whack you." If you read the wrong book you went to the back of the room or stood in the corner. If homework was wrong, you redid it many times or got extra assignments: the work could not be entered on their regular homework paper, so students begged butcher paper from meat markets. On the rare and horrible occasion that a sister sent a note to the parents, it often went by some other student to guarantee arrival. The sisters were remembered, however, mostly for the corporal punishment they meted out. Individuals or even the whole class had to stick out their hands and get hit on the palm with ruler or pointer, a sting Stanley K. described as "quite a sharp feeling." There were more serious offenses and more serious punishments, too. Ted P. claimed, for example, that "if you missed Mass on Sunday and the nuns found out, that was unforgiveable. They'd kill you. You couldn't live through that." Other interviewees supported this contention, providing specific details such as ten lashes from a leather strap on the hand.[31]

Almost everyone involved in this exercise of authority supported it. The priests backed the sisters and cautioned parents, "Do not criticize the teachers or school at all within the child's hearing." Parents agreed that the nuns' power as their proxies was absolute. To bring school problems home "would have been the silliest thing," according to Evelyn Ostrowski and others. Your parents gave you twice what the nuns did for getting out of line and, as Stanley K. pointed out, "it was always better to get one instead of two." Even the students felt that the punishment administered by the sisters was for their own good and it helped to strengthen their character. Anthony W., a self-educated scientist who got into trouble for reading a book on radios at the wrong time while at St. Joseph's, said fervently, "I thank God and thank those nuns today that the strictness has taught me a lesson . . . throughout life," adding, "A little pain'll make you think." Thus, Catholic schools earned a reputation for being better than public schools because they "pushed" students more, got more from them, and were generally stricter.[32]

The students' major goals, besides the diploma and a life of virtue and probity, were the ceremonies of Holy Communion and Confirmation. Confirmation was the final sealing of the convenant with God begun at baptism, plus a rite of puberty similar to the Jewish bar mitzvah. Celebrated by a bishop or higher official of the church, it came after First Holy Communion, the exact date depending on the schedule of the archdiocese's leadership. First Holy Communion was the more important rite for celebrant, relatives, and community. Father Vito Vikolaitis described this occasion, when the child partook of the sacrament of the Mass for the first time, "as a grand and glorious day for the whole family." Girls wore "the most beautiful white dress they could afford," with a white veil, and boys acquired a dark suit, white shirt, and tie. Family and godparents attended the church ceremony and the parents gave a big party afterward. Someone with a camera would snap pictures, or else the child went to a commercial photographer who provided souvenirs and something to send back to the old country.[33]

The alternative education was in the public school. Some children began with public schools and never attended Catholic school except for after-school religious classes. Parochial schools cost money and public schools were free, and this decided the matter for some families. Raymond K., for example, did not attend Catholic school because "we didn't have no money." Some children attended Catholic school until their confirmation, then were transferred to a public school for the last years of grammar school, to save money. And some parents withdrew their children from the nuns' care after an incident, as Lillian K.'s folks did when a sister inflicted a bloody nose; but such action was relatively rare.[34]

Parochial and public education were broadly similar. Some of the course work—basic subjects like math, reading, history and penmanship—was the same. The teaching methods were also similar. There was great reliance on corporal punishment and discipline. The quality of the instruction varied along the same lines, as well, many public school instructors being old and crabby men and women. Mary S., long an assistant principal at Fulton School, said that most of the teachers there were "older than my mother" when she took up her post. An occasional public school teacher was remembered with gratitude. Genevieve N.'s brother in his last year of grammar school developed an enlarged heart and died shortly after. His teacher came to the house, always with a fruit wrapped in gold or silver paper, brought his homework, and helped him study. She promised the family the young man would graduate, and he did.[35]

There were big differences, as well as similarities, between the public and the Catholic schools. In public schools, the children had to serve as interpreters between their teacher and their immigrant parents, projecting the youngsters into a position of unusual responsibility and providing them with an opportunity to use poetic license in their own behalf.[36]

The major difference was in motivation. Over and over, social workers found that students were leaving public schools because they taught useless skills and course material irrelevant to the world outside. In one Back of the Yards study, a researcher asked two hundred working girls, "What did you learn in school that has helped you to earn a living?" Half answered, "Nothing." A considerable portion of the older girls did, however, give some credit to school discipline. The church schools faced the problem of motivation to a much lesser degree. Their courses were no more relevant, but they compelled learning on the grounds that God willed it and that any failure to learn was a sin. One Chicago youngster informed an interviewer, Helen Todd, that "[Public] school ain't no good. The Holy Father he can send ye to hell and the boss he can take away yer job or cut yer pay. The teacher she can't do nothing."[37]

How much education a child received depended, more than anything else, on the family's income. In most families, after confirmation or graduation from grammar school, a child was a young adult, capable of earning a living. Youngsters viewed the event with mixed emotions. Work was movement from the child's world, a jump into the life of an older person. It meant an income, status, an end to the familiar control of school and nun, a life outside the home. On the other hand, it was also the start of a life of toil, the acceptance of the packers' authority and, often, entrance into a blind alley in which one found one's occupation and even one's employer.

There were several ways to find that first job. One was to look for notices in stores and factories; another, to make written application to businesses. Parents often helped. The parents of William B.'s mother, for example, paid a notary public to sign a form verifying that she was old enough to work, although she was only eleven. She first got a job as a cash-girl at a department store, carrying money to different registers, then worked at Hart Schaffner & Marx sewing buttonholes into suits. "Connections," someone to put in a good word for you, also helped. Joseph G.'s uncle took him to one of the outdoor railroad workshops that the packers operated for their refrigerated cars and other rolling stock. The lad preferred indoor work and left after a few hours. When his uncle found out, he "raised hell," yelling, "Here I had to go into the office and plead with the boss to get you a job and you pull off a stunt like that." Joseph returned and stayed for forty-five years.[38]

These youngsters who were assuming adult responsibilities generally found jobs in factories where brawn counted far more than brains. In one study of 560 youths between fourteen and eighteen, only 35 had skilled jobs; of these, 13 worked in dressmaking and millinery establishments and the rest were apprentices. A similar study of first jobs found that, of 86 girls, 52 started in factories and 9 in department stores; of 131 boys, 51 began as errand boys, 26 as factory workers, and 15 as messengers. Some of this work was in the slaughterhouse; in 1900 just over 2 percent of all employees were younger than sixteen. Other kinds of work were of the sort described by Anne J., whose first job, as a fourteen-year-old, was at Kirk's Soap House, where she "put the shine on the bar of soap"— that is, buffed it—for $3 a week.[39]

Three dollars a week was fairly standard pay. The average wage of the 86 girls surveyed in the study just mentioned was $3.61 a week. Schooling did not necessarily help. Though the researchers disagreed on this point, they accumulated enough evidence to bring into question the notion that a grade school diploma meant higher pay for its possessor. Ernest Talbert, for example, found in 1912 that "a longer stay in the elementary school does not help financially," and that "on the whole . . . a higher grade and a greater age do not guarantee better positions and better wages." Only a high school diploma enabled one to escape the back-breaking jobs. Without it, a year or two more of schooling made little difference; with eight years of grammar school, it was almost as difficult to become a skilled laborer as with six.[40]

The lucky ones were those able to go on to high school, either a four-year institution or a two-year business course. According to Monsignor Plawinski, the only ones who sought work outside the neighborhood—a move of great independence—had a high school education, and they looked down on their less-advantaged peers.

1
St. Michael Church (Slovak)
Courtesy of Joseph B. Meegan

2

Pauline Gelatka, Maid of Honor, and Bill Novorolsky, Best Man,
1917. A year later they were married.
Courtesy of Joseph Gelatka

3

Slovak Bride and Groom
Courtesy of Joseph Gelatka

4
Priests of Back of the Yards
Courtesy of Back of the Yards Neighborhood Council

5
The Gelatka Sisters, Catherine and June, at
Their First Holy Communion, 1922
Courtesy of Joseph Gelatka

6
First Holy Communion, 1916
Courtesy of Joseph Gelatka

7

Graduation at Hedges School, a public grammar school, 1925
Courtesy of Sue A. Nemec

8

Graduation at St. Michael's Grammar School, 1930
Courtesy of Sue A. Nemec

9

Wake in Home in Back of the Yards

Courtesy of George A. Becvar

The ultimate status came from a job downtown: "that was class." There were two-year commercial high schools in the neighborhood. One, at St. Augustine, was founded in 1910 and became a four-year institution in 1940. Another was at St. Michael. Its curriculum was:

First Year	*Second Year*
Religion I	Religion II
English I	English II
Shorthand I	Shorthand II
Typing I	Typing II
General Mathematics	Civics I (Semester I)
Vocational Guidance (Semester I)	Bookkeeping II (Double Period)
Bookkeeping I (Semester I)	Physical Education
General Science	Secretarial Studies (Semester II)
Physical Education	

The local public high schools were Tilden, founded in 1889 and rebuilt in 1905, and Lindblom, which opened in 1919. Attendance at any of these schools, parochial and public alike, was determined by sex. Parents believed business courses the proper training for girls; the four-year diploma, considered career training, tended to be a male prerogative. Thus, St. Augustine, a two-year course, began with a class of six girls and no boys. At Tilden, on the other hand, males predominated; when, in 1920, it became a technical school, only boys attended. Males were also in the majority at Lindblom. Similarly, the graduating class at Tilden in 1914 had thirty men and fourteen women; but the two-year course still operated by the school at that time sent out nine men and nineteen women to a life in business.[41]

Enrollment in these schools meant a lively existence. The students were special, out of the ordinary, and they knew it. Their chances to succeed were better than most of the friends they grew up with, and they would soon move on to a different rank in society. As a result, they had plenty of school spirit. Nicknames abounded and descriptive comments were conferred on seniors in the schools' yearbook. There were jokes at the teachers' expense also: the May

1920 Lindblom *Eagle* contained some favorite remarks such as Mr. Boulin's, "Why aren't you in your division room?" and Miss Francis's, "Every lip still now." Entering youngest students were the butt of pranks, purchasing such goods as steam-heated and refrigerated lockers, study hall seats, and passes for nonexistent elevators.

The other factor that tied students to the school were the clubs. Typically, Anna Belle Boyd, nicknamed "Migs" by her classmates at Tilden High School, was a member of the Dramatic Club and Senior Girls Club, and served as Toastmistress of Football Championship Spread in 1914. There were choirs, debating teams, Camp Fire Girls, and Societas Latina. In 1920, the Lindblom *Yearbook* listed eighteen student organizations.[42]

Most teen-age recreation in Back of the Yards, however, and throughout Chicago, was in the neighborhood. Particularly important were sports: local teams played basketball, football, soccer, and especially baseball on fields and streets all over the neighborhood.

Sports were dominated by the social-athletic club, or SAC. There were dozens of these: the Larks, the Wigwams, the Mundanes, the Robeys, the Incas, the Settlement Feds, and many others. When the *Town of Lake Journal* organized a Council of Clubs in 1937, thirty-six societies joined. Some of these local fraternities started as social clubs, and turned into street gangs. The Regan Colts of Bridgeport, for example, were a gang, and a group known as the Hearts, probably because they came from the Polish Sacred Heart Church, became the terror of Lithuanian students at nearby Holy Cross.[43]

Most of the groups, however, were exactly what SAC implied, an association for cameraderie and sports. The clubs gave their teen-age members a place to go and, moreover, a place where they made all the rules themselves. John D. remembered, "I would come home from work and I'd go over to the Club [St. Michael Young Men's Club] . . . You always got something to do." The Lemars, a typical club, had about seventy members in its heyday. The member's dues of 75¢ a month paid the rent of $8 a month for a clubhouse equipped with punching bags, wrestling mats, boxing gloves, weights, card tables, and a phonograph. The name, like all of the teams' names, had its own unique origin. Joseph T., one of the founders, chanced on Lemar, Colorado, in his reading, though it catchy and colorful, and his fellows agreed. The University of Chicago Settlement House sponsored the Settlement Feds, and over at St. Mary's, a Rusin church, everyone joined the Tyrones, since many parishioners had once lived in Tyrone, Pennsylvania. The Tyrones functioned as a sports team, maintained a clubhouse, and held picnics for which they rented a truck, put people, food, ice, and a couple of barrels of beer aboard, and drove to Cedar Lake.[44]

Many other teams were financed by William Fuka, who opened Fuka Men's Clothing in 1923. Promoting teams was good business, because loyalty required that members shop exclusively at his store. This relationship was also a stabilizing social influence, because it tied young men to local institutions. Whatever his reasons, Fuka's devotion to sports was fanatical. He sponsored a football team that won the Interstate Championship, a baseball team, boys and girls basketball teams, several bowling leagues (including the Fuka Pilgrims and Fuka Pequods teams), the Fuka Bullets softball team, the Fuka Boosters Athletic Club, and the Fuka Boosters Ladies Auxiliary.[45]

Another favorite activity was going to the movies, or "to the show," as Chicagoans said. "Movies were the thing," Bruno N. remembered. The family responsible for bringing movies to Back of the Yards was the Schoenstadts, father Herman and sons Arthur and Henry. Herman met the owner of a Loop theatre in 1907, and the entrepreneur urged him to enter the trade. A year later, someone else opened the Little Ashland Theatre, just south of 47th Street. Father Schoenstadt saw the customers filing in and watched the owner collect money without working. "Would you believe it if you didn't see it?" he mused. Moving two blocks south, he took a ten-year lease on two large vacant stores and on Easter Sunday 1908 opened the Palace Theatre. It was a grand emporium, with padded chairs for two hundred and fifty patrons, a pitched floor, smoking rooms, spitoons—and he provided piano-roll music and vaudeville acts as well as movies.[46]

Schoenstadt had competitors. The owner of Guinea's movie theatre, at 47th Street and Ashland Avenue—admission was 5¢ at all the movie theatres—used to stand outside and ask kids walking by how much money they had. Even if they had only 2¢ or 3¢ he said "Gimme it" and let them in. Another hall, on Winchester Avenue, earned the nickname "Dumps" because, as Stanley K. explained, that was the proper description. People brought bag lunches and ate during the show: "All you heard was crackling of papers and everything like that," but apparently everyone had a grand time.[47]

The programs were extravaganzas, even by modern standards. Typical fare included a two-reel feature, a live comedy team, and a vaudeville show. Later there were also newsreels and, on Saturday, a serial. Friday-night audiences witnessed amateur talent competitions: the losers got the "hook," the winners a part in next week's performance. Between reels of the silent films, the projectionist showed slides with messages like "Don't Spit on the Floor" or "Ladies Take Your Hats off" while he changed the reel of film. Next to him, an assistant with a crank-operated machine rewound the previous reel.[48]

The programs sometimes seemed addressed to two different audiences. In 1939, the Olympia Theatre showed *Scouts to the Rescue*, starring Jackie Cooper and advertised as offering "adventure . . . thrills . . . breathtaking exploits by daring Boy Scouts." On the same bill was *Dark Rapture*, produced by Armand Denis of *Goona Goona* fame, offering "Secret Rituals! Signalling manhood of forest boys! and, "Men Welcoming Flogging! Subjecting themselves to punishing agony to win female esteem!"[49]

On rare occasions, a film was shown "for adults only." The audience consisted mostly of young men who hoped that "this is going to be something." One such film showed a woman in her bedroom, the camera focused on the mirror so the audience saw her reflection clearly. When she undressed down to her bra and panties, the finale of the act, everybody in the theatre went "Oooh, ooh . . . You'd think it was really something. And that was for adults only," Ted P. recalled.[50]

The most important type of recreation, however, was dancing. In the dance hall, the young acted independently to find a spouse. In consequence, dance halls dotted the neighborhood. Every tavern had a hall behind it where dances called shindigs competed with weddings and other parties for open evenings. Local high schools, including Tilden and Lindblom, also opened their doors for dancing from 6:45 P.M. to midnight. Admission was 10¢, which included a lesson for those in need of training. Churches also sponsored dances, including St. Rose of Lima, whose hall became the Rose Ballroom for the night. Those who sought a larger stage and more elegant trappings made an easy trip to White City, a combination amusement park and dance hall, or to the Trianon on the South Side or the Aragon on the North. The Trianon, which opened in 1922, was a project of the Karzas brothers, Greek immigrants who made a fortune in the movie business. It was palatial: imported tapestries and chairs upholstered in brocaded velvet decorated the lobby and Corinthian marble columns lined the sides of the dance floor, which measured 100×140 feet. Colored lights illuminated the blue cobalt ceiling, boxes draped with velvet accommodated observers, and rest and refreshment were available in the tea room, which seated 560 people. Its cost was estimated at up to $1,200,000.[51]

Most of the dances in Back of the Yards, however, were sponsored by the clubs, further evidence that youth controlled this part of their transition to adulthood. Every SAC had a fund-raising dance at least once a year. The club rented a hall for the evening and hired a five or six-piece band. The members acted as hosts, as bartenders if drinking was permitted, and did anything else necessary. They handled all the arrangements and all the finances. Indeed, these dances were remarkable displays of organizational ability, independence, and business acumen, far superior to the Junior Achievement programs for middle-class youths. Clubs had reciprocal arrangements: if your members went to their dance, their members came to yours. Some clubs had rules governing attendance—the Lemars, for example, fined any absent member and collected 50¢ from each member before entering the hall. The fees were deposited at the bar as a lump sum to pay for drinks. Even when they did not go as a club, teens usually went in groups, the local crowd traveling together.[52]

There were various traditions at these dances, all originated by the participants. At some halls, when the members of a club entered as a body, the band leader announced their arrival from the stage and they marched around the perimeter of the dance floor. If a young man brought a date, he expected every member of his club to treat her with respect. At some of the more formal dances, girls had dance cards. Local celebrities emerged, such as Vince Mack, who did a dance called the Frisco. There were also fistfights, mostly over a female, usually in the alley behind the hall. Sometimes, however, whole clubs clashed and turned the event into chaos, a spectacle fondly recalled by Joseph T., a scraper who observed, "We used to have some good battles."[53]

One wore Sunday clothes to the dances. The required attire for men was a suit, usually dark; a crisply starched shirt, usually white; and a tie. Frances W. warmly remembered of her male companions that, when "they went out on a date they were *dressed*." The women wore dresses or skirts and blouses, again usually dark, and those who could afford them wore a hat and gloves. Most dresses were cotton, but the more affluent women sported silk. Preparation for these dates was long and sometimes arduous. For an early form of the permanent wave, mothers rolled their daughters' wet hair around a column of paper, much like the roller used years later. One-inch strips were torn from bedsheets and tied through the paper and around the hair; when the hair dried, the fabric and paper came out, leaving a head of curls.[54]

The entire community turned out for these dances. One study of the Back of the Yards in 1913 found that 75 percent of the sixteen-to-twenty-four-year-old females went to public dances, "where there is practically no supervision." The older people attended local celebrations behind the taverns, but the youngsters went to every possible ball. Paul J. danced two or three nights a week from the age of nineteen to twenty-nine, and Stanley K. claimed, "I danced seven days a week." Mary M , who spent her early years learning how to cope with hunger on a European farm, said of her new life in the United States, "I have to dance because I am no good if I don't . . . it's best for your mind."[55]

The dance hall was the most popular place to meet potential mates, but courtship patterns were in flux. In Europe, family and village ties, short courtships, and essential needs were stressed; in the United States, people met at dances, dated longer, and chose as a spouse someone they loved and were attracted to. Many couples of the older generation grew up in the same village or town in Europe, including the parents of Evelyn Ostrowski, Father Vito Mikolaitis, and James T., and their courtships were brief. Ella V.'s parents, for example, met when he boarded with her mother's family. The young man chose the eldest daughter and they married after two or three dates. The bride, only sixteen, knew nothing of the facts of life and did not even realize she was pregnant until she became ill and a doctor broke the news. Ella was a premature baby, about three pounds in weight, and remembers being told that her mother was "scared to handle me."[56]

Some residents followed their parents' European patterns. Mary Z.'s father would not let her date; when she served in a girlfriend's wedding and the flower boy brought her home, her father opened the door and commanded, "Now you get out of here. I don't want to see you around here again." The husband chosen for her was a distant relative from the same village as her parents, who went to Mary's father, declared his love, and asked for her hand. At the time of the wedding, said Mary, "I really wasn't in love with him. I liked him but there was no love."[57]

The young people raised in the United States made their own matches. They dated longer and had many more opportunities to meet the opposite sex. Genevieve N.'s mother told her that sewing was the key, that she should "sit on the steps and stitch, and if a guy wants you he'll find you," but Genevieve met most of her beaus at work. Young people also met in the park or at a carnival. Church functions permitted much association with proper companions, specifically members of one's own nationality and church. Weddings were common meeting places: ushers and bridesmaids often wound up sharing their own ceremony soon after.[58]

Dating went on for six months to a year, much longer during the Depression of the 1930s. Couples went to the movies, the park, the ice-cream parlor, a show at the Settlement House, or to Riverview amusement park. Excluded from much of this activity was Genevieve N., whose mother told her "never go in a car. I never want youse in a car," although she "never told us why." Her mother's attitude reflected traditional standards: preserving a girl's reputation was a delicate business. Any hint that a girl was loose meant social ruin. Three of the surest ways to be ruined were necking or petting in public, common knowledge of loss of virginity, and dating someone of a different race.[59]

Many interviewees did their wooing at dances, the most popular date of all. Stanley K. was talking with a friend when he saw his future wife on her way home from the movie theatre called the Dumps. He decided to ask her to join them in an excursion to O'Henry Park, on the far Southwest side, to hear the featured band and to dance. He asked, "Kid, do you want to go to O'Henry Park? She says, 'no,'" he recalled, "'I wouldn't go with you because I'm not dressed.' I says 'Kid, you're good enough for me.' I says 'You're going the way you're going if you want to go, and if you don't want to go I'll never . . . dance with you or anything.' So finally I convinced her and she came with me to O'Henry Park and we danced that night and I brought her home . . . And I guess from then on that was it . . . and it's forty-nine years."[60]

Stanley's decision symbolized the goal of youth in Back of the Yards, to move into a world where one could act on one's own judgment. For all young people, this freedom embodied the transition from adolescence to maturity. In this neighborhood, though, other changes were taking place as well. Independence also meant weaning oneself from the European experience, a shift from the world of the immigrant to that of the native-born.

It also became a challenge to the packers' control. Young men and women might be treated like machines at work, but in their private lives they were free and independent spirits. The new generation created its own definitions of survival and success, altering the old ways to suit new conditions. Exercising the right to date whom one pleased was thus a big step on the path to freedom and a democratic social structure.

3

Arenas of Life:
Women and the Household

Two Women Out Shopping in Back of the Yards, 1904
Chicago Historical Society DN-960

he world of the woman was centered on the household. This was her domain, where the community granted her total control. In this world she had power and a place to devise and use creative solutions to problems, manipulating its resources so as best to perform her job—caring and providing for her family. Her movement outside was limited to visits to family, to the store, and to that extended version of the nurturing hearth, the church. In these places, women retained their social identity as head of the household, merely moving their authority to a larger stage, and the community granted them a voice and a will in these areas. When women ventured beyond, to the workplace, acceptance was tentative and freedom unattainable. Not surprisingly, the females who had the choice chose to stay where they had sovereignty, where they found the autonomy and stability that was every resident's goal.

In Back of the Yards, the event that transformed a girl into a woman was her wedding. Much care, devotion, and expense went into it. The first step was the publication of the banns of marriage at least a month before the ritual. On the morning of the wedding, the bride knelt before her parents while they blessed and prayed for her and made her an offering of bread, salt, and money. Sometimes the groom's family came over and did the same. On this day, the bride wore white and a veil; the groom wore a black suit. Weddings usually took place on Saturday afternoon; the yards closed at noon and stayed shut on Sunday, so the couple had a day off. Several couples chose the same day and time, and often more than one wedding occurred during the same service. It was one of the great events in a family's history, and memories of it and forever-retold stories provided entertainment for years.[1]

The reception took place at home or in a hall behind a tavern, depending on the family's finances. The bride's mother and sisters and her godparents or other relatives bought and prepared the food. The feast might include beef, chicken, ham, sausage, sauerkraut, boiled cabbage, soup, bread, and cake. Two crucial ingredients were music and liquor. Any true celebration must provide a physical outlet for emotions, and few outlets are as good as raising both feet and voice. "Polish people," testified one Polish woman, "dance like Indians; the more noise they make the better they feel." Alcohol also relaxed people and fostered this release of feelings. Joseph G. brought five gallons of illegal grain alcohol to his wedding in 1929. He diluted it with an equal amount of distilled water and added burnt sugar for coloring and taste, producing a local whiskey. Five

gallons of red wine were also consumed. Joseph T.'s remark, that at
weddings, "they used to drink like crazy" and "had a hell of a time"
was most accurate.[2]

Besides the eating, drinking, singing, and dancing, there were
games to raise money to pay for the wedding. The family might
supply a barrel of thick restaurant china plates, and each young man
would try to break one with a coin. If he succeeded, the family returned the money; if not, they kept it. The size of the coin varied
with the prosperity of the company. In Back of the Yards, the standard was a silver dollar, usually more than one. In another version
of the game, the guests paid for a dance with the bride. The most
common version was a combination of the two practices; the men
threw the money on a plate for the privilege of dancing with the
bride. As Stanley K. said, "when that day was over, that
bride . . . she was dead. She danced with everybody in the place, all
night . . . Some of the fellows had fifteen and twenty silver dollars
and . . . they'd throw one dollar at a time." The final ceremony,
usually at midnight, was a ritual that linked the bride to home and
children, her new spheres of social responsibility. The linkage was
stressed throughout the evening; it was common to call out, "that's
for the crib" or "that's for the cradle" when throwing the silver
dollars. After the last dance, someone, usually the bride's mother,
removed the veil and gave it to the husband. The bridesmaids put
an apron on her, perhaps with little baby dolls embroidered on it, or
handed her a broom. At Catherine I.'s wedding, they sang "Yester-
day you were a girl, now you are a woman."[3]

There were no honeymoons in those days, but a practice known
as *popraveny* (literally, "re-do" or "do over" in Polish) kept the party going for a long time. Every Slavic nationality practiced it, and
its effect was to prolong the wedding an extra day or two, sometimes even a week or more. In the old country, relatives traveled
long distances to get to the wedding, and transportation was unre-
liable. Guests might show up at any time and, to accommodate
them, the celebration sometimes continued for two to three weeks.
Besides, only a long visit could justify the difficult trip. In the
United States, the trauma of getting to the wedding faded, but
there were other reasons to continue the custom. Meeting for a day
or two after the wedding still meant a longer time with the family
and an opportunity to talk in a more relaxed atmosphere than the
charged one of the celebration. For the mother, especially, this was
important. It was a time to sit and catch up on news of the family
and to pass around stories. Another reason was to eat up any left-

over food, especially when a sizeable amount remained. Small amounts the couple might save, but ice boxes were nonexistent or tiny, and it was better to feed the extended family than throw out food. Of course, it created a raucous turmoil in the home, where bodies were piled all over and people grabbed catnaps when they could find a space. After Stanley K.'s sister's week-long wedding, he remarked, "I was so tired that I wanted to die because I didn't have any place to sleep. Everyone was sleeping in your bed, cross-wise, and everything like that."[4]

The wedding left a tired bride in charge of the household. The husband's job was to procure the necessary physical resources; the woman's was to provide emotional strength and take charge of the distribution of both food and love. Historian Leslie Tentler felt that "the mother was the more authoritative parent in many working class families and held the family together." The attitude in Back of the Yards was reflected by a girl of St. Augustine parish who wrote in 1925, "It is a woman, and only a woman, who can turn a house into a home." Marie K. averred that "everything was the child and recipes"; this, plus the church, "was our life."[5]

The life of working-class women everywhere was a career of hard work. Angeline D. mapped out her mother's weekly routine in Back of the Yards:

Monday—soaking clothes
Tuesday—wash all day long
Wednesday—clean house
Thursday—ironing
Friday—finish up all chores
Saturday—shopping, baking, cooking for Sunday meal
Sunday—recreation: meet with other women and "exchange
        hardships"

"A woman always has a million things to do," Evelyn Ostrowski's mother often said. Faced with enormous difficulties, some women could not, or else refused to, maintain their homes according to the community's standards, but most managed somehow. Mary M. "paid attention for every little bitty thing I did. . ." and women like Mrs. M. were more the rule than the exception. Nevertheless, they all felt like Catherine I., who, well past her ninetieth year, said "I was working hard all my life."[6]

The family's most important need was food, and the woman's workday began at 5 A.M. when she rose with her husband to make his lunch and cook breakfast. This meant going to the store for fresh food and then preparing a small meal—a larger one, of eggs, salt pork, potatoes, and toast if the family could afford it. Much of the other food was prepared in advance. Food was not only cooked, it was raised and processed as well. Every family, if it could, kept a garden, plus chickens, ducks, rabbits, geese, and even small pigs for slaughter. Many families ground their own sausage and made their own sauerkraut, usually by the barrelful. Each barrel held one hundred pounds, enough to last a family of six or eight through the winter. If nothing else, one could steal food from the stockyards. There were guards, so people had to sneak it out in their pockets or under a coat. One woman was caught with a ham dangling from a rope around her neck. Nevertheless, the thefts continued because, as Charles H. remembered, "they had to steal to survive."[7]

The staple cooked food was soup. Joseph T. described his diet as "Seven days a week, my friend, soup," and Lottie K. added, "Your meal wouldn't be complete unless it started with soup." There were obvious reasons. Soup was filling. Second, it was a practical way to stretch the food: everything went into the pot, including inexpensive vegetables. In John Sanchez's family, for example, they called beef soup *caldo de visita*, "visitor's soup," because you could always add water to create new portions if guests stopped in. Third, it was flexible and did not require using exacting recipies; this eliminated the possibility of not having some small, crucial ingredient. Fourth, it was easy to make soup. The cook simply put the ingredients into a pot of water and boiled it, stirring occasionally. In the meantime she could bake, attend to the children, clean, or perform other chores.[8]

The ingredients for the various soups included pork or beef, usually cheap cuts like chuck, blade, cheek, or muscle; plenty of vegetables, including barley, carrots, onions, potatoes, cabbage, or sauerkraut; pigs' tails or knuckles and neckbones. For thickening, the housewife added flour, sour cream, or buttermilk. A final ingredient was home-made noodles "as thin as paper" and sliced "so you'd swear that a machine did it." After cutting the noodles, the women dried them in pillowcases placed near the stove. At dinner time, the housewife stuck the big fork into the pot and took out the largest chunk of meat and gave it to the father. Then she served the rest of the family.[9]

This diet also illustrated the key components of most meals— vegetables, starch, and whatever little meat the family could afford. Stretching the food budget with vegetables and starch was a standard technique; a transfer of knowledge and skills acquired in Europe to help the immigrant survive the hardships of the industrial United States.

There were also meals for special days. Friday, according to the laws of the Catholic Church, had to be meatless. The mother served fish that day, but also prepared distinctive dishes, like *blynai* ("potato pancakes"). Father Mikolaitis felt that Friday's foods "were always delightful"; his menu could include *blynai* served with sour cream; blintzes made from special pancake batter and stuffed with cheese, or even better, jelly, which was sweeter, and sour milk and potatoes. On Sunday there was chicken, a special treat because meat was cheap near the yards, and chicken was expensive unless you owned some. The prices at Adam's Meat Markets, listed on 28 January 1937 in the *Town of Lake Journal*, verify Ted P.'s recollection that chicken "was strictly a Sunday dish":

Veal Roast	7½¢ lb.
Pork Roast	12½¢ lb.
Pork Loin	16½¢ lb.
Veal Chops	12½¢ lb.
Cottage Cheese	4½¢ lb.
Rolled Steak	15½¢ lb.
Round Steak	15½¢ lb.
Pot Roast	10½¢ lb.
Roasting Chicken	18½¢ lb.

With the coupon that accompanied the advertisement, a patron also got a free pound of sauerkraut. Another Sunday dish might be duck or goose or pigeons, the last raised in rooftop cages. A few were occasionally killed and added to the soup as a special treat.[10]

At Christmas there were dishes served only on that holiday. The typical Polish celebration, for example, included placing hay, symbolic of the manger, under the table. The father sat at the head of the table and passed around *oplatke*, a holy wafer blessed by the priests. As each member of the family took a piece, they wished the male parent good health and good luck, and he returned the sentiment to symbolize the sharing of family life. The elaborate meal that followed featured many courses, including *zurek*, a soup made of fermented oatmeal and sour bread, with mushrooms and potatoes.[11]

Next to feeding the family, the woman's chief responsibility was to take charge of the house and guarantee its cleanliness. This was a serious job, performed with almost religious fervor. Evelyn Ostrowski's mother "was a very, very meticulous housekeeper who worked from day to night in her own home. . . . Nobody ever came to her house at any time of the morning or night and found anything in disarray." A tenant who lived in one of the upstairs flats owned by Genevieve N.'s father, a woman with ten children, stayed up all night scrubbing the floors. In time, the neighborhood acquired a reputation for this spirit. A frequent sight, claimed Walter S. Kozubowski, was "little ladies in babushkas . . . sweeping these sidewalks and sweeping the streets with the little cornbrooms. . . . They wanted their area clean."[12]

This goal was amazing considering the obstacles to its accomplishment. Soot from the packing plants came up in rolling clouds, described by an early union organizer as "great volumes of smoke" that "roll from the forest of chimneys at all hours of the day, and drift down over the helpless neighborhood like a deep black curtain." One young lad at the University of Chicago Settlement House explained that God's powers included the ability to see everything: "He sees inside of you. Why! He can see down through the smoke, God can." Soot and dirt also came from the constantly passing trains and from the coal-burning stoves used in every household; and, when oil burners arrived, they left a greasy residue. In winter, the snow "would just turn black from the soot." All in all, the words of Sister Mary D. of Guardian Angel Day Care Center ring with understatement: "Everything was pretty hard to keep clean."[13]

Immigrant women overcame these conditions not only because of tradition, but also because they needed to express some form of mastery over their environment. Cleanliness in the United States followed a pattern brought over from Europe, where a woman prided herself on good housekeeping. In the United States, where soap was so much more available, cleanliness seemed more attainable than ever. But cleaning the house was also a challenge; the sheer implacability of the dirt made it even more important for women to win. Cleaning allowed them to rise above the harsh new world and demonstrate their power to overcome even amidst the factories. It also built self-esteem, by reinstating old skills and re-proving their efficacy. Finally, there was pride, as Evelyn Ostrowski explained: "They had so little, I think they knew that no matter what you had, as long as it's clean, you don't have to have anything beautiful, or a lot of something, but what you have is clean and dusted and polished. . . . You can be proud of what you have."[14]

Cleaning the house was a full-time job. Once or twice a year, everyone took rags and washed down the walls and ceilings. The floors were a constant task. They were boards of white pine, bare, with no varnish or floor covering. The mother drew two buckets of water, one for clean and one for dirty water, took out the bristle brush and the Fels Naptha soap: the same brown, hard, all-purpose product was used for laundry and for bathing. Cleaning the floors usually involved several participants—the mother and the children—and a few tricks such as adding fine sand to the soap and water to work out the dirt. Mostly, it was just hard work. They got down on their knees and scrubbed, over and over again—"on my knees, boy, boy" Catherine I. lamented. The results were guaranteed: "that place had to sparkle. . . . It was like entering a church," in the words of Josephine K.. The floors were scrubbed once or twice a week, and the most important work was done on Friday or Saturday. Sunday was visiting day, when relatives and friends stopped by, so everything had to be spotless by Saturday afternoon. After the floor dried, the mother threw down newspapers to keep it clean until after Sunday Mass. Slavs called these newspapers "Polish carpets" and Hispanics called them "Mexican rugs." John Sanchez's family always bought the *Chicago Tribune*, not from respect for the paper's editorial policy, but because of its larger format and consequent effectiveness as floor covering. It was also handy for wrapping his father's lunch.[15]

Clothing was another part of the woman's domain. Mothers sewed garments for children and sheets, pillowcases, towels, napkins, and tablecloths for the household. They made pillows and blankets from down, creating huge, incredibly warm comforters called *kuchina* in Polish. Every time a goose died in the cause of a meal, the mother threw the feathers in a bag; at intervals, she went to the attic and stripped them, later stuffing and sewing the finished item.[16]

Most of the work on clothes was keeping them clean, a long and laborious chore because of the dirt in the air, the filth on most jobs, and the poor facilities for washing. The entire process, from the soaking to the final steps of starching and ironing took three days. The woman usually started on Sunday, when the clothes went into a tub filled with soapy water. Early Monday morning, the mother put a large tub filled with water on the stove and left it to boil, fogging up the whole house in the winter. In a similar tub, which rested on two chairs, sat a washboard. The housewife sliced her Fels Naptha soap into this second tub or rubbed it directly on the clothes. Then came the scrubbing, then the rubbing, then the clothes were put through the wringer and into a third tub of clear water, and then into the huge tub of boiling water, to be stirred with a wooden paddle. After this, the job began all over again—the soapy water, scrub board, and the wringer, but now the clothes went into a cold-water bath which contained blueing, and then into a luke-warm rinse. Then they were hung on a line outside, or in the attic, to dry. Charles H. swore that when father "had a gleam in his eyes . . . the only way she could avoid it" was to take out the scrub board. According to this Slovak offspring, laundry was a form of birth control.[17]

After the clothes dried, they were starched. The woman boiled a pot of water, put Argo starch into it, and dipped in certain parts of the garments, like collars and cuffs. To starch entire garments, she sprinkled the starch on the material, then rolled it up and let it sit overnight. Certain items, like trivets, ribbons, and doilies, especially those that went under lamps, were treated with sugar instead of starch. This made the item stiff and shiny after ironing, and thus enhanced its beauty as a showpiece.

An early form of fabric softner was the mangler, a rolling pin about twenty inches long and two inches in diameter; one side had been flattened and then carved into a row of teeth three-quarters of an inch deep. By rubbing this over the cloth, the owner loosened the fibers. It was especially useful for softening rough underwear. The heavy flatirons were heated on stoves. The extent of ironing varied. Some women ironed only the man's shirts; other added aprons or other items; but most, like Evelyn Ostrowski's mother, ironed "every single thing" except socks. Sue N.'s mom starched and ironed dresses for six daughters, "a tremendous job. . . . She spent hours."[18]

Being in charge of the household also meant guarding the family's health. People avoided the medical profession because of its cost and its lack of reliability. Operations were especially to be shunned, since few returned from them, perhaps because most residents turned to health professionals when it was too late. The few available dentists mostly performed extractions. Anthony W. recalled one who always had a long line of patients that moved quickly because "he was sorta working on piece work." Patients were given novocaine, but it never helped because the dentist refused to wait for it to take effect. In a neighborhood where "they were more or less their own doctors," according to Sister Mary V., the mother became the master of concoctions and potions. Home remedies, particularly salves, usually consisted of Fels Naptha soap, salt, turpentine, herbs, roots, and plants. Boils were common, and it was not surprising to see someone with three or four on his neck. A standard treatment consisted of dandelion leaves, salt, and Fels Naptha wrapped in a rag that was tied onto the neck to draw out the pus. If home remedies did not work, the next step was to see the druggist. Many residents went to the druggist only to purchase patent medicines, "pain expellers," and cough syrup that gained their popularity partly because of their high alcoholic content. More often, people sought out druggists for medical advice, and pharmacists dispensed a wide variety of cures. Every store had eight or ten chairs for customers and the pharmacists listened to each and made up whatever seemed proper. One advantage was that he charged only for the medicine.[19]

If all else failed, the mother or father sent for the doctor. The medical man was on twenty-four hour call. Late-night emergencies were common, and the reason for the summons was always extreme. Stanley K. said that "you almost had to be ready to die" before the call went out. Tuberculosis was common; any lesion in the chest that was not pneumonia could be TB. Packinghouse workers contracted anthrax and various animal diseases, and residents considered influenza or pneumonia fatal.[20]

One physical condition that rarely received a doctor's care was pregnancy. In most working-class districts, this was totally the realm of the midwife. According to William B., "some people thought more of a midwife than a doctor," and everyone used her services. Father Mikolaitis reported that from the founding of Holy Cross Church in 1904 through the 1920s, virtually every birth was assisted by a midwife. Only in the thirties and forties did women start going to doctors and hospitals for childbirth. The midwives had little or no formal education, but learned by assisting older members of their craft. Since they had to be members of the same ethnic group as the mother, and known in the community, it was not uncommon for one woman to deliver every child on the block. Mothers sent for them not only because they could not afford doctors, but also because midwifery was traditional in the old country.[21]

A pregnant woman often hid her condition. Sue N.'s mother "never talked about it. She always concealed it. She'd hide all the baby clothes." It was unheard of to have a doctor check on the woman's condition, and the midwife arrived only at the time of birth. She vaporized water and made the room humid, prepared clean cloths, and worked with the mother to further the delivery. A midwife assisted at all of Catherine I.'s births; "She tried to help you . . . you in pain . . . then she's there, she's pretty good . . . some of them just got the good nerve, to stand that, what one woman goes through when she's giving birth to the baby." If there were any complications the midwife could not handle, she did not hesitate to call the doctor. Dr. Michael V. knew many of the midwives in the neighborhood, one of whom was his patient. If she spotted "anything unusual" during delivery he got the call and came over.[22]

While all this went on the children usually left the house. When Ted P.'s youngest sister arrived, his father told the eight-year-old boy, "Here, take your sister to the show." Ted was dumbfounded: "For him to give me the money and send me out, but it was dark outside, I couldn't believe it. I was afraid." The father insisted, yelling, "Take her to show, go to show." When they returned, "There was the midwife, my father, my mother . . . with a baby sister." Sometimes a child believed that the midwife brought the baby in her bag; but Genevieve N. left the house during the birth of a sibling when a boarder told her to go out and watch the chimney. He insisted that "any minute the stork's going to fly over." Genevieve waited—"I'm watching . . . for four hours"—but no stork appeared. The boarder explained, "Somehow you missed him."[23]

After birth, the midwife cleansed the woman and washed diapers. She returned every day for a week or more, bringing the mother healthy food like cheese or chicken soup, bathing the baby, cleaning diapers and clothes, and washing the house, although she had less work if there were daughters to help out. She also was supposed to register the child with the Board of Health, but occasionally this chore was neglected, so in later years the grown person had to search church files for a baptismal record. Neighborhood women also brought over food and helped, but the midwife was in charge. Dr. Michael V. expressed his appreciation of her role in these words: "She was a family friend as well as a midwife. And she was a good one."[24]

The woman who bore the children and kept the house, the wife and mother, had an important place in the family life. There was no question that the male ruled in a final sense, but his command was often attenuated. With her husband away at work, the actual day-to-day care fell to the wife. The father became a kind of absentee monarch, or "overseer," as one son described his father. In truth, *lord* would have been a better term. He was always served first, made the important final decisions, but left the management entirely to his spouse.[25]

Within the household itself, the woman reigned supreme. She reared the children, made all the decisions, ensured that the home was run efficiently, and provided essential goods and services. Carl Degler wrote that "The wife and mother was the heart of the home." Housewives knew they had this power and brooked little opposition; one female interviewee declared, "I was the boss" and when it came to decrees about children, "Whatever I said was law." One scholar reported that the kitchen is "the kingdom of mothers and daughters, into which space the ruling husbands and sons are begrudgingly admitted and lavishly served."[26]

This control reinforced a European role that was equally acceptable in the United States. Throughout Western society, the home was the woman's domain. In working-class districts like Back of the Yards, however, this arrangement took on new meaning. The household lent stability to the social order. It was a haven from unpredictable packers and the industrial system. It was also the private place where the old ways remained in force and where people were most at ease. Women, therefore, were the custodians of tradition. Thus, they performed a socially useful function by creating a secure environment for themselves, their husbands, their children, and the other members of their households. They paid a terribly high price, however, because their own adjustment to the New World was sharply curtailed.

Part of her power in the house stemmed from her control of the family's money. Earning an income was the father's responsibility, but spending it was the mother's. She did all the shopping, including buying large items like furniture. Both husband and children turned their pay envelopes over to her unopened, and she doled out the necessary funds and spending money. Since written budgets were nonexistent, this was a remarkable achievement. The women figured out how to stretch a small income to maintain the household, pay bills, and provide savings for new homes and other future expenses, all in their heads. Degler found this arrangement typical of most immigrant households.[27]

Other forms of power derived from control of the household's resources. The mother decided who got food, and of what kind. All material objects came under her sway. She allocated space, and therefore privacy, within the walls of the dwelling. Since nurture was also her right and her task, the children looked to her for affection, which she distributed as well.

These women had great inner strength. Experiencing hard, rough lives, they developed immense talents for survival and were conscious of their own abilities and hardiness. Mary Z., a tiny woman who endured many tragedies, explained, "I am a real tough person. I was brought up so tough, that's why." This self-awareness enabled many women to accept their right to rebel and to use it. Mary's husband was a coal miner who came to Chicago to find work, and there he met and married her. Factory work, however, did not appeal to him, so he went back to Pennsylvania. Mary refused to follow. He kept asking her to join him, but the answer remained the

same: "I am not. I've got my family here and I refuse to go." When
she discovered she was pregnant, her father commanded her to join
the husband, and she did. Tragically, the baby arrived prematurely
and died within fourteen hours. After that she was "lonely" and
wanted to return to Chicago and her kin. Her husband, making good
wages, said no, but Mary replied, "If you don't let me go, I've got
people around here who'll borrow me money and I'll go myself." He
finally agreed to go with her and took a job on the loading dock at
Swift & Company when they returned to Chicago.[28]

The world of women extended beyond the hearth to visits with
friends, which also affirmed the social role of housewife. Sunday
visits were important events. With a house to clean, food to cook,
and children to tend, women rarely had time to go out. Sunday afternoon brought a break in the week's toil for the whole family. It
was standard practice to visit a relative or a child's godparents and
enjoy a chicken dinner. The next week the visitor reciprocated. Men
and women separated after the meal, the females playing bunco, a
game with dice, or just sitting and talking. Sue N. overheard these
conversations at her aunt's home as a young girl; they were "nothing exciting, but it was just getting out of the house."[29]

Women also came together for their household chores, such as
the making of the down comforters. They gathered in attics to strip
the feathers, and met in sewing circles to make quilts. The clothes-
line was also a convenient place to meet and chat with a next-door
neighbor. Stephanie M. explained that "You'd get out in the
yard . . . your neighbor came to his fence and you'd come to your
fence, you'd converse and before you know it you forgot about your
work." Then, there was the porch, the front steps, and the backyard. As soon as the weather warmed, families flocked outside,
which inevitably lead to long conversations and strong ties.[30]

But the first step into the outer world was the shopping trip, a
woman's errand. A 1934 survey showed that the neighborhood had
549 groceries, 100 butcher shops, and 28 dairies. There were spe-
cialty shops for butter and eggs and coffee, and women brought
their own pitchers or cans for the milk. The owner of the store
bought large cans fresh from the farm and placed them in a huge pit
in the middle of the store, three feet deep and packed with ice.
Using measuring cups, he poured the proper amount into the customer's vessel.[31]

The mainstay of every neighborhood was the corner grocery
store. No one ever shopped downtown, at least for food, and few in
Back of the Yards even traveled to 47th Street and Ashland Ave-

nue, the central shopping district, for these commodities. Every
street had its grocery store. As Paul J. said, "There was a store in
the middle of every block and each one had its own community."
Each store had a small, local clientele, always of the same nationality as the shopkeeper. Only there could one expect to find the
right ingredients and people one could communicate with. In a
world of immigrants from many cultures, the storekeeper had to
speak the customer's language. Thus, each store was an integral
part of its immediate neighborhood, a typical pattern in urban ethnic districts. Ted P., son of a Polish grocer, said, "If my dad had
fifty customers that's all he had, fifty. If he got fifty-one one day it
would be an odd thing. Somebody from the next block was passing
by or got mad at his butcher that day."[31] Other interviewees spoke
of their friendship with a shopkeeper and his family, or of problems
when they rented an apartment from one and he found that they had
shopped elsewhere and then raised the rent.[32]

The relation of storekeeper to patron was "very close-knit." Merchants gave their customers small gifts—a piece of candy to a child,
or a couple of extra buns when a little one bought at a bakery.
Butchers asked "You got any cats?" and handed over liver, or
"Your mother making soup today?" and produced some bones, even
some with a little meat on them. They gave advice and even referred customers to other stores. They supported community enterprises, sometimes those sponsored by different ethnic groups, by
buying ads. When the dramatic club of St. Rose of Lima, an Irish
parish, produced *The Bells of Shannon* in 1924, for example, its
program contained many ads with German and, especially, Slavic
names. Some of the owners of larger businesses also watched over
local residents. Mary Z. was walking home in a pouring rain with
her husband and baby when Henry Patka of Patka Funeral Home
offered them sanctuary. Though the Zibidas were total strangers,
the undertaker dried them off, gave them coffee, and offered her
husband a drink. Leo M., co-owner of one of the two major department stores in the area, was friendly to his patrons: "We were always on the floor, meeting our people, talking to our people." He
felt that "the personal touch put us over." He knew many of his
customers by name, and there was usually a bond of mutual trust.
People came, discussed their troubles, and sought advice: "They felt
like they could come in and talk to us." Even though these men were
Jews, priests stopped by to chat, and the owners sent them and the
nuns a bottle at Christmas. They gave the church across the street a
free set of furniture each year for its raffle. When homes burned

down and local committees came to solicit help, "we opened up to them," reducing prices and providing credit.[33]

The grocery stores offered personal service and met special needs. Self-service was unknown; the man or woman behind the counter took down every item from the shelf and weighed out the flour, sugar, salt, cheese, lard, or butter. Food was sliced manually by experienced hands that could cut bologna as neatly as a machine. The range of products and services was enormous. Finding poppy seeds, an important ingredient in Catherine I.'s Rusin pastries, was no problem. The corner store stocked two kinds and ground them as well. Many stores also kept live chickens; no self-respecting woman would buy one that was not freshly killed. Ted P. used to "have to go into the coop, bring the chicken out and show it to the woman. And she would feel around, 'Nah, I don't like this one. Take it back and bring another one.'" When she finally selected one, Ted's dad weighed it, slaughtered it, drained the blood, and wrapped it up. Every store also made its own stuffed meats, especially sausage. A wooden bench with a large backstop prevented the raw material from falling off. After grinding the meat, the owner or his son kneaded it, added salt and pepper, and garlic for the Polish version or onion for Lithuanians. Then he stuffed it into a casing machine and tied off the finished product.[34]

Another type of merchant, peddlers, sold or bought fabric and hawked dishes, umbrellas, rags, metal, fish, fruits, and vegetables. They came down alleys and side streets hollering their wares. Some had regular routines, such as the fruit peddler who always stopped before one house where the children brought him a pitcher of water. This he would "down in one sitting" and then he would put a few bananas into the pitcher, and return it. Another purveyor, who bought rags, had a scale with a hook, and children occasionally tried to cheat him by putting rocks in the bag of worn garments they were selling. Experience prevailed, however, since he usually dumped the contents on the floor before weighing them. Some peddlers traded soap for grease and bones. All these men worked long hours. In the 1930s, young John Sanchez sought to earn extra money by helping a peddler on Saturdays. He started at 7 A.M., then spent the day unwrapping fruit, selling it, and cleaning up the paper and the boxes until midnight. For this John received 25¢, all the fruit he could eat, and two hot dogs. He did not go back.[35]

The women shopped every morning because there were no refrigerators. Very little cash passed over the counter; everyone used a system called the butcher book or *carta* (Polish for "card"). When the storekeeper tallied up the total he wrote the figure in the book in indelible ink. On payday, the first stop was always the grocery to clear the book for another week. At this time, the owner gave the customer a little gift—a can of peaches, some soap or other household item and, to the children, a hot dog, a piece of herring or sausage, but usually candy. Some stores gave away a dish, thus enabling families to acquire a whole set.[36]

The daily trip to the store supplied the woman's principal social contacts. Since the shopkeeper waited on everyone individually, there was time to stand around and talk, often a half-hour or more. As a result, the grocery store became a social center and the "family gossip center." The topics discussed were local news and events— the family, the children, a husband and his work, illness, problems with the house, pending marriages, and the events of last night and that morning: in Phyllis H.'s words, "it was all neighborhood stuff." Sometimes there was an argument between women who worked outside the home and women who stayed home with the family; the women with jobs wanted to go first.[37]

The trip to the store was itself sociable. Women met other women and they would stop to talk. Their children became impatient when, after ten minutes or so, they discovered that "they were just getting started." Ella V., for example, would return home alone, her mom following two or three hours later.[38]

The women also went to church. In Back of the Yards, they were more observant than the men. As Ann P. put it, "There is more piety in a woman than there is in a man." It was the mother who made sure the children said their prayers in the morning before they went to school and again at night. Women could, and did, go to Mass every morning while working men could not.[39]

For women the church represented an organized form of nurture based on a powerful authority. It served as an extended form of the hearth, an institution that helped take care of the women's charges, their men and children. The women made sure that their house of worship was clean and orderly, and that it functioned properly— tasks that enlarged their legitimate realm of concern beyond the household to a larger part of the community body. After Mass on weekday mornings, the women would stand in front of the church and talk for a half-hour or more. Even on Sunday, when their husbands joined them, they engaged in conversation. Some spouses rebelled: Ella V.'s father told his wife one Sunday, "If you're not coming, I'm going" and went home alone.[40]

The church also provided a network of organizations for women.

Every church had at least a half dozen groups—a young ladies
sodality, a rosary society, an altar society, a mothers' club, a literary and sewing circle, or a choir, plus groups to support the school
and an auxiliary chapter of such national societies as the Polish
Women's Alliance. For some groups like the national societies, the
church provided only a meeting place and some spiritual sanction,
such as a priest's benediction before the meeting. Most of the clubs,
however, were designed to support the church. They raised funds
for the parish, sometimes for general revenues, sometimes for specific projects; the Ladies Aid of St. Martini's Evangelical Lutheran
Church once worked to finance a new rug, for example. The *Klub
Osadnicek*, or Club of Lady Parishioners, of St. Michael was typical. Its members were mostly married women who organized to
gain income for the parish, the school, the Benedictine teaching
order serving St. Michael, and the needy. Other groups assisted
specific aspects of parish life, such as St. Ann's Society, later the
Ladies Altar Society, at St. Augustine, which provided vestments
and altar decorations, including sewn materials and flowers. Holy
Cross was among the first schools in the city with a movie projector,
courtesy of its ladies' society.[41]

The clubs worked for self-improvement as well, since preserving
their moral stature was necessary to the women's role as the family's ethical guardian. Every parish had a young ladies' sodality, designed to bring women together for sanctification and to save souls.
Members prayed together, attended Mass in a body, and discussed
religious topics. Quite a few ended up choosing a life of religion and
entering various orders. Some societies, like Sacred Heart's, provided a white carpet for the aisle, silk coverings, and a framed picture of the Virgin Mary when a member married. Immediately after
the ceremony, two women took the bride to a separate Altar of
Mary, where they prayed for Mary's protection and intercession
and offered a bouquet of flowers. At the same church, young girls
joined the Children of Mary after First Holy Communion and at
sixteen, when they joined the sodality. All this was to "develop a
sincere devotion to their Heavenly Mother" and make sure they
"followed the path of her virtues." Thus, the church provided a complete path of socialization for women. Many groups also had insurance plans. The St. Ann's Society of St. Augustine collected 10¢ a
month from its members plus an assessment of 25¢ when one died.
The death benefit was $70 when there were 280 members; when
there were 300, the sum became $75, but never more.[42]

All the activity of these clubs followed an amenable, social path.

Fund raising meant parties, carnivals, bazaars, dances, raffles, bingo, and sewing circles. Most popular was bunco; it consumed women's time like mah jong or dominoes would in different eras. No party was complete without a bunco game, which was also the favorite after a meeting, and it was the most preferred method of fund raising. The affair held by the St. Augustine Young Ladies' Sodality on 12 January 1936, for the benefit of Franciscan Chinese Missions, was, of course, a Bunco and Card Party; the church doors opened at "8 P.M. Sharp," tickets were 35¢, and door prizes were awarded. This kind of activity was the heart of the social life of the women in Back of the Yards.[43]

There, as in other working-class neighborhoods, women moved furthest from the home when they went out to work. Female labor was nothing new; the European peasant farm could not have existed without the women's toil. Of 600 women immigrants surveyed in 1918 in Back of the Yards, 570 had worked in Europe; of these, however, 520 knew only the fields and meadows of the old country. In the United States, their work was much more diverse. Many helped support the family by taking in boarders; others ran grocery stores, restaurants, catering halls, and even saloons. They usually worked alongside their husbands, but some ran the shop themselves while the man worked in the yards. Occasionally, a division of labor developed, as in candy stores where the wife served the children who came in during the day and the man came in for the evening customers who bought newspapers and tobacco.[44]

Women's work was considered secondary because the men had to be the breadwinners. In the store, the wife assisted but rarely managed, unless the store was a second source of income yielding less than the husband's wages. Even in the church, priests had more power and received more respect and material benefits than nuns. Rectories, for example, were always grander than convents. James Farrell had a sister tell Danny O'Neill, his fictional self, that "the happiness of any nun is nothing compared to that of the priest."[45]

Despite this dichotomy, however, women did hold jobs elsewhere than the family business. Most of all, they went to the factories. Young women worked until they married, and the majority of female workers were between sixteen and twenty-two. They returned to the packers only when widowhood made them single again. But this was the *preference* of the community, not always the reality. Many wives and mothers joined the work force so that the family could survive or prosper.[46]

The women who worked in the yards have been described as "a

curious blend of real tough and stereotyped feminine." In 1905, the Chicago packing plants employed 2,477 women, 11.1 percent of their work force. The figure changed seasonally, however; other investigations found as many as four thousand women on the premises. The work they did was deemed unworthy of a man's labor—these were the least skilled, the most mechanical, and the lowest paying jobs. There was little chance for promotion except to forewoman, and even less of advancement into a skilled trade. Butchering, for example, was a man's job, and no females came near the killing floors. Their work began in the trimming room, where the hog went after being sliced into sections, and where the women separated the fat from the meat and both from the bone. In the sausage room, the men stuffed the ingredients into a mechanical stuffer; the women measured the length of the casing against a board, and tied off the links. More of the women worked on cooked food, especially in the canning department, handling the machines that carved and chopped the meat and forced it into metal receptacles. Women also painted and labeled cans and wrapped and boxed such foods as bacon.[47]

They earned much less than the men. In 1910, 57.25 percent of the women, but only 18.61 percent of the men, made $6 or less a week. The packers paid most women 10¢ an hour or less; men generally earned between 13¢ and 20¢. At Fairbank Canning Company, some girls painted and labeled a hundred cans for 5¢. Many handled 2,500 a day, earning $7.50 for a six-day week. This was considered a good wage; Charles H.'s sister worked for Armour & Company in 1912 and brought home $8 every two weeks, earning 66¢ a day.[48]

Working conditions varied. The women's stations were usually cleaner and drier than the men's, but the starched uniforms and caps they wore were paid for out of their own pockets. Workers in certain rooms wore aprons and boots, also their own expense, even though some of the chemicals on the floor ate through a pair of heavy leather shoes in a month. Acids in the pickling solution ate away fingernails. Steam was everywhere in the cooked-beef room, and "some of the women would pass out," according to Victoria Starr, a yards workers also known as Stella Nowicki. Women often had to carry someone to the rest rooms; Miss Starr was a country girl who weighed 166 pounds and could literally shoulder the burden. The excessive lifting of heavy weights, like cans of lard or oil, terminated pregnancies. Machines were a constant cause of accidents, especially in the high-pressure atmosphere the bosses created. One woman recalled how she and her co-workers were standing around waiting for the clock to strike the hour so the shift could start, and one girl was picking at something in the dry corn-meal machine bin. The supervisor, wishing to stretch the workday, turned on the machinery a minute early. The girl at the cornmeal bin screamed, her thumb sliced off. A final indignity was that the women had to "cotton up to" the foremen to get ahead; and it was commonly known that the girlfriends of these men got better jobs. Victoria Starr reported that the forewomen were often "people who were quite attractive and who seemed to be getting along with the boss very well." One woman said, "You could get along swell if you let the boss slap you on the behind and feel you up. I'd rather work any place but in the stockyards just for that reason alone."[49]

There were ways of fighting back. The workers talked among themselves whenever possible, to pass the time and to share helpful information. If someone had to go to the toilet other than at break time, others covered by doing her work. The group also controlled production levels, revolting against the packers' regimen. Although the older Polish women pushed the younger ones in the drive for a bonus, telling Genevieve N., for example, to "keep working," an energetic lass who showed up the senior workers was taken care of. The others made sure her work arrived in such poor condition that it took far longer to process. This turned the newcomer into the slow-est worker on the line.[50]

Another method was to unionize. In 1900 four girls, led by an Irish woman, organized a strike at Libby, McNeil & Libby that quickly ended with all dismissed. Two years later, the leaders went to Mary McDowell of the University of Chicago Settlement House, who got in touch with Michael Donnelly of the Amalgamated Meat Cutters and Butcher Workmen, the leading union in the yards. Lo-cal 183, all female, was born. Originally consisting of only fourteen women, all quickly dismissed, the organization reached a mem-bership of over one thousand by 1904. The highpoint of early femi-nine activism in the yards was reached in 1904 at the union's conven-tion. Packers had brought in women to replace men during an un-successful strike of sausage makers the year before, and the men wanted the women displaced from these male jobs and relegated to their usual positions. Women delegates asked for equal pay for equal work, which was agreed to by the assembly. They also argued against any arbitrary line between men's and women's work, claim-ing that "the use of the knife" opened the door to all jobs, but about this there was less agreement. The convention asked the executive board to try to confine women to work that was less "brutalizing" and in which they had been employed before 1902.[51]

In 1904 the union struck and lost, and much of the hope for women's labor organization dimmed till the rise of the Congress of Industrial Organization (CIO) in the 1930s. Small, ethnic groups of women existed, but most were engaged in slim educational efforts. Women had stepped out of the home into the world of jobs, but the move was opposed by the packers and by the male workers. Leslie Tentler has reported that "the work community . . . failed to support a vision of adulthood where women could achieve individuality and autonomy." To find these, they turned instead to the familiar spheres, home and church. In these places they found pride and power, stability and freedom. There they could demonstrate their expertise and win respect. Thus, the hearth, in all its forms, became the arena in which women took their stand in the struggle for a better community back of the yards.[52]

4

Arenas of Life:
Men and the Workplace

Workers in a Meat-packing Plant
Chicago Historical Society ICHi-14232

The man's role was to earn a living for the family, to work outside his home, and somehow return with sufficient income to provide for all his dependents. To do this, he sought employment with a company, where he was expected to submit totally to outside control. The men's efforts to counter this requirement took the form of sporadic guerilla warfare and rare outbursts of unionization. Neither method was very successful until the late 1930s.

To achieve some independence, men created their own world, one apart from both the workplace and the woman-dominated household. Unlike the women, they did not seek to extend their social role so much as to escape from it. The job of wage earner was one they accepted but rarely enjoyed; freedom meant being able to escape its demands for a while. To this end, they developed meeting places, networks, and rules of conduct—areas of comfort and respite in which they could make their own decisions.

The most important part of a man's life in Back of the Yards was work. Mary McDowell of the University of Chicago Settlement observed that *job* was "almost a sacred word," meaning "food, clothes, shelter, and a chance to be human. It is the first word learned by the immigrant. The children lisp it and the aged cling to it to the end." As soon as he arrived, the man began to toil. Konstanty G., a Polish immigrant, described his arrival in Chicago succinctly: "I come on Friday, I go to work Monday." The men shunned any complication that forced them to take time off the job. James T.'s father, a Slovak immigrant, worked in a Chicago stone quarry. One day he fell and broke his leg. Speaking no English and fearing to call out, he dragged himself to a railroad track where he could be seen. The leg healed well in the hospital, but on the way home, his crutches slipped and he fell and broke it again. If he went back to the hospital, he believed, they might cut off his leg and he could never go back to work. He limped home, where his family treated the leg until he recovered. Jobs were precious and getting one was not easy. One needed either luck or connections. "Big Louie," an overseer who hired at Swift & Company, felt the applicants' biceps to see who was fit for work. They avoided him whenever possible and got jobs through a friend or relative's recommendation.[1]

The jobs these men sought were, at the time of the influx of Slavs, mostly unskilled. By 1900, the packers had instituted a considerable division of labor. Whenever possible, they dropped a skilled man and replaced him with a brawny laborer with no skills. This policy had several advantages. The packers lowered their labor costs, of course. Also, the unskilled jobs required little training and scant command of English. Further, workers in a few key, higher-paid trades could set a fast pace. These benefits, combined with those inherent in breaking down the work process, resulted in tremendous efficiency and enormous profits. Splitters, for example, did fairly skilled work. They had to deliver a smooth, straight cut down the middle of the backbone every time. Although every work gang included only a few splitters, the history of their wages illustrates the rising productivity and decreasing pay of the workers in the yards. In 1884, five splitters processed 800 cattle in 10 hours, or 16 per hour per man, for 45¢ an hour. In 1894, four splitters handled 1,200 steers in 10 hours, 30 per hour per man—an increase in productivity of nearly 100 percent in ten years. Moreover, their pay had dropped to 40¢ an hour. Most of the workers were even worse off. In one gang of 230 men in 1904, wages varied from 15¢ to 18¢ an hour up to 50¢ an hour. Only eleven men, however, earned that top figure; 139, or 60.4 percent were in the poorest-paid category, 15¢ to 18¢, and 184, or 80 percent, received 22½¢ an hour or less.[2]

Factory jobs covered a wide range of skills and abilities. Highest-paid were the cattle butchers, a small percentage of the work force, who earned the title "butcher aristocracy." Their superior position stemmed from the relatively high cost of a mistake. A cut in the hide decreased its value by 70¢ and rough carcasses might not even sell. Whereas the sheep butcher could peel off three-quarters of the hide, the cattle worker needed his knife for all but 2 percent of the animal's covering. He had to cut it off neatly, leaving the fell, or mucous covering, on the carcass so as to insure good appearance. Other job classifications included head holder, leg breaker, ripper-open, gullet raiser, breast breaker, and trimmer of bruises. Most of the work was hard physical labor requiring strong hands. Pulling hind toes on the hog kill, for example, meant using a hook attached to a wooden handle, held so the hook protruded between the fingers. The worker grabbed the foot of the dangling hog and quickly extracted the nails. Sometimes a large animal, taller than the pulley chain, came by and the man had to stoop and lift the weight to get at the toes. The men who pulled leaf lard needed very strong hands, since the fatty material was soft and slippery, and grabbing it out required a tight grip. Some jobs were just plain dirty, with few redeeming qualities. Work in the fertilizer plant fell into this category, as did removing blood from the beds with a squeegee or squeezing hog kidneys to get the urine out.[3]

Other workers maintained the diverse industrial complex. Each packer had its own railroad yards and shops, its tanneries and wool houses, as well as its subsidiary plants for by-products like margarine, soap, and fertilizer. The stockyard owners hired cowboys to herd the flocks. These men never saw Texas or Oklahoma; they had learned their skills on the farms of Poland, Slovakia, and Lithuania. According to Joseph T., they never looked like cowboys in the movies, but "they knew how to ride a horse and how to lasso."[4]

The wages these men received in exchange for their labor were low. In 1900, Charles Bushnell found that the wages of unskilled laborers varied from 9.6¢ an hour to 27.1¢, that weekly wages varied from $6.12 to $8.95, and that the average annual wage was $347.36. In 1910, J. C. Kennedy found that one packer paid just over half his workers $600 or less a year; at another factory, 75 percent of the workers at another company earned the same yearly wage. In both plants, only 2 percent earned $1,000 or more. An analysis of hourly wage rates at a third company showed that less than half of 1 percent earned the top rate of 50¢ an hour and that four-fifths earned 20¢ an hour or less.[5]

"Slack time" made real wages even lower. The workers arrived every morning, but did not begin until the cattle arrived after the daily buying. The men stood around for hours, unpaid. When work started, how long it would continue was known only in the front office. The guaranteed forty-hour work week was unknown; during 1910, one of the factories Kennedy studied worked its cattle gang an average of 37½ hours a week; the sheep gang, 36½ hours a week; and the hog gang, 34½ hours a week. Mondays and Saturdays were usually half-days, and extra hours might be required during the week. Moreover, the company shifted workers to different jobs and pay scales daily, as the need occurred. Until the start of each day, therefore, a worker could not tell with assurance what his hourly rate would be.[6]

Unemployment also plagued the workers. At any given time, a quarter of the work force might be out of work. The packers took men on as they needed them, and laid them off when they did not. Bushnell found that unskilled workers were laid off an average of 8¼ weeks a year. Kennedy took monthly readings of the number of employees at one plant and found that employment reached a peak in October of just over seven thousand and slumped in June to 5,641. Victoria Starr and her co-workers always had to save so they would have something to live on during layoffs. "You just never felt secure," she explained, "There was tremendous insecurity." Sometimes the packers laid workers off deliberately, to guarantee that no one would gain enough seniority to qualify for benefits like paid vacations. By the 1920s, workers were supposed to get a vacation after five years of employment, but before they accrued this time the company would drop them for a week or two and then start counting all over again. Herbert March, district director for the CIO in the 1930s and 1940s, knew workers who had been employed for twenty years without a paid vacation.[7]

The men's earnings, thus, rarely sufficed to maintain the household. A comparison of figures developed by the Department of Labor—beneath which "a family cannot go without danger of physical and moral deterioration"—and actual wages revealed that workers earned between 35 and 49 percent of this amount, as table 2 reveals.

Once on the shop floor the pace was maddening. Tillie Olsen, a novelist with experience in Chicago packing plants, painted a picture of this horror: "Their clothes . . . cling; tighten; become portable sweat baths as they work. Aitch Sawyer Crowley, the venerable, faints. Prostration . . . In Casings it is 110° . . . Indeed they are in hell; indeed they are the damned." Evelyn Ostrowski, a compassionate resident of Back of the Yards who became a social worker, said, "They just used you till they got everything out of you and then they dumped you when they didn't need you anymore."[8]

Different job environments created individual problems. Wool pulling meant "you were always full of lice." The shop floor was "slipperier than hell" from blood; and "an almost overpowering volume of steam" was reported in 1903. In places like the hide cellar, no ventilation was permitted because it spoiled the product. There was always the stench; workers on the killing floor found that "that stink just stayed with them." The stench in the fertilizer works was the

Table 2. Comparison of Department of Labor Minimum Levels and Stockyards Workers' Yearly Wages, 1914–21

Year	Department of Labor Budget	Average Annual Wage at Stockyards
1914	$1405.00	$ 546.00
1916	1678.98	582.00
1918	2419.41	1015.68
1919	2818.43	1158.00
1920	2715.86	1327.44
1921	2508.52	1163.52

Source: Samuel Naylor, "The History of Labor Organization in The Slaughtering and Meat Packing Industry" (Master's thesis, University of Illinois, Urbana, 1935), p. 80.

worst: in one week during November 1900, one plant hired 126 men, but by Saturday all but 6 had quit. At lunchtime, the men rested in front of the buildings, winter and summer, and rinsed off their fingers "so we could dip them into our lunch pails. The rest of our hands and arms and clothing were covered with the grime of the slaughtering houses."[9]

Danger abounded. Within one eight-month period, Swift & Company's medical department treated 2,371 cases, and within one year half of Armour's work force was ill or injured. Cattle broke loose and ran through the killing floors, bumping into men clutching sharp knives. Casualties were frequent. One study of 2,871 accidents in Chicago's meat-packing plants found that 19 percent resulted from knife cuts, 16 percent from being struck by falling objects, 7 percent from becoming caught between objects, 6 percent from burns, 5 percent from objects in eyes, and 5 percent from nail wounds. Ted P., for example, worked with a wooden paddle that shoved beef into a cutter. When the paddle stuck it smashed his finger. He lost eleven days of work; the compensation awarded was $3.85. After that he worked at a vat filled with boiling rosin, used to remove bristles. Hogs went into this liquid, came out black and received a cold water bath. A worker then peeled the rosin off, leaving the hogskin clean. Sometimes the hog slipped off the hook and fell into the vat, forcing men to scatter in all directions to avoid the spray of boiling, sticky liquid.[10]

Disease was commonplace. Workers in many areas suffered an inflamed irritation of the hands, similar to a severe eczema, medically termed *dermatoconioses* but known locally as "pickle hands." Appendages became red and chafed, then thickened and broke open, often cleaving to the bone, leaving hideous sores on the palm and the back of the hand. Ulcers followed, and great amounts of pus. The disease responded to treatment slowly, even if the patient left work—which, because of need, he avoided whenever possible. According to the major study of maladies in the stockyards, this affliction "in some form is probably the most frequently found disease in the yards." Similar to this was a kind of ulcerated foot found in workers in the hide department, where salt and other chemicals ate through leather and formed sores on unprotected skin. James T.'s father came home daily from the pickling rooms with his boots white from salt. He stayed healthy, however, because of adequate precautions; beneath the frequently replaced shoes were heavy stockings and stout rags wrapped around the foot like a diaper. The worst fear of workers, because it seemed incurable, was any kind of

pulmonary disease. Dust in the wool, fertilizer, and soap departments was infectious. Workers in the coolers contracted pneumonia
easily, a result of moving in and out of frozen rooms.[11]

Like the women, sometimes with them, the men fought back as
best they could, trying to regain control of their work environment.
Their goal was to control the shop floor and the work process via
improvement of wages and of working conditions. Although their
attempts to increase their remuneration were rare displays of
unionism, their efforts to change the conditions of work were continuous and private, a day-to-day sniping against the packers to make
the job more tolerable.

Thus, the usual kind of guerilla warfare erupted. Workers added
to their income by stealing food or by overestimating the amount of
parts needed in the car shops and later selling them. Smoking in the
plant, an illegal act, became a way for the workers to express their
independence. Companies posted signs all over, but they never
seemed to work. One displayed a carelessly thrown butt starting a
fire and cautioned, "Be careful where you throw lighted cigarette
and cigar stubs." A worker, hauled before the superintendent, told
his supervisor he thought the notice meant he could now smoke as
long as he made sure to dispose of the stub properly. The leading
industry personnel expert pointed out that "it is rather difficult to
accept such an explanation as being made in entirely good faith."
Workers figured out ways to cut the workload and restrict their
output. Even the messenger boys learned to pace themselves: instead of delivering each single letter separately, they waited until a
reasonable amount of mail had collected, and then one boy made the
rounds. This way they sat for most of the day, taking turns, instead
of constantly running.[12]

Efforts to unionize were at first piecemeal and ineffective; the
major study of worker's organizations in the packinghouse reported
that "labor organization counted for next to nothing in the industry
before 1900." The packers had wealth and power at their command,
and the support of the government and the middle class. The workers were hampered by their plethora of different nationalities, their
poor English, and their poverty. There were sporadic strikes during
the days of the Knights of Labor in the 1870s and 1880s, but no real
organization developed until the Amalgamated Meat Cutters and
Butcher Workmen entered the yards in the 1890s. Even then, the
few strikes they attempted failed miserably. Not until the new century dawned did the Amalgamated begin to form an effective union,
recruiting local leaders fluent in the language of the immigrants.

During the 1904 strike, for example, Mary McDowell heard a Polish
worker tell his colleagues in four different languages to hold out for
a proper raise since without it, "You know that you can't give your
child an American living." The union leaders also extended democracy by creating new locals for women and by organizing indus-
trially, by company, rather than by craft.[13]

In the summer of 1904, the union entered into negotiations with
the packers. The packers granted increases to skilled men but refused to discuss a minimum wage for common laborers. The butchers and other skilled workers rejected this offer and agreed to fight
for the right of all to earn a decent living. Finally the companies,
bargaining as a unit, agreed to the concept but rejected the union's
proposed minimum of 18½¢ an hour. On 12 July 1904, the Amalgamated struck and packing plants across the country shut down. In
Back of the Yards, the community united to seek redress of the
economic grievances. The residents made sure that every aspect of
the strike was orderly, and even improved their personal conduct.
Arrests for drunkenness, disorderly conduct, and quarelling
dropped by 90 percent during the strike. The district police commander reported: "The leaders are to be congratulated for conduct-
ing the most peaceful strike Chicago has ever had. Compared with
other big strikes . . . there was no violence."[14]

Eight days after the strike began, Michael Donnelly of the Amalgamated called on other unions—like the teamsters, railway switch-
men, and machinists—to strike in sympathy. On 20 July, the
engineers, firemen, car workers, steam fitters, electrical workers,
millwrights, and other members of the Allied Trades in Chicago
asked the packers to meet with the workers or face a sympathy
strike. The companies consented and that day signed an agreement
to have wages arbitrated. They also agreed to rehire all the men,
and on 22 June, most of the packers did so, although some foremen
seemed to pass some men by, prompting grumbles about discrimination. At Armour, however, the prejudice was flagrant, especially
against the cattle butchers, who constituted a stronghold of unionism. There, the foremen ignored all the union stalwarts when choosing the new crews.[15]

The union immediately called a walkout, and within hours the
strike began again. This time the packers were better prepared:
they vigorously hired the unemployed, affected by a severe reces-
sion, and also recruited blacks, creating an atmosphere of distrust
and fear. By 4 August the companies reported that they had 29,000
men at work in Chicago, including 9,115 at Armour and 8,623 at

Swift. The strike continued through August. On 29 August, President Donnelly asked for an interview with the packers, but they refused to see him. A few days later, a delegation including Jane Addams and Mary McDowell called on J. Ogden Armour and convinced him to end the strike. On Saturday, 3 September, committees reached a settlement that kept wages at pre-strike rates and that called on the "packers to take all men back as fast as needed." On 8 September, the union, defeated, called off the strike.[16]

The workers licked their wounds and looked to the future, to a house with no mortgage, to a child with an education and a foreman's job. In 1914, the beginning of World War I, conditions improved. Hours of work and thus income increased as demand for meat grew and the supply of new immigrants dried up. In 1917, when the United States entered the war and a strike was threatened, a federal administrator, Judge Samuel Altshuler, took over the industry. Wages were raised immediately, but still were barely adequate. In 1914, common laborers had received 18¢ an hour, which was raised to 20¢ in March 1916 and to 27½¢ in September 1917. In March 1918, Judge Altshuler granted an increase of $1 a day to all workers, equal to a 10¢ to 12¢ an hour raise. Still, in 1918, the federal government estimated that a family needed $1,177.95 a year for subsistance; $1,434.64 for minimum health; and $1,551.30 for minimum health and comfort. The United Charities budget for a family was $1,106.82. And wages in the yards averaged $800. Altshuler stated: "If the ten hour workman received 27½¢ an hour or the eight hour man at correspondingly increased rate worked 300 days a year his wages would be $825. . . . I do not believe . . . this sum is adequate to the ordinary needs of the average workingman's family." He granted further raises in 1919, 1920, and 1921.[17]

In 1921, the packers reacted. On 26 February the Big Four meat-packers—Swift, Armour, Cudahy, and Wilson—told the government they planned to drop out of the wartime wage-arbitration system. In March, they bowed to governmental pressure and agreed to remain till November, but they lowered wages and lowered them again in July. In November 1921, wages were again lowered and the Amalgamated called a strike. Picket lines were formed and the entire neighborhood rallied. On 8 December at Davis Square Park, one thousand police, many of them mounted, fought a local brick-throwing crowd.[18]

The riots continued for several days. The women threw bags of paprika into the policemen's eyes and the houses of strikebreakers were stoned. The entire community rallied to help those out of

work. Donations to the strikers' fund came from pastors like Father
Louis Grudzinski of St. John of God; bankers like J. J. Pesicka, president of Depositor's State Bank at 46th Street and Ashland Ave.;
commercial representatives like the Businessmen's Association of
the Town of Lake; and lodges like the Polish National Alliance and
the Polish Roman Catholic Union. The outpouring of popular support was vivid evidence of the importance of the packers to the
neighborhood's existence. By early January, however, the strike
was broken as cold and hunger forced workers back to their jobs. On
9 January 1922, a spokesman for Armour & Company asserted that
"There is no matter of dispute between the management and employees." The Amalgamated was crushed, never to rise again. Not
until the 1930s and the rise of the CIO would labor organizations
again enter the yards in strength. The workingmen returned to
their families and community to seek solace and freedom among
familiars.[19]

Thus, workers searched for stability, democracy, and control in
shifting arenas. One of these had to be the workplace, but victory
there was often impossible, requiring a well-prepared assault. The
factory hands turned, therefore to an area where they did have
power—their homes and their community. Their goals remained
consistent, but their focus shifted constantly from factory to
neighborhood.

The first refuge was always the home, where the men found their
wives and offspring, beds and chairs for rest, and the mandatory
bowl of hot soup. The pleasures of this environment stemmed from
its psychological distance from the workplace and from the intimacy
of the family.

The males, especially, found one other comfort at home, the
newspaper. As noted earlier, Back of the Yards was a community of
people who read. Books were expensive, and men rarely had time to
visit libraries, but the journal, either daily or weekly, had a regular
place in each worker's life. Stanley K., a paper boy for the *Dziennik
Chicagoski*, said that "every person in this neighborhood would get
a Polish newspaper." And every night, Genevieve N.'s father returned to a familiar chair and a familiar position to read his newspaper: "He'd sit a certain way with the light a certain way . . . with
the cigar always going."[20]

Many different papers served the neighborhood. Each nationality had at least two or three foreign-language papers, often a
dozen. The churches published some, political groups others, fraternal orders still others. Many of the periodicals came from out of

town, the products of strong ethnic pockets elsewhere; others came from the City of Big Shoulders; and still more arrived courtesy of parish or club enterprise.[21]

People bought these papers all over the neighborhood. Newsstands carried the large circulation journals like the Polish *Dziennik Chicagoski, Narod Polski,* and *Zgoda;* the Lithuanian *Dragus* and *Naujienos* (published at Holy Cross Church in Back of the Yards from 1913 to 1920); or the German *Abendpost.* Other papers, especially those from other cities, arrived by mail or were delivered by a boy who worked for a neighborhood or a Chicago distributor. Stores, usually the small groceries, sold newspapers. Since each catered to a distinct national group, they were a natural source for papers in that language. One could also obtain news sheets at meetings of the sponsoring organizations, and many men picked up the weekly Polish Roman Catholic Union paper *Narod Polski* when they went to pay their dues.[22]

Whatever the method of obtaining the papers, men bought them in large numbers. A survey of the circulation of some foreign-language papers in the area, conducted by the University of Chicago Settlement House in 1934, reported the following figures:

Naujienos (Lithuanian)	1,200
Vilnis (Lithuanian)	500
Dennik Hlasatel (Bohemian)	3,000
Dziennik Zjednoczenia (Polish)	5,600
El Nacional (Mexican)	150
Staats Herald (German)	500

At that time, the area's population was 87,103—18,763 families. The total circulation of the papers listed above was 10,950, indicating that 58 percent of all families received the foreign-language press. This list, however, was only a small fraction of the available publications; even some of the major journals were ignored. Furthermore, there was no mention of English-language papers such as Chicago's *Tribune, Sun,* or *News* which, by 1934, the year of the survey, must have become popular among an audience increasingly literate in English. It is therefore quite possible that, at the time of the survey, most houses in Back of the Yards received at least two papers, one in English, and another or even two more in the language of parents and grandparents.[23]

The foreign-language press was very important in neighborhoods like Back of the Yards. It provided a link to individuals of the same nationality in other parts of the country, sustained ethnic cultures, supported community institutions, and helped to socialize immigrants. It also delivered material in the most personal manner possible. As Morris Janowitz put it, "The world . . . of the community press is a mass of parochial details." Immigrants wanted information, not about abstract issues, but about people, places, and institutions they knew, cared for, and often missed deeply. Much of the news they read was about the activities of the parish, or a coalmining town in Pennsylvania where everybody had relatives, or the church or club sponsoring the paper. Genevieve N.'s father, for example, always read the death notices first.[24]

This personal touch achieved its fullest development in the local papers, one of which was an English-language publication. From 1931 on, west of the stockyards, that paper was the *Town of Lake Journal*, which changed its name in 1939 to the *Back of the Yards Journal*. Aaron Hurwitz, who became co-publisher in 1935 and remained with the paper for forty years, said that his first issue was a perfect example of how personal involvement could guarantee success. He and John Haffner, his partner, worked all through the night to get out the first paper, and as a result they were "woozy." The captions for two photos—one of Joe Brabec, owner of Brabec's Department Store, the other of a local monsignor—were switched. The publishers figured that the paper was finished. "We thought there would be a cry against the paper for such a blunder," Hurwitz said. Instead, "It helped. . . . Everybody was walking around laughing their heads off." Brabec announced to everyone, "I am a monsignor," and the man of God walked around telling people, "I now own a department store," and laughing.[25]

When a man left his home for recreation, he had only a few possible destinations. One was the social club. Every Sunday, meetings took place all over the neighborhood. A wide-ranging series of groups clustered around every church and the parish itself sponsored many societies, including Holy Name societies, young men's sodalities, and choirs. In addition, the churches were the meeting ground for many national and fraternal groups such as the Knights of Columbus, the Polish Roman Catholic Union of America, the First Catholic Slovak Union, the Ruthenian Burial Society, and the Federated Russian Orthodox Clubs. Other clubs—like the Mexican League and El Frente Popular Mexicano—met at locations such as the University of Chicago Settlement House, and veteran's societies such as the Zientak post of the Veterans of Foreign Wars met in their own halls. The club system that developed had two central foci. One was ethnicity. Each society was comprised of only one group, so their members had no problems with different languages or customs. The other was the church, far and away the most common meeting place. A large number of organizations were religiously oriented, but others met in the church building because it was the social center of their community. As a result, each church hosted an enormous number of activities. At the first meeting of the Back of the Yards Neighborhood Council, for example, St. Michael enrolled twenty-eight different clubs, including the societies of SS. Peter and Paul, St. Joseph, St. John the Baptist, St. Catherine, St. Martin, St. Elizabeth, St. Michael Archangel, and the St. Agnes Falcons.[26]

The church was a place of worship, where devotion to the moral guides of the community was practiced; it was also, as we have seen, a men's social center. Few of the men's religious societies were directly tied to church work; most had secular purposes. Males viewed the church as part of the world they could escape to, away from the packers' might. The majority of the clubs represented a way of declaring the males' autonomy, of designing an environment to meet their own needs. Meeting at church also bolstered their role as the breadwinner. If the women donated money and cleaned and adorned the edifice, it was still the men who earned that money, at least, according to local beliefs.

Certain church groups were of paramount importance to the men. One was the Holy Name Society. In 1916, Cardinal Mundelein asked each parish to create such a group, in large measure to combat juvenile delinquency, and each group had a Big Brother committee for this purpose. The society's primary purpose, however, was religious. First and foremost, the society worked "to spread respect to the Holy Name of Jesus" and to make sure the title never became associated with blasphemy, according to a description by Sacred Heart's chapter of the society. The church expected the members to behave in exemplary fashion and serve as its finest representatives. To help maintain these high standards, the entire membership attended Mass once a month and received Holy Communion together. The society had two other important functions. One was to help the church by fund-raising or in any other possible manner, including working as ushers, commentators, or maintenance helpers. One interviewee summed this relationship up succinctly: "The Holy Name is a part of the church." The other was to watch over the youth of the community by sponsoring athletic and social programs as well as counseling. Members at St. John of God took on the supervision of problem boys, gave them guidance and brought them into the church, so as to provide a solid base for the socialization of the youngster.[27]

10
Drovers Rounding up Cattle in the Streets, 1904
Chicago Historical Society DN-976

11
Workers in a Canning Factory, 1917
Chicago Historical Society ICHi-03286

12
Line of Men Waiting at the Central Time Station
during Stockyards Strike, 1904
Chicago Historical Society DN-1000

13
Women Involved in the Stockyards Strike, 1904
Chicago Historical Society DN-984

14
Police Keeping Back Crowd during the Stockyards Strike, 1904
Chicago Historical Society DN-940

15
Vacant Lots, Viewed from a Window of the
University of Chicago Settlement House
Chicago Historical Society ICHi-15015

16
Guardian Angel Day Nursery
Photograph by Casey Prunchunas. Chicago Historical Society

17
Immaculate Heart of Mary Vicariate Church (Mexican)
Courtesy of Back of the Yards Neighborhood Council

The other groups that met at the church were combined national and fraternal clubs like the Polish Roman Catholic Union or the Knights of Lithuania. These groups stressed nationalism and celebrated European traditions. In this way they supported their members' sense of security and self-esteem, badly needed in a new world where the value of men's lives seemed to have shrunk. Lillian K. described lodges as places "where they keep the people together."[28]

Many of the clubs had benefit plans. For a small monthly sum, a member could sometimes be insured against illness or unemployment, but death benefits were the most common. The clubs' plans generally paid funeral expenses, supplied pallbearers, and gave the widow a small sum. Typical were the following regulations of a Slovak society:

1. Benefits in case of death—$1.00 from each member to the family of the deceased. An announcement to be made in a Czech newspaper, for which $2.00 is allowed. For flowers at the funeral, $3.00 is allocated. Expenses for the carriage are paid from the treasury.
2. Sick and accident benefits are $3.00 a week for a maximum of 13 weeks.
3. Membership dues are 25¢ a month.[29]

Another advantage of the men's clubs was cultural. Ethnically oriented societies offered a way to pass language, customs, and heritage on to the next generation. Many had young peoples' auxiliaries or fellowships specifically for junior citizens. Numerous programs sponsored by the senior clubs included youngsters in choral reading, dramatic, or other European-language activities designed to foster ethnic pride.

The most important benefit the clubs offered, however, was companionship. Every Sunday, in halls, churches, and taverns throughout the Back of the Yards, people gathered to enjoy "the closeness of familiars, the pleasures of smallness regained." Meetings seemed to "last interminably," according to Msgr. Edward Plawinski. Members sat over coffee and cake, and discussed their world: the parish, the neighborhood, the yards, the old country, sports, politics, and any other subject they chose. Sometimes members would refuse to pay dues more than a month in advance just so they could come to each meeting and sit and talk. Helen Zand thought that these clubs "furnished a hearth for the homesick and disoriented; they gave interest and objectives to the aimless. Little wonder then, they were a powerful force of life in the community."[30]

Men also went to the tavern. This was their own world, a respite from the packers, and remote from the female realm of the household. In the corner bar, men created their own social network and made all the rules. The tavern was a primary component of autonomy in Back of the Yards.

Bars dotted the neighborhood. In 1900, according to one survey, there were 500 saloons in Back of the Yards; even in the thirties a researcher found 372. There was a saloon for every 221 inhabitants, seventh highest of the seventy-five districts in Chicago. The other six, however, included a minute, undeveloped area that was a statistical anomaly; the downtown section, which had a small population and many establishments for entertainment; and the Bowery section of Chicago.[31]

Many workers wanted to own taverns and saved up to do so. At the turn of the century, 3 percent of Chicago's Polish population were tavern owners, their second largest occupational group (common laborer was the first). Besides providing a good income, being a saloonkeeper conferred status. The saloonkeeper was an important figure in the community, a businessman and his own boss. His operation was in an old-country tradition—the innkeeper, a man of distinction. And the breweries provided considerable assistance, often the building and some beer and glasses. When James T.'s father built a tavern, the Monarch Brewing Company rented it and paid half the water bill and the insurance fee for the front window. Often only an investment of $500 was needed to start in this new career.[32]

Saloons were usually in large buildings that included apartments as well as storefronts. Inside there were tables, chairs, and brass spitoons. The beer stayed in the basement and every day someone chopped ice and packed it around the barrels. Often a kettle sat in the heating stove, filled with boiling water for hot drinks. Few brand names existed, but some locals were known, like Old Quaker Whiskey, and Nectar or Kohler beer. The standard was a shot and a beer, no brand names asked for; "Nobody drank martinis or anything. They never heard of that."[33]

In Back of the Yards there were two kinds of taverns. One catered to workers in the yards who were on the job; these were open to all nationalities and were particularly good hangouts for union organizers. Customers entered these saloons on their way to or from work, but particularly during lunchtime. There was little business in the evening or on weekends. These establishments clustered close to the work site and created two notorious sections. One, Whiskey Point, followed Gross Avenue from Ashland Avenue into the yards on a diagonal route. In the last block before the yards, bars lined the street. The other was Whiskey Row, on Ashland Avenue from 41st to 45th street, especially from 43rd to 45th. There were, in 1910, forty-six bars on Ashland Avenue between 42nd and 45th streets, "one on top of another." Van Gordon Sauter, now a broadcast executive and then a young boy recalled that "All you could see, one saloon after another, each one jammed . . . the lights and neon signs with wonderful beer names . . . Ashland, there by the yards, was a paradise."[34]

Lunchtime was these establishments' busiest period. Many workers came with pails and took out their refreshment. Charles Bushnell, an intrepid researcher from the University of Chicago, watched the "noon can rush," as it was called, and somehow managed to count the number of pails leaving the saloons between 40th and 41st streets. There were 1,065. Runners arrived carrying long poles from which the beer pails dangled, and brought the beverage back to the yards.[35]

It was more common, however, to drink in the bar. For the price of a beer, a worker could come in, sit down with his lunch pail, and eat in peace, or at least protected from the elements, since the packers provided no dining facilities. Some tavern owners even had benches in the back for those who brought their own food. Many customers ordered several drinks, which made them eligible for the free lunch. One beer would not do; any attempt to grab food in exchange for one nickel's worth of refreshment was met with a request to leave, or even eviction. For the price of a few drinks, however, hot food was available—dishes like boiled cabbage, soup, sausage, ribs, roast beef, or roast pork. Workers sometimes brought in meat pilfered from the yards, and everyone ate that for a week. When the leftovers became too small to display anymore, the tavern owner or his wife might give them to poor children who came calling at the back door. Buying a few drinks also qualified one to cash a paycheck: the packers paid by check and the families needed the money immediately to pay bills. One researcher claimed that 95 percent of all checks issued to the laborers were cashed in this way. It thus became standard practice to stop on the way home on Friday and hoist a few. Sometimes the women had to go and "pull their husbands out . . . Some of these guys blew everything." Their children often met such fathers at lunchtime and collected the check to ensure its safety.[36]

Another kind of saloon was located off Ashland Avenue, always on a side street. In 1910, Sophonisba Breckenridge and Grace Abbott found, in their survey of Back of the Yards housing, that their chosen ten blocks held thirty taverns, practically one to a corner. This situation was typical of working-class neighborhoods. Historian Jay Dolan, for example, reported that New York's Sixth Ward, an Irish neighborhood, had one grog shop for every six residents in the 1860s. He referred to the Irish saloon as "a neighborhood club," a description equally true of the Slavic taverns in Back of the Yards a half century later. This was the classic neighborhood tavern, strictly the province of one group, or clique, or block, vigorously segregated by ethnicity. Walking into one of these places meant entering a tight circle of friends who used their native language exclusively—a virtual trip to the old country. James T., for example, ran his father's tavern for many years and told how 90 percent of the customers "were talking their own language, you didn't have to know English too much."[37]

Unlike the bars on Whiskey Row, these places did little business during the workday. The evenings were busy, but not all the patrons came to drink on the premises. Some men stopped on the way home with their pails to purchase a "bucket of suds" to drink with dinner. More often, they went home first, sometimes calling upstairs to have a youngster bring down the container, but more often sending one of the children on this errand. Saloonkeepers got to know these responsible offspring, who especially enjoyed running for a mixture of root beer and beer, which they sampled. The last part of the ritual was enacted at home. Before drinking the beer, the father put a poker into the pot-bellied stove, then plunged it into the pail, because drinking cold beer was supposed to chill the insides and cause influenza. Evelyn Ostrowski described it as "such a big ritual." According to Dr. Michael V., "Drinking something cold was supposed to be bad for the chest," and Stanley K. explained that "these people were all afraid of colds." The medical man said that cold beer could not produce pneumonia, but that the procedure did have "a cleansing effect, a sanitary thing." But even the doctor admitted that the body is not used to sudden changes in temperature, and that such shifts do lower resistance. Most of the married men stayed home weekday and Saturday evenings with their families. Single men did not have this society, so the tavern became their hangout and clubhouse, the saloon keeper their friend and confidant.[38]

The big day at the tavern was Sunday. The men stopped off for a drink after Mass, then returned home for the special afternoon meal with relatives or friends. Father Joseph Kelly of St. Rose of Lima described the scene: "It was almost like somebody rang a bell. The tavern after Mass would be jammed, then all of a sudden there would be no one there." After the meal and some dinner conversation, however, the men and women separated and the men headed back to the bar. What they did there, more than anything else, was talk—about "basically anything they wanted to talk about, anything that relaxed them." During the early years of the community, and for a long time after, the most frequent topic was Europe. Patrons at James T.'s father's tavern thought the young man came from Slovakia, even though he was born in the United States, because he knew so much about the old country, knowledge acquired behind the bar. They also talked about work: "Mostly everybody was moaning and groaning about conditions," hard work, and low pay, discussing fellow workers, and how they got along, and condemning the boss. Other major concerns were sports, friends, neighborhood news, politics, and women. These conversations, in James Borchert's words, were conducted by men who "shared a common past and present." They strengthened friendships and group ties, and helped advance the neighborhood's social structure.[39]

They played card games like poker, pinochle, and sixty-six. As the hours went by, the tavern owner's wife put out some food, perhaps sausage and pickles, so the men would not drift back home for a meal. Card playing furnished an evening's entertainment at remarkably low cost. Paul J. spent many hours at a local tavern, playing pinochle. The team that lost the hand bought a round of beer. He would enter the bar between 7 and 8 P.M. with $1.25 in his pocket. When he left at 1 A.M., he usually had 85¢ left, having spent 40¢ for five or six hours of recreation.[40]

Their saloon group was many men's basic unit of mutual social support. This is different from the explanation Perry Duis offers in *The Saloon*. Duis argues that the tavern (and other public spaces like the grocery store) were "extensions or enlargements of inadequate living spaces," but this explanation ignores the existence of different spheres of life. The house was a place of succor and relief, a female and child-oriented place of unique warmth, whereas the tavern was male-dominated, a center of friendship and a place for escape, with its own rules of conduct and solidarity.[41]

Father Kelly believed that "their club houses were the taverns" and James T. recalled times when owners refused to serve intoxicated customers or those who spent too much money, even if "the guy got kind of wild about it." Such thoughtfulness, though not the rule, was far from uncommon. And in the long run, it was good

business, especially if the clientele included married men. Funds for
the sick or needy were collected at the bar. It was a place to take
care of "their community business." Father Kelly recalled Chip,
who hung around one particular tavern: "Everybody loved Chip."
One day Chip got into a fight and had his teeth knocked out. The
other men who frequented the bar took up a collection, organized a
raffle, and bought him false teeth. He had them about a year and a
half, until blind drunk one night, he threw up in a toilet and washed
them down. His friends therefore held another lottery. When the
priest came around an evening or so later, he learned about the
raffle and asked what it was for. He was told, "Don't ask what it's
for, just buy the tickets, Father." He purchased his share, and
found out later it helped buy a new set of dentures for Chip.[42]

The advent of Prohibition hit the neighborhood hard, and many
institutions, including much of the ethnic press, the Catholic clergy,
and business community condemned it as a deprivation, a denial of
the workingman's rights. The *Narod Polski* said that "Prohibition is
needed as much in America as a fifth leg on a dog." A survey of the
effect of Prohibition on the neighborhood showed that priests were
"unanimous in their opinion that prohibition had created a deplora-
ble situation within the community." One Slovak priest told Norman
Hayner that, "Prohibition is the biggest crime a person can imagine. God will punish the country!" One real-estate dealer felt that
"It is human nature to have some kind of stimulation. A man works
from 7 to 12 and gets nothing but water. He needs a can of beer to
brace him up."[43]

The residents adapted. In Back of the Yards all who wanted to
drink soon did so. Home brew was common and speakeasies replaced saloons. But prohibition had some ill effect. As drinking took
on the allure of an illegal activity it became more fashionable among
certain groups, particularly the young, and more prone to abuse.
Hayner learned from one teacher that "Some are drinking now that
would not have drunk before Prohibition." The hip bottle began to
appear when young men got together, behavior at dances got
rougher, and guns became more common. Decent liquor was hard to
come by, so people began drinking alcohol in any available form,
including dangerous brews. As one priest declared, "They give the
good stuff to the sewers and the bad stuff to the people." Women
complained that "My husband used to get drunk. Now he gets
crazy." A typical substitute, especially for women, was Hoffman
Drops, a product consisting of 60 percent alcohol and 40 percent
ether, which left the breath etheric. One druggist sold a gallon a day

before Prohibition, two gallons after its passage and, twenty-two months later, only one-half gallon a day. The reason for the dropoff, he felt, was that people were making their own moonshine. One police captain estimated that every block contained at least three to five stills, and on some blocks they were only a house or two apart. A worker at the University of Chicago Settlement House, walking on Sunday afternoon, "smelled home brew all the way." Stills blew up sometimes, and according to Father Vito Mikolaitis, "You'd see the brew start floating out. . . . You could smell it." The industrial relations departments of the packing plants found that inefficiency, absenteeism, accidents, and charity and welfare cases increased after Prohibition.[44]

As elsewhere, liquor was for sale back of the yards. Saloons were far too important a social institution to become extinct. Only 12 percent of the taverns closed during Prohibition; the rest became soft-drink parlors that served alcohol covertly. One study of 250 pre-Prohibition saloons found that only 16 went out of business, and 7 of these became a nursery funded by the packers. Some of the saloons made little attempt at concealment. Father Vito Mikolaitis saw cars pull into the alley and men carry out five-gallon cans, presumably full of grain alcohol. But some owners hid the product off the premises. Evelyn Ostrowski's parents, for example, permitted a relative to store his liquor in their attic or garage. Drinks in the speakeasies included beer, or whiskey of 80 proof and more. Prices, compared to the old nickel glass of beer and dime shot of whiskey, were outrageously high, 35¢ to $1. Some local drugstores sold grain alcohol under the counter. The smart customer tested it in the store, by filling a spoon and lighting it. If everything burned, it was 200 proof, 100 percent alcohol. He then took it home and diluted it with fruit juice before drinking it. Pharmacies also sold tonics that were 35-to-45 proof, and pain killers similar to Hoffman drops. Bootleggers and beer runners like Joe Saltis and Dingbat Oberta, local boys, became heroes; residents fondly recalled growing up with these men.[45]

The most elaborate ritual in which a man joined with his companions was his final one—his funeral. Funerals were a special concern of the men. They were a product of that masculine universe, with its clubs and meeting halls and rules. Their splendor depended on the club's income from its benefit plans. The procession, especially, brought together the social club and the church, both isolated in ethnicity and removed from the packer's control. It was at the funeral, therefore, that men in Back of the Yards performed their last ceremony, their last joint statement of self-won freedom and self-imposed order.

These were huge affairs. A lavish celebration assured the family of company in time of sorrow and of a public demonstration of affection for the departed. Guilt also entered into this, since the funeral was the last gesture anyone could make for the departed. Many people participated in the funeral—friends, neighbors, acquaintances, co-workers, lodge brothers, and anyone else who ever knew the deceased—a collection of mourners built up over the years. It also reflected the man's status: the cost of the funeral was a declaration of relative affluence. And, of course, it provided the socially acceptable way to pour out one's grief. In the words of William B., a mortician, "It always hit the people."[46]

The undertaker had to be of the same nationality as the family, in part because he had to speak the language, in part because tradition dictated that ethnicity be maintained, even unto death. Thus, opposite each church was the office of at least one appropriate funeral director. The funeral director was "an important man in the neighborhood," according to Anthony W. and others. He did what he could to show sympathy for the customer. Bruno N. compared the undertaker to "a family healer. . . . He consoled you." The undertaker also handled all the money. Most residents paid for funerals from their lodge benefits; so they turned the papers and the lump sum over to the man in charge of the ceremony and expected him to handle everything. This made it easy to swindle people, and some did, but the ones who stayed in business were aboveboard. Their honesty made their reputation, brought in new clients, and resulted in the esteem in which many held their profession. Encarnacion Chico, speaking of the undertaker who buried Mexicans, said, "That's a reasonable man."[47]

The funeral director's main job was to prepare the body for burial. Rarely was this done in a chapel, which was usually unavailable or inadequate and much less comfortable than the home. Any such work done at William B.'s premises took place in the barn; his family's sitting room, only 20 by 15 feet, doubled as the chapel. "They had more room at home," he observed. Most of the time, therefore, he prepared bodies for the wake in the person's house, which was also where the death usually occurred. Sometimes the coffin was bigger than the windows and they had to be removed. A funeral on the second or third floor was always a problem, especially if there was a sharp turn on the stairs. There were also difficult sights and smells. One interviewee watched blood drain from a dangling arm into a jar, and Genevieve N. remembered that the undertaker kept going to the toilet to spill out liquids.[48]

In the home, the woman in charge covered all the mirrors, stopped the clock, and turned off the radio. Candlesticks, often rented from the undertaker, were placed in the main room. On the front door hung a spray of ribbons and flowers made by the funeral director. The color symbolized the age of the deceased: white for a baby, beige for a woman, purple for a man, and black for the elderly. One trick of neighborhood hooligans was to move the arrangement to someone else's home.[49]

Funerals lasted two days. The body rested in a coffin equipped with a metal liner for ice, complete with a spigot. Even though the undertaker drained the lines and repacked the ice, the odor became very strong. For the wake, which went on around the clock, the funeral director brought extra chairs. Some men stayed up all night, watching and playing cards. It was usually the women's job to check the candles to make sure no fire was started. The women also sat up through the night, crying, talking, and singing hymns. The Lithuanians had a special prayer book, a *kontichka*, two inches thick, that contained songs and prayers for the occasion and which the women used "endlessly." Female friends took care of the family—bringing food, cleaning the house, and taking care of the children. Most of all, they cried, thus providing the proper atmosphere. William B., an undertaker, said "There are always a lot of crying. If you didn't cry, you didn't pay your respects."[50]

The formal service was stricter and masculine. The family had an honored place, of course, but the priest officiated. The pallbearers, males, were indispensable participants. To Evelyn Ostrowski, a funeral without pallbearers was "completely unthinkable. You would find somebody. Even if you had to pick them up someplace and bring six strangers, you would get them in there." There were actually seven, three on either side of the coffin and one more in front. Each wore a badge indicating his lodge or affiliation, for it was one of the chief functions of such societies to provide this service. The reason was the expense: few workers would afford to forfeit a day's pay to attend a funeral. The clubs paid their members a standard fee for this duty: Joseph T.'s Lemars paid each pallbearer $3.50.[51]

When the funeral procession moved outside, passing from house to church, church to buggy or funeral train, it displayed its richest trappings. First there was a coffin, usually of pine. Less expensive material was covered with white silk. When William B.'s father bought his first oak casket, it was such an event he displayed it in the window of his funeral parlor. When an infant died, a white hearse took the family to the cemetery. Sometimes there was a special carriage with a hole cut in it for the coffin, and the family sat with their feet next to it. Sometimes the father or the funeral director carried the dead infant's coffin, as they did when babies were stillborn. The stillborn and premature babies of poor families were buried in shoeboxes donated by the undertaker; the more affluent clans paid $4.50 for a child's coffin and a burial plot.[52]

The vehicles were important symbols. The hearse, the family's carriage, and all the horses had to match in color: white for youth, grey for middle age, black for elderly. For this purpose, the undertaker kept a stable of at least six horses, and undertakers traded or lent horses or, when necessary, turned to delivery companies for assistance. At least once, however, William's father had to send out a team composed of one black and one white horse. The family "never forgave him." There might be, at extra expense, a thick, wide netting for the steeds and the hearse, or even plumes for the corners of the wagon carrying the body. A band of at least three instruments—drum, trumpet, and tuba—led the way. At some funerals, especially of young women in their teens, white-clad damsels led the procession.[53]

The price of an adult's funeral depended on the ceremony and the trappings. In 1913, families paid anywhere from $16.60 for a one-carriage funeral to $304 for sixteen-carriages, but $80 was a typical charge. The embalming cost $5; the hearse, $10; carriages $8 to $10 each, depending on the nets and other decoration; the grave site $10 and up; and the casket $7 to $37.[54]

The trip to the cemetery was long, the nearest burial sites being on the far Southwest Side of Chicago. The body could be transported in the baggage car of the train that stopped at Ashland Avenue and 49th Street, while the mourners took regular seats. The standard means of transportation, however, was horse-drawn carriage, and this turned the trip into an all-day affair because just getting there took three hours, more if the weather was bad. Sometimes the passengers had to get out and push. On cold days, the driver put coals into a small stove under the riders' feet and a boy at the cemetery replaced them. Opposite the graveyard was a tavern where the family and guests went, after the burial, for a meal and drinks arranged by the undertaker. The horses were watered and fed at the same time at stables attached to the inn. After this stop for rest and nourishment, the long journey was resumed, and the cortege finally returned home, often in darkness.[55]

The burial grounds were segregated by nationality. Residents in Back of the Yards marked these difference in life and preserved them in death. The Irish went to Mt. Olivet Cemetery; the Germans, to St. Mary. Lithuanians rested at St. Casimir, which was opened in 1903. Father Motiejus Kriauciunas bought a forty-acre tract in 1903 and Bishop Muldoon consecrated the land that year; all the Lithuanian societies participated, complete with banners and badges. Other Slavs, especially Poles, Slovaks and Bohemians, went to Resurrection Cemetery. The Patka family, which owned one of the oldest undertaking establishments in the neighborhood, started this cemetery by buying a farm of twenty acres and asking a priest to help raise funds to buy the surrounding land. Father Adalbert Furman, a Polish priest, and his fellow clerics did so; he blessed the ground in 1904 and Resurrection Cemetery became a reality. That year there were 348 burials, all but 10 from three parishes. One, St. Joseph, was in Back of the Yards. Early support also came from four other churches, two of which, St. Michael and SS. Cyril and Methodius, were in the neighborhood. These churches served three of the major ethnic groups in the area—Poles, Slovaks, and Bohemians. More than any other place, therefore, it was in Resurrection Cemetery that people from the community west of the Union Stockyards ended up after their long toil on earth.[56]

5

The Creation of a Social Order: The Segmented Group

Priests of Back of the Yards. *Standing, left to right,* Father Roman Berendt of Sacred Heart, Father Louis Grudzinski of St. John of God, Father Thomas Bobal of SS. Cyril and Methodius, Father Edward Plawinski of St. John of God; *seated,* Father William Ward of St. Rose of Lima, Bishop Bernard Sheil of the Archdiocese of Chicago, Father Anecetus Linkus of Holy Cross

The greatest goal of Back of the Yards residents was to create a community. This was what Oscar Handlin called "the central social problem of the city . . . developing the means through which great agglomerations of humanity . . . could act toward . . . common goals." Building a community was a long and complicated process, conducted over many years, and in certain stages. No two individuals, or even groups, went through these stages simultaneously, but the sequence remained consistent.[1]

The first settlers all had the same concerns. Alone, facing a changing and fragile environment, they sought survival and then stability, an established place where they could grow and proper. As a first step, they developed a social system consisting of small segmented groups. These groups enabled them to regulate their lives—providing social assurances, enforcing morality, and defining membership. Such an organized social structure was the "crucial factor," according to anthropologist C. J. Calhoun, "which may make a community . . . out of a mere aggregation of people."[2]

This segmented social order was the immigrants' first step in the long and convoluted process of community development. It was a major change because, to the earliest immigrants, Back of the Yards was a chaos, an environment totally lacking social structure and one in which each individual was forced to forage alone for the means of survival. From this chaos the residents slowly built a society which guaranteed trust and dependability, and whose small scale fostered democracy.

This segmented social structure was typical of industrial neighborhoods throughout the United States. Historians and sociologists have long debated whether or not these areas developed into communities. In fact, each neighborhood included many such entities, similar in form yet separated, with little communication among them. For scholars to argue the lack of community is therefore, a macro exercise in futility. The urban landscape abounded with them, each powerful and in control of its members' actions. And in the early years of the Slavic immigration, these groups were very small, which perhaps explains the failure of the academics to perceive them. Nevertheless, their structure and method of operation were crucial, for they were the first forms of social organization in these districts, and thus the building blocks for all future community growth.

The motive for creating this structure stemmed from the heart of the immigrant's experiences. Next to economic catastrophe, immi-

111

grants most dreaded fraud. The New World they entered was a strange one, a world whose rules they did not know and where they had no means of redressing grievances. They were prey to all manner of swindlers and confidence men. Even before they left Europe, people tried to sell them phony steamship tickets, rail passes, and accommodations in the United States. The hunt for jobs in the new country led them into further traps. There were employment bureaus which took a fee and gave nothing in return, or even worse, sent men to far-away places where the jobs had been filled long before. Ten Poles, for example, paid $10 each for jobs in a Wyoming lumber camp. When they got off the train there were no jobs, but a railroad offered temporary work. When this ended, they started to walk back to Chicago. One man's foot froze. With no money to pay for medical attention, he wrapped it and continued hiking. By the time he got to Chicago, blood poisoning had set in and doctors had to amputate the leg. His reaction was shame, and an acknowledgement that "everyone cheats a greenhorn." Until one learned about the corner store, shopping was baffling: shopkeepers wanted cash and did no bartering, nor did they speak the immigrant's language. There were fakers in Chicago who sold magic carpets to cross the seas, magic caps that made wearers invisible, and secret machines that printed money. Even worse, there were cheaters among the local merchants and small tradesmen, immigrants themselves and thus supposedly worthy of trust. One Back of the Yards woman paid a tailor $25—three weeks wages for a packinghouse worker—to train her daughter for a year as a dressmaker. Six months later the girl still sat, pulling basting threads, a preliminary to the instruction yet to come.[3]

One fundamental reason for social organization, therefore, was the need to identify friends, people who could be trusted and depended on. By establishing rules of social order and by defining a membership that would abide by these, the Slavic immigrants started to create a useful social structure out of the prevailing chaos. The first step in building this system was to determine the size and composition of its basic unit.

The size of the group developed by Slavs in Back of the Yards was crucial. The group was small, fifty or a hundred at most. It had to be kept that size to be sure it was manageable, homogeneous, and democratic. But such a miniscule scale meant that Back of the Yards was not a single community; it was, instead, an industrial neighborhood dominated by one form of community structure of which there were numerous examples. Over the years, the defining characteristics of the units changed, as did their social boundaries, but the pattern of multiple, divided units persisted until 1939 and the rise of the Back of the Yards Neighborhood Council.

The initial foundation of all these groups in Back of the Yards and across the United States was kinship, or the extended family, stretched even further by marriage ties. For centuries, the most trusted bond was blood. Fundamental rules of morality and social order supported the family, a power buttressed by every societal institution and by fearsome powers of social and psychological rejection. Marriage was the next most important link. In the early days of the Slavic communities, this method of expanding membership was also kept within narrow confines. As we saw in chapter 2, many future spouses met at weddings of mutual friends, thus keeping the new addition within the same social circle.

But the family unit was too small, its resources far too limited to provide aid and assistance, or even that most fundamental of services, friendship. The immigrants needed a broader social circle, with greater resources, but one that they could still comprehend and control.

The perfect social bond was the Old-World village. It was small enough to guarantee face-to-face recognition but large enough to provide a full range of services. And immigrants from the same village had grown up with, and thus shared, many of the same rules and understandings necessary to create a new social order. The village became, therefore, the basis of the first major form of community organization, the segmented group.

This system worked because most peasants were already accustomed to identifying themselves as members of a specific village. There were few independent nation-states in Eastern Europe; most ethnic peoples lived within one or the other of the empires that dominated this region. European peasants later learned to become nationalistic, but the first immigrants defined themselves simply as villagers and had a great deal of experience in using that personal and social identification to create ties of community.[4]

It was in the village, for example, that men and women earned their social standing, where each member gained what Poles called *okolica,* "reputation." In the United States, these characterizations became crucial pieces of knowledge, information that went a long way when one was evaluating another's dependability. By using the village as the basis for community, therefore, residents in Back of the Yards made sure everyone was aware of everyone else's character.[5]

The compactness of the European village was another factor creating a manageable social order in the United States. It ensured that every member of the group in the New World *personally* knew every other member or at least knew about him or her. This meant that the segmented unit, its rules and activities, would be as predictable to its members as is humanly possible. It also ensured a remarkable closeness, buttressed by the many overlapping social functions each member attended. Stanley K. compared each segment to a "clan," the members of which "stayed together and partied together and met together." In the midst of migration and change, this was the kind of stability and reassurance that the residents sought.[6]

The village traditions also provided a preestablished set of rules, guidelines, and predilictions—antidotes to instability. Emily Balch, writing of her travels through Europe in the late-nineteenth century, said, "Each little village is a tiny world in itself, with its own traditions and ways . . . the neighbor from the next town, even, is an outsider." Residents of any one of these villages, transplanted to Back of the Yards (or any other U.S. setting), automatically held similar views and were logical candidates for membership in a new joint community. There were so many areas of agreement that communication was easy and discord relatively small, conditions that contributed to the slow but steady rise of new communities.[7]

The Old-World tie was also a basis for group effort because communal support was common in Europe. Farmers often helped each other in difficult times. In Lithuania, if a man could not harvest his crops because of injury or difficulties with the authorities, his neighbors cleared his fields. According to one researcher, "misfortune was keenly felt by everybody."[8]

Moreover, this kind of connection had social and psychological advantages. The group's members spoke a common language or dialect, without which no common ground would be possible. Within each of these groups, English remained a second language, difficult to manage at best. A survey of six hundred families made in 1918 by the Stockyards Community Clearing House, a social-service center started by the packers, found that 67 percent of the women and 32 percent of the men spoke no English. Another study, by the Immigration Commission, found that in Chicago, only 19 percent of the Lithuanian males spoke English, 25 percent of the Poles, and 13 percent of the Slovaks. The figures for females were even lower: only 4 percent of Lithuanian, 15 percent of Polish, and 4 percent of Slovak women were able to speak English. The rest could communicate only in their native tongue. When Charles H., a Slovak, appeared for his first date with his future wife, a Pole, her mother looked him over and asked, "You Polish?" He said no, then added *in Polish*, "but I can understand it," and the mother gave him a big smile.[9]

Another reason for using the old village as a basic link was homesickness, the need to find people who could help one recapture a memory, a piece of the world one grew up in and missed dearly. Only those from one's own village could be expected to show an interest in discussing the old ways, to commiserate with one about the problems of the new or, with luck, have some news from overseas to share. It was only natural that such people would stay together and provide each other with company.

The village tie also served as an inducement for further immigration. As we saw in chapter 1, newcomers came to their compatriots when they arrived in the United States, receiving advice or aid and sometimes staying on as boarders. This kind of linkage, therefore, not only eased the strain of adjustment but permitted the community to grow along acceptable and predictable lines.

The social units that grew out of these Old-World ties served several functions. They provided a way for residents to create and enforce social values. Sociologist Elizabeth Bott, in *Family and Social Network*, a study of English family structure, reported that both individuals and kinship groups played "an active part in developing their social ideology." They shaped values and defined acceptable behavior on the basis of their own experiences, adapting to their environment and finding ways to understand and manipulate it. In so doing, they provided a set of social boundaries for members, an important form of order and security. C. J. Calhoun quotes Elizabeth Colson as writing, "Communities . . . do not leave their members free to go their own way and explore every possible avenue of behavior. They operate with a set of rules." In time, the small units established by the residents in Back of the Yards performed these same functions, establishing values and norms of proper conduct and enforcing them among their members. A small group, therefore, guaranteed nearly universal participation, and thus the growth of democratic procedures and widely accepted standards.[10]

A second important function was the management of resources. Wellman and Leighton, who defined the "community saved" concept mentioned in the Introduction, state that within such a system "community members do not have many individual personal resources." Furthermore, they had limited access to "external ties" to power. As a result of these deficiencies there was great interest in "Conserving, controlling and efficiently pooling those resources" the community already possessed. This description clearly fit Back of the Yards, a poor, working-class area where material goods were minimal, which had little connection with the city's movers and shakers, and where survival depended on cooperation and the creative management of slim resources. The development of a network of community ties helped, both by defining membership and by setting the forms and limits of collective activity. This in turn produced an informal but effective system of mutual aid and assistance. This adaptation was typical of urban communities. James Borchert, for example, describing alley life in a black section of Washington, D.C., wrote that "One of the key functions of the alley community . . . was the granting of aid and support to those . . . who needed it."[11]

The forms of this mutual aid were many and varied. The mother of one interviewee owned a washing machine that was operated by a crank. On wash day she invited over a nephew who was training to be a wrestler. He spent the day doing the laundry, getting a workout and a meal for his efforts. When Stanley K.'s dad started painting the house, neighbors came over with brushes and ladders. Joseph G.'s daughter once had colic; it was summer, the windows were open, and the woman next door heard the baby crying and came over to offer advice.[12]

Mary Z.'s entrance to the neighborhood illustrates the kind of support this network offered. In 1918, the fifteen-and-a-half year-old was working in Pennsylvania, earning $3 a week in domestic service. Her grandfather resented the low wages and took her to Chicago, where her brother worked in the yards. Grandpa took her to a saloon run by a woman he had known in Europe and told her that Mary was sixteen, the minimum for work in the yards. It was hard to believe, since she weighed only seventy-nine pounds at the time, "just a little bitsy . . . freckled thing." Another woman, the saloonkeeper's friend, took Mary to the foreman: "She's kind of a puny thing, but she's real active. . . . She does all my work. . . . She works just like a twenty or thirty-year (old) girl." The foreman agreed, and woman and girl got on the elevator. Mary, however, had never been on one before and began screaming: "I got down on my knees because I was afraid." The woman scolded her: "You get up here. You're going to act like a lady. Cut out this comedy." On the job, Mary was terrified; she did not know what she was doing. Another woman kept slapping her hands and saying, "You're going to learn. You're going to learn because I'm going to make you learn." In a week she knew her work perfectly. Within a month, the woman who brought her in asked the foreman to give the young employee a better job. By the end of the year, Mary was a forelady.[13]

Third, each small community screened its potential members to make sure they shared the group's values, thus reducing the possibility of discord and deviant behavior. In Back of the Yards, the standards for admittance were strict, and rigorously enforced. To enter a group one needed a sponsor: as Raymond K. explained, "There was such a thing as vouching." A period of probation followed, during which the members watched the newcomer carefully, checking and double-checking his or her qualifications. Transgressions led to expulsion, no matter who the sponsor was: "If something got out of line, you'd be told, 'Look, this guy is a little pain in the dootbop, get him back somewhere else, we don't want him'" The group also defended itself against rules breakers, both within the group and from outside, and developed a code of action appropriate to infractions. Gossip might be followed by expulsion. In this way, the members acted collectively to guard their safety and placed limits on the activities of their own guardians.[14]

The group's fourth function, protection, was extended especially to children. Lillian K. learned of the gypsies next door when the woman who owned the store across the street came over to instruct Lillian to watch herself and tell her mother about the danger. When Kitty S. was seven, a man grabbed her on the street. She escaped into the nearest tavern. At first the men were angry and asked what she was doing there, but when she told them, the drinking crew immediately came to attention. One man walked her home and the others ran out to look for the aggressor.[15]

There were more general forms of protection as well. An elaborate sequence of checkpoints and mobilization areas protected the area. Raymond K. came from Brighton Park and had to travel through Back of the Yards to get to Tilden High School. "Until they got to know me . . . it was kind of rough. They didn't like outsiders in Back of the Yards." Residents would "look at you and they knew you weren't from the neighborhood and . . . they questioned you, 'Where you from, man?' I'd say, 'Up west.' They'd say 'What are you doing around here?'" For a long time his responses were never good enough; since he was from outside the neighborhood, his explanation that he went to Tilden was insufficient. They merely replied, "Take a bus." Later, when he visited friends in Back of the Yards,

"There always used to be two or three guys sitting on a porch here, or two or three there," always checking him out. "After a while, if they seen you running around they'd wonder what the hell you're doing and say 'What are you doing round here, pal? You looking for somebody?' . . . This is the way they'd put it to you."[16]

The fifth function of the segmented group was to provide information, a form of collective protection and solace. Information was exchanged in all the little hangouts, the bars, the stores, the barbershops, the churches, and the lodges. Most important however, were the back fences and the front steps. The people in the neighborhood spent a good part of their lives there, talking, sharing news, giving psychic support, extending social pressure, measuring and reaffirming relationships over and over again. When a letter came from overseas, the whole block might gather on a front porch to hear the news. Many people stopped on the way home from work or shopping to greet a neighbor and wound up relaxing, a luxury in that world of toil, while cementing a friendship.[17]

The groups also organized or fostered various institutions. Mutual-aid societies, for example, had a wealth of purposes—to provide benefits in the event of sickness or death, to promote political aims, to offer companionship, or to sponsor sports. These societies were the beginnings of institutional growth, a necessary step in the transition from chaos to order that produced the neighborhood's most enduring social structures. Some of these were informal, like the bar or the back fence. Others, like the lodge, had elaborate rules of order. The most important, however, a force that dominated the entire neighborhood, was the church.

The central institution of the segmented society as well as the later forms of community was the church. Generally, the church was the Roman Catholic faith, although Lutheran, Methodist, Greek Orthodox, and other temples also existed. Evelyn Ostrowski described the area as "a community which was highly religious with a great reliance on the church." Even Saul Alinsky, a Jew and perennial enemy of any power structure, admitted that "it is the Catholic church which serves as the medium through which these people express their hopes, desires and aspirations." Every Sunday the neighborhood churches, which had a seating capacity of many thousands, were filled to overflowing at each of the several Masses which were necessary in order to accomodate the large number of parishioners. Walter S. Kozubowski said that, "No matter how poor you were, when Sunday morning came . . . the whole family went. . . . If you were poor, you were poor, but you went to church." Indeed, the parish automatically became the community's center because it was the one institution most easily carried over from the old country. In the peasant farmlands of Europe, the parish and the village were concurrently the major social, economic, and political units: the church district, therefore, was easily perceived as a reasonable, similar basis for organizing community life.[18]

There were several ways of founding churches. A group of residents might band together and petition the governing body of the area for a new parish. Holy Cross got its start in March 1902, when a group of Lithuanians created the St. Vincent Ferrer Society for spiritual and charitable purposes, as well as for a benefit plan. The members asked Archbishop Edward Quigley of the Archdiocese of Chicago for permission to start a local parish, and his excellency agreed on condition that there be at least sixty Lithuanian families to join the parish, thus guaranteeing a minimum of support. In 1904, the condition having been met, the archbishop sent a letter to Father Alexander Skrypko in Westville, Illinois, inviting him to organize the new unit. Sometimes the central body, the archdiocese, started a new church. When local pastors reported that churches had become overcrowded, the bishop might respond by sending a priest to launch a new congregation. Sacred Heart began with a letter from Archbishop Quigley to Father Frances Karabasz dated 1 July 1910. The missive's opening line was: "I hereby appoint you to organize a new parish in the territory of St. Joseph's parish." This indicated that Father Cholewinski of that church had reported on the crowds and the need for a parish in the western sector of his area.[19]

People quickly learned which church to go to. They made the selection on the basis of nationality and the parish boundary lines, and the segmented group that welcomed and evaluated new arrivals helped steer them to the proper institution. Once a part of the group, each citizen supported the church, the center of the family's life, to the fullest extent possible. The cathedrals of Back of the Yards grew from the nickels and dimes of immigrant stockyard workers and, as Stanley K. pointed out, those early arrivals believed that any money they gave to the church was really going to God.[20]

The church performed certain crucial functions. Foremost was the development and maintenance of a social order independent of the packers. As a religious institution, the church promulgated rules of morality, reinforced them at services, and taught them in the schools. The priest was the moral leader of the community, setting an example, explaining the ways of right and wrong, and often acting as an arbiter of disputes. His teachings extended to the most commonplace level; the priest not only spoke about good and evil but told his parishioners to "keep their homes nice and clean and their children behaving."[21]

The churches also advanced the stability of society by accepting some degree of democracy and by suffering through periods of awkward familiarity and even irreverence. In 1895, the parishioners of St. Joseph protested against the pastor, Father Michael Pylpatz, for his arbitrary use of church building funds. At one point, matters became so tense that opponents called a mass meeting at Columbia Hall to condemn the priest. Over a decade later, at St. John of God, religion celebrates the turning points of life in its rituals; in Catholicism these are the Sacraments. They brought forth the neigh-parish history reported that "a sort of religious indifference arose among certain members of the church." At St. Mary, the community exercised even more control. Most churches had a powerful building committee, but this Byzantine Rite edifice had a parish council, the *koratori* ("committeemen"). The council could even ask for a new priest, but since this request might be refused arbitrarily, they were not above using trickery. Father Max Relich, pastor from 1910 to 1928, rarely got into arguments with his flock; he was, however, an old man, and they wanted a new, young priest. One day at the parish house the men sat and drank and talked. Father Relich joined them for a few drinks, became unsteady, and then fell down during services. The local society used this incident as an excuse to get a new priest. His successor, Father Milan Hranilovich, eventually got into a dispute with the *koratori* over church property and found his way to Mass blocked by a crowd of women parishioners carrying large, slogan-filled banners. After this, the Father acceded to the wishes of his community.[22]

The church was also the social center; as Anne H. explained, "there were so many doings in everybody's own church." Every religion celebrates the turning points of life in its rituals; in Catholiusm these are the Sacraments. They brought forth the neighborhoods great parties, like the ones after Communion or a wedding; Father Joseph Kelly of St. Rose of Lima observed that "the liturgy of the church dictated so much of the social life." There were also festivals, carnivals for fund raising, a parade for a saint, or some other festivity. The church clubs and the national lodges that met in the hall also had parties; and Msgr. Edward Plawinski thought the neighborhood's entertainment "centered around the church." The churches also contained the area's works of art. Although affluent matrons from Chicago's Gold Coast traveled to Europe and to Michigan Avenue's Art Institute to view cathedral architecture and religious art, at least three of Back of the Yards' churches—Holy Cross, St. John of God, St. Joseph—were august structures with fine artwork. Others, while not as grandiose, contained important paintings and stained-glass windows.[23]

From church, rectory, and convent came service of many kinds. Monsignor Plawinski portrayed his pastor at St. John of God as "a pioneer in social work." Father Grudzinski was the leader in founding the Guardian Angel Day Care Center and Home for Young Ladies and helped to start the Mid-West Grocers Cooperative. Many parishes had a St. Vincent DePaul Society that raised funds for the poor and distributed charity. The priest also gave more personal assistance. People came to him for advice of all kinds, including business matters, and asked him to settle family and neighborhood disputes. William B. said that "Priests were more like a lawyer than a priest," but at times the parish leader must have felt most like King Solomon.[24]

As it did in Europe, the church helped people deal with the incomprehensible. Eschewing knowledge or solutions, since the former was often unavailable and the latter frequently unrealistic, priests gave succor. The priests "always said, 'Pray together and God will take care of you.'" Supporting this was the Catholic belief that any sinner, no matter how bad, who accepted the sacraments before death would find salvation. Joe Saltis and Dingbat Oberta, notorious beer runners, came regularly to Father Charles Florek's St. Michael church. On Sundays before Mass, Saltis lined up his men and told them to contribute when the plate came around. Saltis came because it was his church; he was Slovak, he grew up in the neighborhood, and he had been a boyhood friend of Florek's. Also, he knew that if he repented, even on his deathbed, the father would take him back to the fold. Parishioners described Florek's philosophy as, "If a man comes to me and he gives me fifty cents . . . from his heart, I'll bury him."[25]

And religion offered solace. In this secular age, in a world where most middle-class people exercise a fair degree of control over their lives, it is hard to realize how irrational and capricious the immigrant's life was. One never knew when a disaster, an accident, or a layoff might occur. The church represented stability and serenity; it was both awesome and comforting. Even the relationship to the deity was expressed in a set of familiar, repetitive, and therefore calming rituals. It is difficult to imagine how an Eastern European peasant felt, going into the cathedrals of Holy Cross or St. Joseph after a long week in the slaughterhouses. There must have been respect and wonder, but also a feeling of tranquility. As James Farrell wrote, "It was so quiet in the church . . . here it was so peaceful, so like Heaven must be."[26]

One reason the church functioned so well was because of the special relationship between the individual priest and his community. The priests made the church seem like home, by their very presence. Good or bad, they were invariably from the old country. Father Stanislaus Cholewinski, pastor of St. Joseph, a Polish parish, was born in Poznan; Father Thomas Bobal, of SS. Cyril and Methodius, a Bohemian church, was born in Luzkovice, in Moravia; Father Alexander Skrypko of Holy Cross, Lithuanian, in the town of Pabalis. Thus, people responded to their priests with a strange mixture of deference and familiarity. On the one hand he was the man in charge, the overseer of the flock, the man whom God and the archbishop entrusted with the keys to the church. Father Kelly reported that "they held the priests in the highest respect" and compared his status to that of nobility. Yet the poverty and poor conditions of Back of the Yards affected everyone, including the clergy, and there were frequent casual and informal meetings which reduced the distance between the people and the man of the cloth. People got to know their priests intimately, catalogued their characteristics, and reacted accordingly.[27]

There were many forms of contact between the clergy and their parishioners. Priests shopped and bought services in the neighborhood, and pastors often handled some of their chores themselves. Father Cholewinski of St. Joseph cleaned the boilers and took all church deposits to the bank. When Father Bobal of SS. Cyril and Methodius went out, Phyllis H. recalled, "You saw him in the snow, his little footsteps, you knew it was Father Bobal that went to the barber." Priests also made regular visits to the home to conduct the parish census and take up collections. In the Polish churches, priests always appeared before Christmas with the *oplatke* ("holy wafer") which parishioners bought at prices that guaranteed a donation for the church. They also came to christenings or wakes, and sometimes even stopped in just to say hello, without an invitation. The people considered this a great compliment—"A glorious thing," in the words of Ann P. They blessed the house, talked, shared a cup of coffee, gave the children holy cards, and asked a few questions from the catechism.[28]

People got to know their priests well because of this frequent contact. Everyone at St. Joseph knew that Father Cholewinski, a small, wiry man, was very strict, had poor hearing, and was very, very concerned with money and business. There were persistent rumors that he owned quite a few houses himself. Very thrifty, he rarely heated the church. When Stanley K. was an altar boy, it was so cold they had to keep the sacramental wine and the holy water on the radiator to keep them from freezing. He wore gloves while serving Mass. Some priests excelled in their role as community servant. Outstanding was Father Ambrose Ondrak, assistant pastor at St. Michael. Father Ondrak loved children and music, and Sister Mary V. recalled his coming into class to play for the children and lead them in folk songs. He made sick calls. Old women would just come up to him on the street and he would cry with them. According to Mary Z., whose husband served as St. Michael's janitor for many years, "He was so good to the poor. All he was concerned about was families. He would visit every family when he had his Sunday off. . . . He just talked to you and he made you feel good." He went to people's homes, sitting and talking, indulging in his favorite dishes, which were the simplest, like sauerkraut. He loved to play pinball at Trop's tavern. Paul J. thought that Father Ondrak was "something sent down from Heaven to us."[29]

The church, with its rigid structure, offers of heavenly comfort, and idiosyncratic ministers, was a major bulwark of the Back of the Yards' social structure. Even this powerful force, however, had been summoned by the small, segmented group. It was these clusters that organized the people who either specifically requested or indirectly demonstrated the need for religious centers in the area. This relationship illustrates the democratic nature of the early social structure of the neighborhood. Social values and controls sprang from the bottom up, a product of felt needs. From the first, the residents agreed on problems and solutions and organized to make their life better. The result was that the small group, with its intimate and immediate forms of communication, dominated its own society, made all the decisions, and managed the life of its members as they went about the slow process of building a community. Even the church, bound to an international hierarchy, was subject to reproach and local criticism. This was also the level at which women and children exercised the most power.

In no way, however, did this democratic control create a golden age for the neighborhood. Industrial conditions, unmitigated by exposés or worker's unions, were at their worst. The neighborhood's physical development and community services were primitive. The point is not that this early stage was a positive situation, but rather to underline the deep roots of democracy in Back of the Yards and other, similar neighborhoods.

Within the small groups, however, certain individuals eventually acquired resources and power, and a local leadership developed. The leaders were always men and always heads of institutions (the sources of their power), qualifications which linked them to the next, more authoritarian group of chieftains. They also had above-average educations. All could read and write, usually in both the language of the old country and the new homeland, and had specialized training in theology, medicine, law, accounting, or business. Their education offered them advantages and opportunities superior to the typical Back of the Yards resident.

The initial goals of these men were strength and growth. They wanted to expand the capabilities of their own segmented group and of the neighborhood by enhancing old institutions and creating new ones, especially by improving physical conditions. In this way they could improve the lives of their followers and foster stability and order.

The obstacles they faced were formidable. First, they had to arrange a program that did not appear in any way to challenge the packers. It was clear to everyone in Back of the Yards where the power was: any activity, like unionization, that threatened these giants courted annihilation. As a result, these community leaders had to operate in areas the packers either ignored, like religion, or accepted, like business.

A second problem was poverty. As we saw in chapter 4, the packers paid wages far below any governmental or charitable standard of living. This meant that there was little spare capital to work with. The leaders overcame this with a church building drive or a savings-and-loan institution, programs that could slowly accumulate the area's sparse funds and apply it to large-scale projects.

A third obstacle was the transiency of part of the population. Meat-packing was a seasonal industry, its busiest season from late November to early January. Business slowed down in spring and early summer, and picked up again in August. A study of slaughtering in 1921, in the industry journal *The National Provisioner*, showed that during the slowest week of the year, only half the number of animals went under the knife than during the busiest period. The number of employees needed by the packers also fell accordingly. Alma Herbst confirmed the *National Provisioner's* figures, reporting that, from 1922 to 1926, the number of employees during slack time was as small as 51 percent of the peak work force.[30]

Sporadic employment, coupled with bad working conditions, meant that many workers lived in the neighborhood for a short time and left, and that others hung around as floaters. Both Herbst and the U.S. Immigration Commission found that only slightly more than half of all laborers were employed for the full year. There were always large numbers of workers waiting for a job, many of them without community ties or intentions of staying. It was common for hundreds, even thousands, of men and women to stand outside each plant every day, hoping for work. After a while, many left for other neighborhoods and cities in search of a job. The effect of such mobility, which was typical of industrial neighborhoods, could have been catastrophic. Transiency meant a less stable population, fewer people who would become part of the community and invest in it. And temporary residents were not bound by local rules and morality and were thus a potential security problem. The floater symbolized, especially to social reformers, the chaos of the industrial slum and its lack of order.[31]

The local leaders, however, saw beyond the transients to the people that stayed. The situation that developed was characteristic of new and changing industrial communities, and has been documented as far back as the early nineteenth century. Robert Doherty, for example, in a study of such centers in New England, found that each hamlet had two populations, one steady and one temporary. The first maintained long residencies while the second moved in and out with great frequency. The members of the first group became leaders, built institutions, enforced values, and produced stable and coherent settlements; the individuals in the second category never stayed long enough to leave any kind of imprint at all. Doherty concluded that "if community is defined in terms of participation in a network of relationships and institutions, mobility did not have much impact." The leaders in Back of the Yards and in other immigrant, industrial neighborhoods accepted this pattern and worked with it. They handled transiency by ignoring it, and they appealed to the stable portion of the local population. These resident families became their clients, since it was the people who stayed that needed the services these men offered.[32]

The most important community leaders were, of course, the priests. As guardians of God's moral law and the community's social values, they had tremendous influence. They used this influence to improve the conditions in their own parishes. They sponsored or encouraged numerous clubs and societies, and increased the number of links that bound the residents to their community and to the church. This made for stability. The priests also taught residents how to use their meager capital. They frequently lectured on the need for saving and on the importance of buying a home. Some went even further. In the early days at St. Michael, Father Bartholomew Kvitek reasoned that if parishioners bought houses they would stay in the area and support growth and local improvements. In 1907 he called a meeting of businessmen which produced the first savings and loan in the parish, the *Dunaj* ("Danube"). Eleven years later a new pastor, Father Gregory Vanischek, discovered his flock's ignorance of banks. While collecting parish dues, he visited family after family that kept their savings in coffee mugs and tomato jars, forgoing an interest-bearing savings account. When Slovak businessmen organized the Damen Savings and Loan in 1916, he resolved to support this institution. He held meetings, delivered sermons to explain the importance of interest and dividends, and urged parishioners to acquire passbooks; when some families still held back, the priest came to the house, took the adults by the hand, and brought them to the bank.[33]

Thus, the men these priests turned to for help in building stable communities were bankers, individuals with superior education or capital who used their resources to make money and improve the community. The first board of directors of the *Dunaj* Savings and Loan, for example, included a butcher, a building contractor, a tavern keeper, and a real-estate and insurance broker. The savings institutions all began by catering to members of segmented groups. They were small and they specialized in personal service. Many, like *Dunaj*, took their names from a prominent, fondly remembered feature of the old-country landscape, reinforcing the notion of a warm welcome. A Ruthenian society, for example, named its savings and loan institution *Voda* ("fast waters") to commemorate the flow of European rivers. The typical bank was a storefront, had a staff of three to five employees, and possessed few assets. The Slavic Building Loan and Homestead Association listed typical assets, in 1910, of $17,081.81. Relationships with customers were, according to Hemlock Federal Savings and Loan, "very personal"; the tellers knew each customer by name and often by account number as well. This was in the segmented groups' tradition of face-to-face knowledge; in the same tradition, new clients arrived by referral. Among other services, the savings and loan associations sold steamship tickets, rented safe-deposit boxes, and sent money overseas.[34]

The benefits to customers and community were twofold. First, these institutions permitted residents to enhance their physical environment. According to the charter of Prospect Savings and Loan, its purpose was "to promote thrift by providing a convenient and safe method for people to save . . . and to provide for the sound and economical financing of homes." The second benefit was the stabilization of the community fostered by the workers' investment in the neighborhood. Homeowners were the group that all leaders naturally appealed to because they had the most to gain from a stable community, and the savings and loan associations increased the number of people who joined the ranks of regular Back of the Yards residents.[35]

These bankers established the first community-wide institutions in Back of the Yards. Their goals were stability and prosperity, both for themselves and for their clients. To achieve this they used the resources at their command, those of the small group. Though they stood apart, these men still depended on the democratic system of the segmented society and on the village tie to define their sphere of influence, then built on this foundation.

The small, segmented group and its institutions was the dominant early social pattern not only in Back of the Yards, but in urban immigrant neighborhoods throughout the United States. All newcomers feared fraud, and sought comfort and reliability. For these, they harked back to an *old* community across the seas, and the knowledge, trust, and freedom it provided. Time after time, in cities across the United States, the most fundamental community tie sprang from a local European setting, and the most cherished word was *neighbor*. To Jews in New York, praying with *lantsmen*, or to Italians in Cleveland, singing with *paesani*, the village tie was crucial. Given this tie and the security it vouchsafed, they then created *new* communities under novel conditions, in Back of the Yards and its counterparts elsewhere. Their experiences were harsh, but the process was a democratic one, a way of teaching newcomers how to act together to manage their own lives. They learned independence, even though on a small and separate scale: as Robert Wiebe put it, " 'Born free' in America meant born in pieces." This pattern was of great importance for future generations because it formed the core of the urban immigrant's experience in the United States.[36]

6

The Creation of a Social Order:
The Nationalist Enclave

Interior of St. John of God Church (Polish)
Courtesy of Back of the Yards Neighborhood Council

he next stage in the building of a community in Back of the Yards involved larger and more powerful groups. The basic units were enlarged, based on nationality instead of villages. These national enclaves never totally replaced the small groups, but rather they consisted of many allied segmented sections which, with superior resources, became powerful tools for building a strong neighborhood.

These enclaves, and the linkages on which they were based, did not originate in the small segmented groups of the neighborhoods, but in the minds and activities of an elite, leaders of many types who strove to institutionalize their convictions and ideas. They worked in citywide and even national arenas and were acquainted with power far beyond the ken of the segmented group or even the Back of the Yards neighborhood. In order to achieve their goals, however, they needed popular support. This meant that new rules and broader identifications had to be taught to the yards' residents. It also meant that decision making fell increasingly to a small circle from which sizable groups of the population, especially women and children, were excluded. By the time these leaders had finished, they had reorganized the social and cultural framework of the urban immigrant neighborhoods in Back of the Yards and throughout the country.

The fundamental change these leaders imposed on the residents of the Back of the Yards and elsewhere was the adoption of a nationalistic ethnic identity; a new, broader ethnicity. The shift was a long and complicated process, sufficiently subtle and yet eventually so acceptable and all-encompassing that historians overlooked it for years. But nationalism, the public, political expression of ethnic ties, was not the primordial sentiment scholars assumed it to be.

We argue, in this work, that to understand the growth of nationalism in Back of the Yards and other places, one must first accept the fact that large clusters of immigrants belonged to common ethnic cultures. We define ethnicity as Karl Deutsch did in *Nationalism and Social Communication*. Deutsch viewed ethnicity as a shared set of symbols and understandings that permits communication. This explans why people living in the same place, subject to similar conditions, can still belong to different cultures; they have different beliefs, different values, and use different symbols to explain the world and their place in it. Conversely, widely separated groups, with similar values and tokens, can communicate freely and therefore feel a sense of kinship. Eric Wolf described the first situation in an article on two adjoining Alpine villages that shared a common environment but had markedly different cultures. The second phenomenon occurred within many immigrant groups in the United States. Living in neighborhoods teeming with other foreigners, they eschewed contacts with members of other ethnic groups living nearby but maintained close relations with other colonies of their own ethnic group scattered all over the United States. Thus, the Slovaks of Back of the Yards were more familiar with the Slovaks in Middletown, Pennsylvania, than they were with the Poles next door.[1]

Ethnicity, then, involved common viewpoints and guideposts that fostered intercourse. Large population sectors in Back of the Yards, all from the same region of Europe, had some common understandings even if they did not share the intimacy of the small group. And they could use this knowledge to ease relations between individuals or even segmented groups of the same ethnic background, thus helping to preserve order and stability. There was, in other words, an unconscious cultural bond that could be manipulated for unofficial purposes.

Ethnicity, however, was not the same as nationalism. Anthony Smith, in *The Ethnic Revival*, held that the latter term "extends the scope of ethnic community from purely cultural and social to economic and political spheres," or from "private to public sectors." Nationalism was the public, formal statement of ethnic culture, advertised to achieve political goals. In Back of the Yards, this meant that the leaders substituted an avowed nationalism for both the identification with the village and the quiet ethnic bond.[2]

It was not an easy switch, since several factors mitigated against it. The most important was that Slavic peasants were ignorant of nationalism. Vytautas Beliajus, a Lithuanian storyteller, told about the time rumors hit the village of Pakumprys that Lithuania would become "free and independent." The older villagers did not understand the excitement: "They were *Katalikas* (Catholics), hence *Zmones*, 'The People' [of the land]. . . . It never entered their minds that they were also *Lietuviai* (Lithuanians)." This ignorance stemmed, in part, from the fact that many of the Slavic countries had disappeared from the political map centuries before. The one institution capable of keeping peasants informed of national culture and politics was the school, but the lack of educational facilities in Europe halted the spread of this information. According to Helen Lopata, the small Polish landowner of the late-nineteenth century lacked "any knowledge of Polish national literature and art." Complicating matters even further, he remained separate from and suspicious of those who had such knowledge, the intellectuals and nobility of the cities. Moreover, the imperial powers actively repressed the nationalist movements; any attempt to teach national culture was met with stern discipline throughout Europe. In Lithuania, the Czar's government forbade the teaching of the domestic language in any school, and in Slovakia the authorities expelled some theological students because "they smuggled in Mr. S. and talked Slovak with him." These repressions kept the peasants ignorant and also removed those people who were capable of transmitting national culture and who advocated national politics.[3]

Despite all these problems, nationalism became, by the First World War, the defining characteristic for people of Slavic descent in Back of the Yards and throughout the country. Political agitators found an almost complete lack of opposition to their beliefs in this country and they found a host of powerful institutional supporters as well. The industrial United States was totally unlike Europe in that conditions were immensely favorable to the adaptation of nationalist causes.

Nationalism took root because of the weakness of the forces contending against it and the strength of those in agreement. The groups that fought against nationalism were those advocating class identification, such as labor unions and the Socialist Party. These organizations, busy defending themselves against industrial power and middle-class attitudes, lacked sufficient energy to mount an effective opposition to nationalism, which was, after all, not their chief concern. The packers, on the other hand, did not resent this kind of European patriotism because it posed no threat to their interests. They accepted nationalism and even used it to further their own goals. The main reason for nationalism's success, however, was the amazing lineup of institutions that supported it, each for its own reason: it included every bulwark of the community in Back of the Yards and in every other immigrant district. Church, nationalist organizations, intellectuals, and the foreign-language press all supported this definition of community. In so doing, they shifted the basic unit of society from the segmented group to the nationalist enclave.

The most important institution advocating nationalism was the church; its reasons included the European background of many priests and the nature of the American urban Catholic Church, particularly the Archdiocese of Chicago, from the turn of the century to the start of the Second World War. In Back of the Yards, typically, the important Slavic pastors had two things in common. First, most of them were born in Europe. Second, they were all educated men who had completed seminary training. The first meant that they grew up in places where old-country cultures still held sway; the second ensured that they had the necessary background, and possibly the opportunity, to learn about nationalism.

Priestly fervor, in some instances, stemmed both from education and from personal experience of European repression. Such a man was Father Skrypko of Holy Cross. Born in Pabalis, Lithuania, in 1867, Skrypko came from a family of farmers, but his father also worked for the government as a forest ranger. Despite the cultural and political orthodoxy an official position must have required, the father taught his son to read and write Lithuanian. Later he hired a tutor and, in 1881, took the young man to Riga, where the child passed an examination to enter high school. Ten years later, Alexander was ordained a priest and became famous for delivering sermons all over Eastern Europe in native tongues, including Lithuanian, Latvian, and Polish. In 1902 he came to the United States, and in 1904 he founded Holy Cross. Three years before he died, in 1938, the Republic of Lithuania awarded him the Order of Gediminis for service to the national cause.[4]

Other priests had similar incentives to become nationalistic, but found them in the United States rather than in Europe. Father Gregory Vanischek, pastor of St. Michael from 1915 to 1928, was born in Lemesi, Slovakia, in 1884 and emigrated to the United States in 1902. At that time he had no education and knew nothing about nationalism. In 1903, he entered St. Procopius secondary school at the Benedictine Seminary in Lisle, Illinois, and came under the influence of Father Stephan Furdek, the leading Slovak patriot in this country and the founder of his people's two most influential lodges, the National Catholic Society and the First Catholic Slovak Union. Vanischek, in the words of Sister Mary M., another Slovak Benedictine, "hooked his dreams on Father Furdek's," especially dreams about Slovak independence and national unity. But at Lisle, a seminary run by a Bohemian order, Vanischek also suffered from the prejudice of his superiors who were in an Old-World tradition of Czech discrimination against Slovaks. These indignities, "the rubs," affected Vanischek for the rest of his life, so that whenever "the Czechs spoke about their nationalism, he felt hurt." In response, the future priest founded a Slovak literary society at St. Procopius, which published its own journal. He later became the first Slovak Benedictine ordained in the United States and a leader of his people's cause in Back of the Yards and the Midwest. When he died, the

Osadne Hlasy described him as a man who "loved the Slovak language and the Slovak people and worked for them indefatigably."[5]

Clerics in many other cities had similar experiences, especially because many U.S. parishes were staffed by religious orders based in Europe rather than in the archdiocese. The Polish Congregation of the Resurrection, for example, supplied priests not only to Chicago, but to such places as Buffalo and Pittsburgh that also had large Polish populations.

Other religious leaders fostered nationalism because of the internal politics of the Archdiocese of Chicago and other cities. In the United States, the Catholic Church permitted two kinds of parishes, territorial and nationalist. The first, considered "American," were usually headed by Irish priests and could be attended by anyone who lived within the parish boundaries, regardless of ethnic background. National parishes, on the other hand, were established for specific ethnic groups. With the exception of St. Rose of Lima, every Roman Catholic church in Back of the Yards was a national parish.

When the first waves of Slavic immigrants hit Chicago, the archdiocese showed little preference for one kind of parish over the other, but by the latter part of the nineteenth century, Archbishop Patrick Feehan had started many national churches in response to requests from local Catholics. When Feehan assumed office in 1880, there were 38 parishes, 22 national and 16 territorial. Before his death, twenty-two years later, the archdiocese had added 94 new parishes, of which 53—including 15 Polish, 5 Bohemian, and 3 Lithuanian—were national; and more were being formed every year. Feehan was known for giving priests a free hand in running their own domains, and he resisted pressure for "Americanization" on the grounds that an immigrant could love both his birthland and the United States.[6]

By the beginning of the twentieth century there was, however, great dissatisfaction within the national parishes, particularly the Polish ones. Roman Catholic leaders across the United States, sensitive to criticism that they commanded a foreign, impoverished horde and besieged by competing pleas for ethnic units, began to oppose European nationalism within the churches. Archbishop John Ireland of St. Paul, a powerful organizer in the U.S. hierarchy, wrote a letter to James Cardinal Gibbons, in 1891, that "We are American bishops; an effort is made to dethrone us, and to foreignize our country in the name of religion." Cardinal Gibbons of Baltimore, the outstanding U.S. church figure and head of the

oldest Catholic colony in the new world, could not have agreed
more. "Ours is the American church and not Irish, German, Italian
or Polish—and we will keep it American," he later orated.[7]

These bishops sought an end to the nationalization of parish life
and an increase in the assimilation of immigrants into the mainstream culture. They tried, both in their own areas and by pressur-
ing other churchmen, to end the system of national parishes, to
eliminate parochial schools that taught European languages and
heritages, and to punish priests who opposed these viewpoints. In
so doing, they also fought to extend central control and to end the
independence of the parishes. This threatened the power of every
local priest. If the bishop could challenge the nationalist cause, was
there any limit to how much he could interfere? Thus, when priests
rallied behind the banner of nationalism, most in all sincerity, they
were also responding to another issue, the freedom of the individual
priest to handle his flock as he saw fit.

One of the major problems, according to the European nationalist
priests, was the Irish and, to a lesser extent, the German, domination of the U.S. church hierarchy. Until 1908, there was no Polish
bishop in the United States, despite the fact that, according to the
1900 census, they constituted 12 percent of all Catholics in the
United States. Proportional representation would have given the
Poles two archbishops and eleven bishops, not zero. The Germans,
with only half as many parishes, had three archbishops and fourteen
bishops.[8]

The Irish-dominated church hierarchy left the Slavic pastors
open to attacks from nationalists within their own groups, and such
disputes resulted in the creation of new national denominations, the
most enduring of which was the Polish National Catholic Church
(PNCC). For the Poles the chief points of contention were the coer-
cive efforts of church leaders to eliminate their ethnic culture, and
the fact that all church property belonged to the bishop, which
meant that the Irish controlled the fruits of the Polish workers' savings. Thus the PNCC described itself in the church's sourcebook,
Eleven Great Principles, as "an organized body of free religious
people." The church declared: "Every religious act must evolve
from man's free will; it must not yield in any way to external com-
pulsion." All ceremonies were to be conducted in Polish, not in the
"alien Latin tongue; the language of a dead people." And it contained a statement that "the owners and controllers of National
Church property are the Polish people."[9]

Support of nationalist churches was manifested in many of the industrial neighborhoods across the United States. In Back of the Yards, Polish independents met near St. Joseph's in November 1895, and guest speakers included citywide leaders of the movement. In 1914, Holy Cross, a Lithuanian parish, was also threatened with a nationalist church in its vicinity, although the project was short-lived. In 1928, the PNCC finally established a parish in Back of the Yards, Holy Family, that still exists. None of these nationalist churches became strong, proselytizing forces in Back of the Yards, but they did put pressure on local pastors to engage in nationalist activities. Accused of subservience to foreigners (the Irish bishops), the Slavic priests had to prove their patriotism to maintain their position in the community.[10]

The tension between the Slavic priests and the Chicago chancellery became even more pronounced in 1915, when George Mundelein was appointed bishop. Mundelein was a supreme builder and centralizer, a man who brought diocesan affairs to a modern, efficient level; before he was finished, he had made Chicago the premier Catholic center in the Western United States and a major force in Rome. Charles Shanabruch, in *Chicago's Catholics*, wrote that George Mundelein "ran his archdiocese like a general." The bishop was strong-willed, prepared to fight if necessary, and demanding of total loyalty from his subordinates. In his first speech to his priests after taking office, he explained his requirements: "I am going to make mistakes, but I am your archbishop, and I look to my priests to cover up my mistakes, not to expose, discuss or criticize them. For to whom else can I look for such consideration?" His disputes with Slavic priests were fierce and angry, and directly affected many parishes, some in Back of the Yards.[11]

As befit a great organizer, Mundelein moved quickly to centralize operations and to shrink the parishes' autonomy. First he moved all decisions on building projects to the chancellery office. This step was badly needed for the more efficient use of the archdiocese's capital; at the same time, the pastors lost control of the largest single item in their budgets, the funds used for large, brick-and-mortar projects. Mundelein also moved toward a more unified religious identity. In part he did this by restricting the creation of new national parishes, favoring territorial ones instead. Between 1916 and 1929, Mundelein founded forty-one parishes, only nine of which were national. In 1916 he also began, via his hand-picked school board, to consolidate the Catholic school system. In the future, all textbooks had to be uniform in content and the only language of instruction was to be English. The Irish representative on the board, Father James Jennings, declared that "It is the purpose of this order to thoroughly Americanize the Catholic School System of Chicago . . . there shall no longer be Irish-Americans, German-Americans or Polish-Americans . . . but only real Americans."[12]

Within the chancellery, the major voice for national blocs was the Board of Consultors, a three-man body that advised the archbishop on key issues and which served in lieu of a system of auxiliary ethnic bishops. Each seat represented a major group, usually German, Polish, and Bohemian. This body became the focus of the disputes between Mundelein and his Slavic priests, particularly those of Polish background. From 1915 to 1921, the Polish seat on that board belonged to Father Louis Grudzinski of St. John of God. At the time of his appointment Grudzinski was already an outspoken nationalist, and Mundelein's biographer called him "a loud Polish voice" on the board. Grudzinski opposed Mundelein on many issues, including parish formation and school policy, but the issue that caused the greatest conflict was the assignment of priests.[13]

At first Mundelein permitted each member of the board to act as an ethnic "boss," keeping track of assignments within his own group, which ensured that all new priests of that nationality would be sent to the appropriate church. For several reasons this was viewed as one of the most important rights of each national bloc. First, if a foreign priest were sent, a priest who could not speak the language of his parishioners, he would not be able to hear confession. Second, if Mundelein gained this control, he could punish priests for nationalist activity or any other infraction, simply by reassigning them. Third, any threat to the established system would be a fundamental challenge of the right of every pastor to run his domain as he saw fit, without undue influence from downtown. In 1917, Mundelein assigned several newly ordained priests, including three Poles, to territorial parishes. In response, Grudzinski led sixty-eight of his colleagues in the formation of the Polish Clergy Association of Chicago, which sent a protest to the archbishop. Letters flew back and forth, but the appointments stood. In 1921, Mundelein removed Grudzinski from the Board of Consultors and installed a more compliant Pole.[14]

The case of Father Louis Grudzinski helps to explain why priests in Back of the Yards and other places became nationalists and influenced their people in that direction. There was no question of Grudzinski's patriotism, but he also had more practical reasons for supporting the nationalist cause. For at least a short time, he held considerable citywide power, including the right to assign all Polish priests in Chicago. When Mundelein threatened his power of appointment, Grudzinski had to respond on the basis of nationalism rather than of politics. Pragmatic motives thus joined with idealism to push the nationalist cause within St. John of God and other parishes.

This threat to Grudzinski's autonomy registered with every Slavic pastor in Back of the Yards and in Chicago. If Mundelein could shift priests at will, no parish was safe, no domain was sacrosanct. The only way to fight back was to rally popular support around the national cause and to have large public demonstrations of nationalism. This kind of activity would send a message to Mundelein, warning him not to foment opposition to his authority. Every Slavic priest in Back of the Yards and the other Chicago neighborhoods, therefore, worked for nationalism not only because of deeply held feelings, but in order to secure his realm from the archdiocese's great organizer.

Such events were not confined to Back of the Yards or even Chicago. In every major U.S. city, there arose a church builder akin to Mundelein. The dates of their appearance differed, but bishops like Ireland, Gibbons, O'Connell in Boston, and Spellman in New York all sought centralized authority and diminished local control. In all these cities, priests felt the same pressure from the people below and the chancellory above and turned to nationalism as a way to buttress their power. In so doing, they caused their parishioners to redefine their identity, and thereby helped to restructure the basic units of community in the urban industrial neighborhoods.[15]

There were many ways for the priests and other nationalist leaders to rally the people, but their first job was to teach a new, national consciousness. They did this by attaching additional, secondary meanings to familiar cultural forms. George Deutsch argued that putting "symbols about symbols . . . to items recalled from memory" was the best way to achieve higher levels of understanding. A native costume was no longer just a pleasant memory, but an example of national culture. Thus, the artifact remained the same but it gained a new significance. There were also many specific projects that priests could use to advance the national cause. Besides establishing schools to bolster ethnic culture, they could sponsor a wide range of groups that directly or indirectly advocated nationalism. Father Kulinski of St. Joseph successfully urged Polish veterans to form the Zientek Post of the American Legion, guaranteeing that even U.S. rituals would be carried out under a banner that heralded Slavic pride. Priests offered free use of the parish hall or served as chaplain for a branch of a national society such as the Polish Roman Catholic Union or even small, local groups. Many Slovak priests attended meetings of the Furdek club, the leading social organization of that national group. None played a larger role than chaplain, but Father Charles Florek of St. Michael often held that post, and the society frequently met in his parish hall.[16]

Priests also spoke out to their flocks whenever possible. Father Florek's predecessor, Father Gregory Vanischek, never used the pulpit for national causes, but he often spoke at lodges, picnics, dinners, and rallies. He lectured on Slovak literature and history, and usually took as his theme ethnic pride, admonishing his listeners to "stick together . . . you have lots to be proud of. . . . Throw up your head." Years later, Slovak priests, including Father Florek, made it a habit to speak at the Catholic Slovak Day. St. Michael's pastor served as president of the seventh such celebration, admonishing attendees to "warm their hearts with the flame of patriotism."[17]

There were also special parish projects, such as dramatic clubs and guest speakers. Many pastors invited famous Europeans to speak, and after 1918 the favorites were generals who had fought in the First World War. Father Grudzinski, at St. John of God, was able to arrange for a visit from the most beloved Pole of all, the pianist Ignace Paderewski. In terms of leadership and symbolism, however, the most important event was the awarding of a national honor to a local priest for his nationalism. This happened, for example, when Father Grudzinski accepted the Polish Commander's Cross of Poloniae Restitute from Paderewski. Such occasions showed that the moral guide of the area's national group exemplified proper conduct and patriotism.

All this work helped to shift the basic unit of community in Back of the Yards from the segmented group to the nationalist enclave. The priests and other leaders convinced the residents to expand their circle of trust to those with a common national background, thus reforming their community on this basis. Over and over, priests urged the people to unite on these grounds, and offered countless opportunities to do so. After the nationalist enclaves formed, the priests, as moral guardians, continued to reinforce the values they held dear and that they needed for practical purposes.[18]

There were other institutions urging residents to think in national terms. One was the national lodge, like the Polish National Alliance or the Knights of Lithuania. In Back of the Yards, as in so many other industrial neighborhoods, the local assembly was usually small. The Star of Victory Lodge #46, Polish Women's Alliance, for example, a society of about one hundred and fifty members, was a typical women's club with little interest in citywide or national activities. Such societies were bastions of the small group and its democratic processes; nevertheless, by bringing people together under a national banner and by exposing them to communication from a central, politically oriented leadership, they strengthened nationalism in Back of the Yards and other places.[19]

The sheer number of such groups, each with a national identification in its title, bolstered the new identity. Residents of St. Michael's parish, for example, could join local chapters of the First Catholic *Slovak* Union, the First Catholic *Slovak* Ladies Union, the *Slovak* Catholic Sokol, and the National Catholic *Slovak* Society. Other organizations assumed a nationalist aspect despite their dedication to altogether different purposes; the Slovak sokol, an athletic organization, took as its motto the patriotic slogan *Za Boha a Narod* ("For God and Country"). Some societies sponsored entertainments with historical or patriotic themes. Most national blocs had patriotic days, and every ceremony included the singing of both "The Star Spangled Banner" and the anthem of the European homeland. There were ethnic food, ethnic performers and costumes, and numerous speeches about the glories of national spirit. A leader of the Tenth Catholic Slovak Day felt that one benefit of the event was that Slovak "hearts again become inflamed with a true patriotic spirit towards . . . their Slovak ancestry and traditions."[20]

Intellectuals of each nationality also influenced immigrants to think in national terms. There were two different types of such leaders, each practicing a different type of national reinforcement. One consisted of professionals who organized on a national basis: the Bohemian Artists Society, the Polish Social Workers Club, the Lithuanian University Club, even the Association of Polish Chiropractors. Professionals founded these and many other societies for ordinary reasons—to share similar experiences and work together on common problems. The Polish-American Businessmen's Association held a smoker on 26 May 1917 so that Polish merchants and industrialists could "get acquainted with one another and . . . open the field for organizational work." These groups also launched public-relations campaigns to alert the public to the need for their services: Lithuanian doctors lectured at Davis Square Park on tuberculosis and wrote a health column in *Draugus*. Another reason was to increase their status within the national community by extoling the achievements of their peers, as by such newspaper announcements as the notice that "Miss Mary Dowiatt, one of our Polish girls . . . has received the Doctor of Medicine," printed in *Dziennik Chicagoski*. These clubs also, of course, provided comraderie and fostered friendships. The result, in Back of the Yards and other Chicago neighborhoods, was an increase in national identification. Professionals were leaders and set an example by organizing on that basis. Nationalism permitted even workers to gain status as those less fortunate merged their identity with those of achievement on the basis of a common national ancestry.[21]

Another kind of intellectual had an even greater impact on the communities of Back of the Yards. These were the educated, nationalistic individuals who formed the major patriotic societies, the citywide and even nationwide networks of like-minded people and groups. From these cliques arose the major attempts to foster nationalist education, large enterprises that influenced communities throughout the city and beyond. These intellectuals were classic examples of Robert Park's "marginal man," a person least confined by rules and the need to conform to them and so most likely to become an agent of change. They possessed the desire, the skill, and the resources for these ventures, and became, along with the priests and the lodge presidents, the leaders in restructuring the local community along nationalistic lines.[22]

These people were motivated by their backgrounds, both in the world they entered and the world they left. All had had opportunities beyond those of their compatriots and enjoyed advanced training. George G. was born in Slovakia, emigrated at the age of eleven, and settled in Back of the Yards. A year later, his family in financial need, he quit school to get a job, and went with his mother to the Board of Education to get a work permit. He said he was fourteen, the minimum age for a certificate. When the officer then asked George's mother, George pointed out that she spoke no English, but knew Slovak and was fluent in German. The man was of Teutonic origin and, after a long discussion, gave George not only his working papers but also a letter of introduction to a publisher who ran a bookstore. George started as a floor boy, handling stock in the history and auto sections. He stayed for two-and-a-half years, reading vociferously, and by the time of his departure any trace of a Slovak accent was "all gone." He became an accountant and a leader in Slovak circles, but the early, lucky break was, in his opinion, the reason for his success. "Whatever I am now," he remarked in later years, "that was my start."[23]

The oppression of nationalism in Europe was a second influence on people in the United States. Patriotic immigrants taught their children nationalist ideas. George G., for example, described his parents by saying, "their soul was all Slovak." When asked where he learned about nationalism, he replied, "I was born into this atmosphere." Dr. Peter Hletko, the outstanding Slovak leader of Chicago and a native of St. Michael's parish who became president of the Slovak League of America, attended high school at St. Procopius and was a contemporary of Father Gregory Vanischek. Like the cleric, he came under the influence of Father Stephen Furdek, the founder of American Slovak nationalism, and later became one of the great patriots of the cause. A third influence on intellectuals was the bigotry that was part of the dominant culture in the United States at this time. Outstanding individuals were particulary sensitive to such insults. Because of their achievements, they expected respect, only to be rebuffed by a mainstream culture prone to prejudice. By commanding movements for national pride, therefore, they rebutted these criticisms and achieved the positions of leadership their ability justified.[24]

These leaders served in three capacities. First, by being active in all kinds of national organizations, they served as brokers between different factions and coordinated their efforts. Many leaders joined the entire range of groups and became friends of all kinds of leaders in the patriotic cause, thus creating a remarkably intertwined network of leaders. Dr. Hletko, for example, entered whatever Slovak organizations he could, so that he could attend national conventions and influence policy. He was a close friend of Wendell and Florian Tylka, founders of the *Osadne Hlasy*, the Slovak paper, and all three were acquaintances of both Father Vanischek and Father Florek of St. Michael. Florek was chaplain of the Furdek Club, which Hletko founded, and president of the Seventh Catholic Slovak Day, which the paper trumpeted. Florian Tylka, copublisher of the paper, joined the Slovak League of America, the First Catholic Slovak Union, the Slovak Catholic Sokol, and the Slovak National Society. In Lithuanian circles there was a similar crossover. A listing of Back of the Yards Lithuanian organizations and their leadership in a 1913 edition of *Lietuva* revealed that seven different men served as officers of two or more clubs, and that one, A. J. Bierzinskis, acted simultaneously as president of one group and treasurer of three others.[25]

A second function of the leaders was to act as spokespersons, carrying the national bloc's message to the larger society. They were accustomed to operating in larger circles than the neighborhood, and they represented their people in citywide and nation-wide matters. Dr. Hletko and the Furdek Club wrote frequent letters to the Chicago *Tribune* because that paper used the term *Czechoslovakia*, which Slovak patriots considered a false state. A third function of leaders was to form organizations that created cit-ywide nationalist projects. The Furdek Club was typical. Dr. Hletko organized it in 1929 for Slovak students, as a place where they could work for national independence, and to "support the cul-tural, historical and ethnical [sic] life of the Slovaks." Their original project, which never succeeded, was to create a municipal celebra-tion for SS. Cyril and Methodius similar to St. Patrick's Day, but the club, which eventually numbered one hundred, soon expanded its purpose. It became the meeting place for the Slovak "intel-ligentsia," people who, according to Sister M., were, "very refined, very intellectual." To join you needed at least a high school diploma, and the club sought out professionals like doctors and lawyers. The members worked, not only for the advancement of Slovak culture but, in the words of the *Osadne Hlasy*, to "push forward our Slovak political leaders, stand by them, show the nation we are intelligent."[26]

The club, particularly its senior members, was a close-knit group. Members often belonged to the same church: George G. and the Tylka brothers were fellow parishioners on the West Side of Chicago. Wives often worked together on projects, and small cliques socialized after meetings. One faction, including most of the clubs's guiding lights, went out so frequently and stayed so late they became know as the "night owls" and had their pictures printed in the club bulletin. Included in this group were the Peter Hletkos, the Tylka brothers and their spouses, and Mr. and Mrs. George G. Mr. G. felt that the club was "just like a family; we wanted to keep together."[27]

The club launched most of the citywide efforts at nationalization, thus increasing the number of occasions on which Slovaks from all over the city could meet, exchange greetings, and share in a group activity. According to George Deutsch, these were the key ingre-dients in the development of national consciousness, "promoting more intensive communication among contemporaries" so that they became aware of their joint heritage. The Furdek Club, therefore, held concerts by Slovak musicians, supported Slovak candidates for public office, and were chiefly responsible for the massive Catholic Slovak Days which rallied Slovaks from all over the city to demon-strate on behalf of nationalism. It also helped to create the Slovak Radio Hour in Chicago.[28]

The most important method of communication, and one linked directly to the Club, was the Slovak newspaper *Osadne Hlasy*. Robert Park called the ethnic newspapers "the printed diary of the home community," and although there had been several Slovak papers in Chicago earlier (many coming out of St. Michael), *Osadne Hlasy*, founded in 1928 by Wendell and Florian Tylka, was the most enduring. The Tylkas were immigrants from Namestove, Slovakia, who came over when they were teenagers. Florian worked in the stockyards, but Wendell got a job as a printers devil and learned the trade. When Chicago's Slovak paper folded in 1923, the Tylkas began thinking about starting another one, since no paper in the Midwest was written in their native tongue. They also owned a small shop that printed most of the material for Slovak parishes and societies, so they had the proper facilities and connections. The weekly paper appeared for the first time on 1 September 1928, but money was a constant problem. The first five issues were free; thereafter, the Tylkas charged 3¢. Parishes and societies collected payments, ran errands, and made donations to aid this unabashedly nationalist newspaper. Though the Tylkas printed general news, they specialized in reports on Slovaks in Chicago, across the United States, and in Europe. Dr. Hletko wrote editorials and feature articles. *Osadne Hlasy* declared that its purpose was to "educate our Slovak Catholics" and that its focus was on "the good of the church . . . our homeland and our Chicago people." The paper became the leading Slovak medium in the region, and it supported every Slovak campaign mentioned earlier, including Catholic Slovak Days, Slovak radio hours, concerts, dramatic presentations, parish and national societies and, particularly, the Furdek Club.[29]

The Furdek Club and the *Osadne Hlasy* typified the development of nationalism in Chicago's ethnic blocs. Every nationality had its intelligentsia, its newspaper, and its programs for cultural and national reinforcement. The Polish *Dziennik Chicagoski* organized a radio hour. Intellectuals started the Association of Lithuanian Patriots, and sponsored *Lietuva*, a newspaper which, when asked to present its platform, printed the Lithuanian national anthem.[30]

The result of the work of these leaders was to push Back of the Yards and other neighborhoods into a nationally oriented social structure. They did this by setting up a network of communications that increasingly linked the local communities to their counterparts around the country. By fostering such ties, they bolstered the tendency for immigrant workers to associate with others from their own country. Another result was that representatives of people in Back of the Yards spoke more and more in nationalist voices. When the residents looked to someone to articulate their feelings to the outside world, that advocate tended to explain problems in a national context. Third, the development of an organized leadership meant that people in small communities like those in Back of the Yards were now exposed to more, and better-prepared messages designed to teach them nationalism. They were thus drawn into a citywide and a nationwide web that worked with influential local residents to force them to reorganize their thinking and their associations.

Finally, in addition to the priests, the lodges, and the intellectuals, one other important institution pressured people in Back of the Yards to think in nationalist terms—the packers. The bosses recognized that nationalism was a powerful tool for dividing workers and hindering unions. John O'Hern, superintendent at Chicago's Armour complex, told a Senate commission that the company preferred men to join national societies because it made them better citizens. Even so, it remained a fact that nationalism could be used as a barrier to the unity that the labor unions preached. The foreman, however, was the only plant official who actually understood the differences between the various Slavic nationalities and the only one who manipulated them on the shop floor. Nationalism was a powerful way to divide the men. One method was to pit nationalities against each other in piecework or even wage rates. Often the foreman could simply integrate a department to create friction. According to Ted P., when a foreman wanted to get rid of a Pole all he did was put Lithuanian workers on either side of him. Within a week of this kind of isolation, the Pole would quit. The result of such maneuvers and the resentment they caused was a rise in nationalist feelings.[31]

Because what happened in Back of the Yards took place in every other neighborhood in Chicago, and in many other cities, it is important to examine the ramifications of this shift from the small ethnic cluster to the nationalist enclave.

First of all, nationalism became the major form of identification for immigrant industrial workers, even after the political goals that often justified such activity were achieved. Helen Lopata, in her study of Chicago's Polonia, pointed out that the Polish national associations had to change their purpose after World War I and the creation of a Polish state. After 1920, they created a new ideology based on the view that the United States was a country "composed . . . of sub-cultures and sub-societies," each of which contributed to the "composite which is America." By maintaining their nationalism, therefore, leaders and organizations were sustaining a necessary culture through the next generation and at the same time informing the broader society of the great contribution of each nationality. Since such goals had to be achieved by demonstrations and propaganda, nationalism still met Anthony Smith's definition. It remained a public, political statement.[32]

A second effect was the restructuring of the community into nationalist enclaves. National leaders taught the immigrants to look to shared ethnicity and collective patriotism, rather than to village connections, for dependable associates. This meant that the basic community unit had to be reformed, shifting from the segmented group to the nationalist enclave, which took over many of the functions and responsibilities of its predecessor. People now received their news in a nationalistic citywide newspaper as well as over the back fence. In times of trouble, they turned to the national lodge, to the nationally defined parish, to leaders who spoke for them in nationalist terms. The ties that bound, the associations and linkages that made up community, became redefined on a European patriotic basis across the urban industrial United States. The supplanted segmented groups, however, did not perish. They survived as the basic units of friendship and security, and reappeared later as the core of a new, democratic form of community organization.

Nationalism also mitigated the terrible generational conflict within immigrant families. By constantly teaching and reinforcing ethnic cultures, the leaders of these national enclaves brought the children back into the world of their parents and gave them the tools to understand their heritage. It was not surprising that in 1905 "prominent Polish-Americans" campaigned for the inclusion of "the history of their homeland" in the Chicago public school curriculum. They were working to build a bridge across the chasm that so often separated European parents and their native-born offspring.[33]

A fourth effect of nationalism was that it dealt a blow to the democratic community. The system of national enclaves was an authoritarian one, a formal, centralized structure with remote leaders who elicited little participation from the rank and file. Major groups, including women and children, were excluded from the decision making process.

It was only fitting, therefore, that the one major rebellion against nationalism came from the young, in the dating and marriage patterns of the second generation of Slavic residents. These youth fought for the right to make their own decisions regarding their companions. They went to dance halls to which people of all nationalities went and they communicated in a common language, English. The rules and passions of the old country, while still important, carried less weight. Work meant even more contact with "foreigners," and increased leisure time gave them greater opportunities to act on personal likes and dislikes.

Parents and priests alike tried to prevent "mixed marriages" between children of different nationalities. Poles said that "a Polish Anna look for a Polish John." Girls of that nationality were taught that if they married Irish men they would be slaves for the rest of their lives. Father Stanislaus Cholewinski told a girl who was dating a Greek boy, "You come back with a nice Polish boy and I'll marry you." Despite the pressure, large numbers of the second generation married outside their nationality. Mamie O., a Ukranian, married a Russian. Paul J., a Slovak, married a Pole. Stanley K., a Pole, married a Bohemian freethinker, even though Father Cholewinski asked her, "Why don't you go to a Bohemian church?" Some families went even further. Of Sue N's seven brothers and sisters, only one married within the nationality. The brothers of Theresa G., Germans, all married Poles. In Genevieve N.'s Polish family, one sister married a Swede, another a Lithuanian, one brother a Slovak, and one a German. She married an Irish man and later a Slovak. Genevieve grinned and remarked, "We had the League of Nations."[34]

A fifth effect of nationalism was that it provided a way to deal with other groups in the neighborhood. In order to protect themselves, the immigrants had to know what to expect from others. The sin was never that strangers might cheat or bully; the failure was in not finding out beforehand how they might do this. Such knowledge made it possible to fight back, avoid difficulties and, if need be, roll with the punch one knew was coming. One way to do this, of course was to learn about all the strangers one might come in contact with, measure their strong and weak points, and then figure out how to deal with them. This was exactly what went on within the closed circle. No one, however, could extend this learning much further; it took too much time to discover the good and bad among the entire population of Back of the Yards, a community with tens of thousands of potential challengers. The immigrants needed, therefore, a brief collection of characteristics they could attach to a stranger as soon as they learned some basic piece of information. Nationalism worked beautifully. By language, accent, name, in a thousand different ways, people quickly revealed their nationality. With that identification, a known list of traits immediately became available, and there was now a way of predetermining what to expect and how to deal with it.

Monsignor Edward Plawinski, a Pole, still had at his fingertips a capsule description of all other nationalities. The Irish stuck out "for being in some way underhanded. If you wanted a . . . favor, always you would go to the Irish because somehow or another . . . they got the favor." As to Germans, "The Poles never liked the Germans because of the partition of Poland." Worse yet were the Lithuanians, whom he referred to as "almost natural enemies. . . . They're very hard-headed, very stubborn." Slovaks "are closer to Poles," but Bohemians are "more distant." Even his own group was predictable: "If some issues came up, you always knew where the Poles were going to be." These were, however, only the categorizations used in the Monsignor's circle. Each group had its own understanding of outsiders. Stephen S. knew that the Irish were fighters and that Poles and Lithuanians were peaceful, but if you made them angry you were in trouble. Germans were fun-loving. Anthony W., on the other hand, thought the Irish were all "brawn and brogue" and that Slovaks kept to themselves, acting friendly, but cautious. Each group thus developed its own protective system of identification. Again, this was a method used throughout the United States.[35]

A sixth result of the pattern of nationalistic enclaves was the links it established among communities. Trust was now based on shared ethnicity, rather than on proximity or class. This meant that strong ties bound the national enclave to its sister communities around the country, via a network of newspapers and other types of communication. At the same time, ties between different enclaves within the same neighborhood disintegrated. It became better to associate with your own, even if they were several hundred miles away, than with a neighbor next door whose cultural heritage was different. Evelyn Ostrowski, a Pole who grew up on a Bohemian block, explained that "You were always cordial and friendly towards them, but you would never call upon them to help you." Relations between her people and Slovaks were also merely polite: We "were still Poles and they were still Slovaks. . . . There was no big open enmity or anything like that, but they weren't Polish, let's put it that way."[36]

This was the tragedy of the community pattern that developed in Back of the Yards and so many other places. Unity became difficult, and in time, impossible, despite the need for collective action about so many neighborhood problems. Earlier, when the area was sepa-

rated into segmented groups, people and leaders of different nationalities collaborated. As the nationalist spirit grew, however, the
barriers between enclaves became higher and stronger, until they
seemed unbreachable. By the time of the Great Depression, it
looked as though no power, no institution, could unite the neighborhood. Even the church became a victim of this situation which it
helped to create. By the late 1920s, priests were not on speaking
terms with one another; most of them did not even know one another. There was no communication, no cooperation, no visiting between rectories. It was not uncommon for priests of different
nationalities to cross the street rather than to exchange greetings.
Each priest viewed his parish as a separate national unit, to be ruled
as a private domain, a "kingdom"; as Herbert March said, parishes
were like "little autonomous empires." This, then, was the calamity
of the church in Back of the Yards. The major institution in the
community, which had helped to develop the social system by which
the residents coped with the world, had divided them.[37]

Nationalism worked beautifully as long as the enclave could handle whatever problems occurred. As a general rule, its resources
were phenomenal, its flexibility forged by creativity and necessity.
The nationalist enclave was not equipped to handle long and extreme hardship, however, any more than the village community
could solve the problems of a changing European economy. To solve
the larger problems, unity was needed, the drawing together of
people in a common fight for mutual goals. But the one belief common to all, the one institution everyone shared, became incapable of
leading the residents of Back of the Yards toward unity. Instead,
the church itself was fragmented: "Everybody had his own kingdom
to take care of and there was not too much concern about the other
fellow, the community," Monsignor Plawinski admitted. These men
could not take command of a larger movement. The walls within the
neighborhood were too high and nationalism too imbedded in their
mortar and brick.[38]

7

Spheres of Power:
Politics

Left, Martin H. Kennelly, Mayor of Chicago, 1947–55;
right, Edward J. Kelly, Mayor of Chicago, 1933–47.
Chicago Historical Society ICHi-18890

hicago's politicans used the ethnic conflicts in Back of the Yards for their own ends. The elaborate structure of tasks and rewards they erected offered many benefits to the residents, helped stabilize the neighborhood, and created an area of power apart from the packers. The politicians, however, never considered theirs a platform for fostering independence and challenging big business. Prisoners of ethnicity themselves, they perceived their area of influence as a private domain, ruled by a small and homogenous clique. In so doing, they built the national walls that much higher.

Politics in Back of the Yards was always a lively affair, rough and tumble, with an absorbing cast of characters. Though the neighborhood spanned many boundaries, the ward that came to be identified with the area was the Fourteenth. The adjacent wards, the Eleventh and Fifteenth, were considered the heart of other communities. The Eleventh, north and east of the Yards, contained Bridgeport, the home of Chicago's mayors from 1933 to 1979, and the Fifteenth covered the south and west, including more affluent sections like Brighton Park. The Fourteenth Ward stood squarely in the middle of the stockyards district.

In Chicago's working-class neighborhoods, there were certain rules to politics. The first was that the Democratic Party was the dominant political party, often to the virtual exclusion of all the others. It was the party of the workers, the poor, and the Roman Catholics. John Allswang, in *A House For All Peoples*, called it "the ethnics' real representative in . . . politics." Bruno N., a precinct captain, searched his memory and said, "I can't remember a Republican here . . . at any time." Election figures supported him. In the 1938 election, everyone in the 25th Precinct voted Democractic, even the Republican judges and clerks. When a couple of local Polish boys succeeded in getting sixty-five votes in one precinct for a Republican candidate, "it was almost written up in the *Tribune*," according to Ted P., one of the participants. Years later, in a 1967 campaign speech, Mayor Richard Daley said: "The Democratic Party is the party that opened its arms. We opened them to every nationality, to every creed. We opened them to the immigrants. The Democratic Party is the party of the people."[1]

Another prime rule was loyalty. A feature of the segmented society, this was the other side of the fear of fraud. Loyalty and dependability in politics, as in every other aspect of life, was of paramount importance. Loyalty produced order out of chaos, as important in the political clubs as it was anywhere else. Every group added the word "regular" to its formal title, to imply consistency and dependability. In 1986, the local political party was still formally registered as the Regular Democratic Organization of the Fourteenth Ward.

Politics also meant reliance on individual politicians. People looked to specific officeholders, and they had to measure up. The criteria were not brilliance or constitutional knowledge, but concern for the constituent's interests and an understanding of their way of life. Jane Addams explained, in "Why the Ward Boss Rules," that the residents of areas like the Fourteenth Ward "admire nothing so much as the good man. . . . The successful candidate must be a good man according to the standards of his constituents. He must not attempt to hold up a morality beyond them, nor must he attempt to reform or change the standard."[2]

Years later, David Heffernan, son of one of the first ward committeemen in the area, wrote of his upbringing: "We were respectably poor because everything . . . which might have provided our family with extras went to the desperately poor of the Thirteenth Ward in Chicago, now the Fourteenth Ward." Heffernan's father "never questioned *need;* but he did accept IOUs from the proud." These went into a drawer "in case they should ever be redeemed. His great fear was that he would be embarrassed if he could not find them to save a man his self-respect." When the father died, his widow gathered her children and showed them the pile of IOUs. Their lawyer could collect those debts, and little else remained by way of inheritance. But she also told them that they, the family, were all healthy and could work, while the IOUs were from poor families. The family destroyed every scrap. Charles Merriam, the political scientist, described leaders such as Heffernan as "the Little Father of the Community, who is always there and ready to help as best he can."[3]

The politicians, of course, demanded something in return—complete trust. Back of the Yards was strictly a representative democracy, never a direct one. The politicians defended the rights of their constituents passionately, but did not expect them to play any role in the workings of the ward or the city other than going to the polls. Everyone kept to his or her own domain, again a kind of segmentation. Rarely did the rulers permit outsiders to enter their world and learn how to wield political power.

The men of these early days were rough-and-tumble leaders. Tom Carey, alderman from 1893 to 1906, called his followers Carey's Indians, and Back of the Yards was known as "The Reservation." One labor organizer claimed that "For him they work and fight and not infrequently, bleed and even die." Carey came to Chicago in 1881 and worked in the yards for ten years before he became alderman. He owned the brickyards at 47th Street and Damen Avenue, and his workers dug clay and fired it for use in the new houses. The newspapers nicknamed him King of the Town of Lake. Men like these lived rough lives. At a dinner party, one of the speakers addressed David.

> David, it's a good thing you went into education. Politics would never do for Jim's son. While the people of the Ward worshipped him, by now you know, politics could never survive with many like him. He was good for the Ward when men worked like dogs from six to six and had little money to take home.

The speaker was the man who brought order from chaos, the organizer and leader of the Regular Democratic Organization of the Fourteenth Ward, Judge John J. Sullivan.[4]

Judge Sullivan was, according to Monsignor Ignatius M., "one of the pioneer architects" of the Fourteenth Ward Democratic Organization. Sullivan grew up on the South Side, attended public schools, and was graduated from Chicago Normal College in 1898 and Kent Law School in 1905. Admitted to the bar in 1906, he ran for a judgeship on the Muncipal Court in 1912, won, and reached the Superior Court in 1916. The judge had a remarkable memory and a strong temper, and though he could accept many kinds of intemperance from the voters, he accepted few slips from his workers. Martha Palka claimed that Alderman McDermott could often keep his anger in check and "just lay down the law, that's all. But the judge, oooh, he was a son of a gun." But at no point did Sullivan ever desert his ward. For years, his wife tried to persuade him to move to a better neighborhood, but the judge compromised by constantly moving further along Garfield Boulevard, always promising, "We'll move, we'll find something nicer," and then ending up a block away.[5]

Sullivan loved politics, and was in it "knee deep." His younger brother was personal secretary to Edward Dunne, governor of Illinois from 1913 to 1917, and a close friend of Patrick Nash of the prestigious political law firm of Nash and Aherne. Throughout his career, the judge refused to sit on a bench higher than the appellate court because it would have meant leaving politics. He also "avoided any type of limelight" and "preferred working behind the scenes," which suited his position as a judge. He first entered the political fray in the Thirteenth Ward, as the Fourteenth was then called, in

the mid-1910s. At that time, two politicians, Billy Lynch and
William O'Toole, fought for the alderman's position, draining each
other's energies and permitting an occasional independent Democrat like streetcar conductor Joseph Mahoney to slip in. Sullivan
persuaded Lynch and O'Toole to run in alternate years, thus keeping the organization firmly in control. According to the best account
of this 1914 meeting, the judge told them: "Now there's no use you
two beating your brains out. One of you run this year and the other
support him, and the next year vice versa." The two flipped a coin to
see who ran first, and O'Toole won and became alderman. From
then on, Sullivan was the undisputed arbitrator and boss of the
ward. That very year, he began to appoint precinct captains and
establish a formal ward organization.[6]

Judge Sullivan chose the Fourteenth Ward's alderman and the
ward committeeman and dictated their actions as he saw fit. Before
any big meeting downtown, he told his man, "Give me your proxy,"
and he attended the session himself. He governed his precinct captains with a firm hand and expected them to follow orders. Every
Sunday morning, all the members of the ward's organization met in
the judge's basement to thrash out any problems in their provinces.
One election year, one of his precinct captains did not like a candidate and failed to "get out the vote." Predictably, the total vote
dropped. At the next meeting, Sullivan asked why. The man explained, "I guess the people didn't like him." Sullivan poked his finger at the precinct captain: "It's because *you* didn't like him." Then
he laced into the man. The Fourteenth Ward soon gained a reputation as one of the strongest Democratic bastions in the city, in contrast even to the powerful Fifteenth, where, according to one social
worker, "they kind of let you go on your own and you could even be
a little independent." This was impossible in Judge Sullivan's
territory.[7]

The people, as well as the local politicos, turned to Sullivan. He
controlled all the city jobs in the ward, and eventually many
throughout Chicago. He was particularly efficient in arranging matters for prospective captains of police. One time, so a story went, a
captain wanted a transfer to the Loop station, but there were no
vacancies. The current officeholders told him, "Our clout is better
than yours and we're staying here." The police captain went to
Judge Sullivan, who arranged his transfer. His new colleagues,
amazed, asked, "Who was your clout? It must be a good one." He
replied, "Yeah, Judge Sullivan." Surprised, they responded, "Oh,
that's ours too." But it was not only police captains that he helped

with jobs. People came to his home constantly, asking help of all kinds. He dispensed financial advice and marriage counseling, got people out of jail, and arranged promotions. This went on every night and every once in a while his outraged wife protested the eight or ten people waiting in the house and the line outside.[8]

The Democrats downtown recognized Sullivan's shrewdness, even-handedness and, most of all, his brilliance at slatemaking. The judge was a master at setting up a winning ticket, knowing whom the voters would accept for which office. Jacob Arvey, chair of the Cook County Democratic Party, claimed that five men ran the Democratic organization in the thirties and forties and that Sullivan was one of them. These five men also made up the slates, often in Judge Sullivan's basement on Garfield Boulevard. He was asked to act as arbitrator in the highest political circles, and he was the only man to sit on the Cook County Democratic Party Central Committee without being elected to it. The observation that Sullivan "helped found the whole Democratic Party that exists today" (i.e., the Democratic Party machine) seemed accurate.[9]

Political success in Sullivan's organization required a variety of skills. Someone who was a good campaigner, able to talk up a candidate to friends and neighbors, was noticed by the older, more established figures, who would ask him for small favors—run errands or go to City Hall. Someone who was doing well might be asked to serve as an usher at a rally or escort a speaker to the platform. Escorting a speaker was a real sign of recognition. The excitement would "rub off on you," according to Monsignor Ignatius M.: "When the leader's name was announced and people clapped, well, you became an extension of that applause. You're right next to him. . . . You say, 'Hey, gee, what he has, that's what I would like to have.'" Another route to success was to serve as a precinct captain. And if one had an education, one attracted notice immediately because most of the politicians lacked any advanced schooling. The legal profession was the best to be in, because lawyers gained reputations as smart men and good talkers. Lawyers could create backing by helping people and by word-of-mouth publicity that brought them and their good works to the attention of higher-ups. The profession was respected: "People took an awful lot of pride in somebody in those days . . . who was working his way through school and became a lawyer."[10]

It also helped to be part of the right ethnic, family, and social circles. All Fourteenth Ward politicians were Irish, and they were often related to other ward leaders. James McDermott learned politics from his uncle Frank, the alderman of the Twenty-ninth Ward from 1910 to 1916 and the ward committeeman from 1910 to 1914. The most important fraternity was connected with Visitation parish, on Garfield Boulevard. *All* Fourteenth Ward politicians went there, not only to worship but also to educate their sons in the parish school. Sullivan, James McDermott, Clarence Wagner, and Joseph and Edward Burke—that is, every alderman of the Fourteenth Ward from 1933 to this writing—attended services at that church, and Wagner and Ed Burke were educated in the parish's school. Even James Breen, Republican committeeman of the Fourteenth Ward from 1928 to 1960, was a parishioner at Visitation. It was not idle chatter when David Heffernan remarked, "That whole South Side was such a clannish, tight group."[11]

The job of ward leader was a taxing one and took long hours, sometimes seemingly without end. There were really two positions, ward committeeman and alderman. Committeeman was a party post, and its incumbent was elected by the precinct captains. He handled requests for patronage jobs; chose candidates for the Illinois House of Representatives, Senate, and judiciary; sat on the party's central committee; and ran the election campaigns in the ward. The alderman was the elected representative of the people and sat in the City Council. He handled complaints, dealt with his constituents, and in general was the front man for the ward. In the Fourteenth Ward, the alderman and the ward committeeman were usually one and the same, ensuring a united organization.[12]

The ward's residents turned to the organization for all manner of help—cleaning up dirty alleys, having garbage collected, getting out of jury duty, fixing broken curbs, obtaining food, finding medical help and gaining admission to Cook County Hospital, getting kids out of jail, obtaining financial assistance, appealing real-estate tax assessments, having gutters and street lights put in, obtaining permits and licenses, doing any other kind of business with the city, and especially getting jobs. They wanted to get things fixed, and according to John H., a former precinct captain, they wanted the alderman "to stick up for you." Though the alderman met his public every day of the year, Tuesday night was ward night, the appointed time for citizens to seek assistance. Always accompanied by their precinct captain, the voters filed in with petitions. The alderman and ward committeeman "would sit in the back room, and as the people would come in with their precinct captains they would be handling job requests and services."[13]

Favors were not automatically granted. If someone complained that an assessment was too high, the alderman went downtown and checked it out. If he could do nothing about it, he told the constituent that the assessment was fair. Usually, the constituent needed another favor later, and the score could be evened. The Democratic Party's helping hand was always extended. Richard Daley, Chicago's mayor from 1955 until his death in 1976, instructed his people, "Don't worry if they're Democrats or Republicans. Give them service and they'll become Democrats."[14]

The alderman was always visible and always on call. He attended funerals: Jane Addams wrote of the alderman's "ministering to a genuine craving for comfort and solace, and at the same time . . . assisting at an important social function." Aldermen attended fund raisers for the church and for its organizations. Among the honored guests at the celebration for Father Joseph Forst, long-time chaplain of St. Augustine's Knights of Columbus, on 19 December 1932, were Judge Sullivan, Alderman James McDermott, and future alderman Clarence Wagner. When the Mexican residents began to form a church of their own in the late thirties, Alderman McDermott was there also. Encarnacion Chico, one of the founders of Immaculate Heart of Mary Vicariate, said of him, "A lot of time, he come over here and talk," and he spoke of the politician's friendship with Father Tort, the priest who founded the parish. The alderman's attendance at services also bolstered the priest's influence: as the alderman emerged, he would stop to talk to the pastor, who might introduce and intercede for a petitioner.[15]

The alderman also took care of his people in more formal ways, both within the ward and downtown. The Fourteenth Ward Democratic Organization sponsored picnics and field days; Fourth of July celebrations with fireworks and parades; softball leagues; and a charity show that earned enough in 1937, a Depression year, to pay for clothes for four thousand children. In the City Council, the alderman fought for new street lights and wider viaducts, services that were not always easy to obtain. Alderman James McDermott got streets in the Fourteenth Ward paved in 1937 despite "a heated debate in the City Council."[16]

One of the Fourteenth Ward's great aldermen, and the foremost protégé of John J. Sullivan, was James McDermott. He served as alderman from 1933 to 1942 and as ward committeeman from 1932 to 1948. Judge Thomas Kluczynski, brother of the ward's Polish political leader, described McDermott as "a great, strong-minded lad, good lawyer, good political man . . . and he was a leader." He came from the yards neighborhood and attended grammar school at St.

Gabriel's in the front of the yards, the parish of Father Morris Dhorney, the "stockyards priest." He graduated from DePaul University Law School and was admitted to the bar in 1920. James was attracted to politics early by his uncle Frank. Wisely following the path of aspiring politicians, he attached himself to Frank Bush, a professor at DePaul and, when Bush ran for office, helped with the campaign. After that, he started working with the Fourteenth Ward Organization. A member of Visitation parish, McDermott was also friendly with Judge Sullivan, and eventually they became neighbors.[17]

McDermott used his law degree to advance his political career. Joining the firm of Nash and Aherne, he assisted the defense in the Chicago Black Sox trial. He worked long and hard in the community and placed his knowledge of criminal law at the service of youngsters in trouble with the police. People began to turn to McDermott for help, and they told Sullivan: "Gee, that McDermott's a hell of a guy. . . . He's got a lot of ability. . . . He's well known in the community. . . . He's done this for Mrs. O'Shaughnessy, and this for Mr. White, and he's done this for So-and-So," and they reported, "I heard the judge say, as he left the courtroom, 'that guy's ticketed for something and he's a comer.'" In this way, according to a relative, the citizenry acted like "talent scouts." Sullivan found in the young lawyer qualities he respected and valued—McDermott was outgoing, bright, energetic, and put in long hours—and he decided to foster McDermott's career. Decades later, McDermott told a dinner audience that he owed everything to Judge Sullivan.[18]

McDermott's big chance came in 1933. From 1923 to 1931, the Fourteenth Ward's alderman was William O'Toole. His perennial opponent was Thomas O'Grady, "a fiery person with ability and talent and a good orator," who, according to John C., "could talk his weight in gold." O'Grady was an "insurrectionist" Democrat who fought the regular organization. In 1931, O'Grady ousted O'Toole, so the judge dumped O'Toole and chose McDermott to replace him. In 1933, McDermott, the new regular candidate, won; he remained alderman till 1942 and ward committeeman till 1948. Years later, when O'Grady died, McDermott took care of all the relatives and gave them jobs.[19]

James McDermott was perfect for the role of alderman. He was tall—six feet and three inches—and very handsome, with silver-gray hair. Nicknamed Big Jim, he was a fiery speaker and cut a fine figure. Father Joseph Kelly described McDermott as "a great, beautiful . . . father, victory triumphant figure. . . . He had presence." The *Town of Lake Journal* (now *Back of the Yards Journal*), an independent paper not tied to any political organization, spoke of the "brilliant, powerful, forceful Jim McDermott, known not only on the South Side but throughout the whole city." His precinct captains saluted him, and one described him as "a gentleman. . . . You couldn't find better." At parties, according to Martha Palka, he "used to dance like heck when he had a few drinks," and every Christmas he brought all the nuns a little something. Stanley K. summed it up: "McDermott was a very high-class man."[20]

As important as the alderman and the ward committeeman were, their power lay in the ability of their precinct captains. Judge Thomas Kluczynski described the precinct captain:

> He is the bone of the organization. He is the unit where the party functions. He's with the people, with the voter, he's the one that's selling, he's the solicitor for the party, he's the one that convinces the people to vote. . . . Without the precinct captain, you don't have much of an organization.

A study of six hundred precinct captains throughout Chicago in the mid-1940s found that most were men between thirty and fifty-five. They settled largely in areas occupied by their own ethnic group, and in poor and middle class districts the neighborhoods they served were the ones they grew up in. Seventy percent held jobs in government; 20 percent of these with the city, 17 percent with the county, 10 percent with the Sanitary District, and 9 percent with the courts. Eighty percent were married and 60 percent had children. Their most important qualification was their gregariousness. Every precinct captain had to like people, had to enjoy talking to them. Tom D., an Irish precinct captain, said, "I enjoyed it all the time. . . . You were good to the people. . . . They were people you lived with all your life." When asked why he was a precinct captain, Edward M., Polish, answered, "I like people, I like talking to them." Other attributes helped, of course. Edward's fluency in Polish gained him entreé into Polish homes. Tom D. had a perfect memory; he could take a poll sheet and add the proper address to any name, or the name to literally any address in the precinct.[21]

Most precinct captains started out in city jobs. The incumbent precinct captain got a worker a city job, and in return the worker started to help out in the ward. If the newcomer showed talent, in time he could take over the precinct captain's job himself. If he was *too* good, was showing up the regular captain, he often got the job faster. Stanley K. started out in politics by supporting an independent. When, owing to his work, the regular Democratic candidate lost in that precinct, the ward office called him in and asked him to join. Similarly, Joseph Palka, challenged by an Irish acquaintance, campaigned for an opponent of the regular Democratic ticket. When his man won, the organization made him precinct captain. At the time he was not even old enough to vote.[22]

Working the precinct was a full-time job. According to Stanley K., "an active precinct captain is out 365 days." Edward M. said that people came to his house "any hour of the night, any hour of the morning." Every day, the precinct captain visited his neighbors' homes to see what services the organization could render. The subject of conversation was usually anything but politics. If they liked dogs, the precinct captain talked about dogs; if they read books, he offered to lend volumes from his own collection; if the voter preferred magazines, these were available. Always he asked: "What can I do to help you?" He would "just rant and rave, never mention a word on politics . . . make friends. It was number one on my list. Make 'em your friend. Kill 'em with kindness."[23]

Women were not neglected by the organization. The politicans recognized the importance of the female's influence at home as well as of her vote, and they organized ladies' clubs. Some precinct captains, like Stanley K., concentrated on the women during the election. And one official position was reserved for women—clerk or judge on election day. It was a woman's job because it paid less than a man made during the day. Women were more likely to be home anyway, the party figured, and the precinct captains chose women who could read and write English. Most of all, they preferred to hire members of needy families, a good way of adding a few extra dollars to the family till. The women chosen as judges looked forward to the election as a "way to get away from home." They sat and chatted about who had come in and who had not, compared impressions, swapped recipes, and always sent someone out to Urbauer's Bakery on 51st Street for rolls and cake to go with the coffee.[24]

This entire structure had one purpose—to win elections. Precinct captains were hired and fired in accordance with the votes they delivered. Their concern was the local, not the national election. Edward M. explained that "you want the home front . . . solidified because, after you got the home front solidified, the national election will come. It'll fall in line." The intimate contact of the ward officials with the voters thus guaranteed Democratic votes for city, state, and national office. The campaigns were large and loud. Parades blocked streets and auto drivers honked horns. Mass meetings were held in school auditoriums, the only halls large enough to handle the crowds. Especially in the early days, these meetings were among the few public entertainments available. The ward provided singers and other performers, and the candidates told the people why they should vote for them and what they would do for the neighborhood. Part of the campaign's funds was raised at parties and through games. Other income came from dues, raffles, and businesses.[25]

During a campaign, the precinct captains and even their assistants held weekly meetings. Workers went from door to door, reminding people of past favors, and used their personal contacts. No one, not even the Republicans, missed a meeting with the Democratic precinct captain; one could never pass up the chance to meet a voter. The precinct captain used information about the candidates, the ward organization, the neighborhood, and the voter himself. "Nine times out of ten," said Edward M., "I'd be invited in and have coffee, rolls, whatever, or a drink." He canvassed two or three homes a night. Tavern proprietors also played their part. The captain approached the owner and presented his side of the issues. The saloonkeeper then spoke favorably about the candidates and displayed posters. A small exchange of business, such as a beer, was part of the encounter. The same conversations were held at other kinds of stores. Posters, on houses as well as shops, cloaked the neighborhood. On election day, large majorities voted Democratic. Most of the money given to voters during a campaign went to poor families, but some illiterates received $1 and a marked ballot. The tie between the citizen and the ward worker was often so close that the voter came to ask, "How should I vote?" This happened because the voters' knowledge of local politics was often dim but their trust in the precinct captain was great.[26]

The major source of friction within the organization stemmed from the ethnic diversity of the ward. Though reformers labeled the Democratic organization a "machine," it was never that monolithic. Each ethnic group had its own political interest and organized and fought for recognition. Each group revered the few kinsmen who succeeded in public life. John Kubina and others, for example, organized a Slovak political club around St. Michael church. It was affiliated with the regular ward organization and, during a campaign, they worked for the regular ticket among their people. Throughout the year the group functioned as a club and performed social services such as taking people downtown for naturalization examinations. There was also a chapter of the Lithuanian Democratic League in the ward.[27]

The archfoes of the Slovaks, the Bohemians, had their own hero. James Kovarik, alderman of the nearby Fifteenth Ward from 1931 to 1947, was the first of his ethnic group to reach this position, and to Bohemians, "he was a saint." William B.'s father used to take Bohemian countrymen downtown for their citizenship exams. One fellow failed over and over and Mr. B. said he would escort him only once more, and only if he attended naturalization classes and studied. After doing so, the man reported that he "knew everything." At the courtroom downtown, they showed him a picture of the flag of the United States, which he identified correctly. "Oh, he was so proud" of that accomplishment. Then the judge asked, "Who is the president of the United States?" The Bohemian replied instantly: "Alderman Kovarik." William's father, angry and embarrassed, called him names in public, yelling, "You told me you knew everything." The fellow could only reply, "Well, isn't he president?"[28]

These ethnic groups resented the Irish domination of politics, but the Irish retained their power through superior tactics. Most Eastern European groups hated each other more than they did the sons of Eire, and the Irish used this advantage. McDermott once repeated a classic political saw to John White: "A Lithuanian won't vote for a Pole, and a Pole won't vote for a Lithuanian. A German won't vote for either of them—but all three will vote for a Turkey [an Irish man]." They also capitalized on jealousies within an ethnic group. If one group put forward a candidate, the Irish asked for nominations from the floor and some other ambitious precinct captain from the same national group usually accepted the bait. When this did not work, a straw horse, previously agreed upon by the ward leaders, entered the fray. The members of the group began to wrangle, the ward leaders would amicably point out that they liked both contenders and didn't want to antagonize either, and then chose their own man. In December 1938, for example, Anthony Wojciechowski announced his candidacy for alderman of the Fourteenth Ward, opposing McDermott. In February he ran against the Irish ward leader and Walter Piotrowski, a staunch member of the Fourteenth Ward Polish Democratic Club, which was part of the regular organization. The plan was to split the Polish vote, but it was not really necessary. Piotrowski received 257 votes; Wojciechowski received 489; and McDermott, 13,410. And the Irish had other ways to prevent the rise of effective, independent action by other ethnic groups. Potential leaders were bought off or controlled through patronage or by controlling their representatives, or power brokers, who spoke for them in the higher circles of the ward.[29]

All of these factors can be found in the story of the Poles, the largest group in the ward, and the source of the most conflict. Their resentment was often great; they felt that "If you weren't Irish you didn't get too much." Nevertheless, they said that when the Irish politicans needed something they always came to the Poles: "The Irish politicians controlled them [the Polish people] completely. . . . They used them and used them and used them for their own purposes."[30]

The leading instrument for politically minded Poles in the area was the Polish Citizens Regular Democratic Club of the Fourteenth Ward, founded on 28 April 1928 and renamed the Polish Regular Democratic Club of the Fourteenth Ward in 1933. Although his name did not appear in the incorporation papers, its moving spirit was State Representative John Kluczynski, nicknamed Johnny Klu. Kluczynski was a precinct captain in the Fifteenth Ward who moved into the Fourteenth and linked up with Tom O'Grady. After sizing up the situation, he switched to the Sullivan organization. John Kluczynski had "a great personality," according to his brother Thomas, and was a good campaigner. In 1930, he was elected state representative, a position he held for many years. Kluczynski became the spokesman, or broker, "the big leader," of the Polish politicians. Sullivan and McDermott accepted him and became "very close" with Kluczynski, "the only Pole out with McDermott and Sullivan and all of them," according to Stanley K. This status enabled the state representative to organize the Polish Democratic Club as a personal vehicle; in it he assembled all the powerful Polish precinct captains, men like Anthony Grabe, Joseph Detloff, Peter Kezon, Joseph Palka, and John Chudzik. They were his clique, controllable and deliverable both to him and to the larger ward organization. He arranged for jobs and other services, he served as the club's honorary chairman, and he helped it to function properly by donating beer for parties and celebrations and by keeping a close eye on its activities.[31]

The club functioned as a social club as well as a political club, a not unusual combination. It sponsored traditional affairs like the Easter Dinner, the Polish Constitutional Day Party on May third, and all the religious and social events celebrated in Poland. There were picnics, Christmas parties for members' children, a large fundraising turkey raffle each year, a New Year's party, and the annual induction of new officers. Members exchanged personal news at meetings and drummed up business. Afterward there was always plenty of conversation, food, and coffee or other refreshments: the minutes of the meeting of 9 May 1941 report that Mr. Burdzinski,

No.

164

Chapter 7

Sr., "said we should adjourn the meeting and drink up the beer that we have on tap." The club also looked out for its members and neighbors. Wakes were well attended, since cards were sent to all brethren asking them to appear. The club sponsored a Polish-language school for young children, and free naturalization classes which were attended by as many as ninety-four students at a time. To help foreign-born Poles in the courts, the club tried to get a member assigned to the local judicial center. An Improvement Committee passed on to the ward office the membership's recommendations for banning peddlers and its requests for street lights, stop lights, street paving, repair of curbs, and improved public transportation.[32]

These social and service-oriented activities served many purposes. Representative Kluczynski once said that most Polish-American political clubs failed because there was too much emphasis on dues and politics, not enough on "social conviviality." The Fourteenth Ward's club became one of the strongest in the city, in part because its wide range of activities acted as glue to bind members to the club and to the ward organization. Kluczynski also felt that a major cause of failure was the lack of organized social events in the summer; again the Fourteenth Ward passed a resolution to "hold meetings all summer or just drink beer on that day."[33]

Like any part of the segmented society, the club had its own internal order. All business remained confidential; any news leaked to the outside created a stir and led to long discussions and recriminations. Such indiscretions included both talking too freely and placing unauthorized articles in the local press. When another social organization used the Poles' clubroom without a member's permission, a "long discussion" in executive session resolved that anyone wishing to use the facilities must have a letter okayed by the executive committee.[34]

The Polish Democratic Club had a woman's auxiliary, founded at the same time; members were mostly the wives of precinct captains and other ward workers. They had, according to Walter S. Kozubowski, "organizational abilities," and they played major roles in raising funds and in organizing social activities. The women's group had interests similar to the men's, but its emphasis varied. The women sponsored few large parties of their own, but they took the day-to-day business of running a club very seriously. There seemed a real joy in participating, in going through the motions of parliamentry procedure, thereby emulating the higher-status organizations outside the domain of the household. Discussions of the exact

procedures to follow when a member died covered page after page
of the minutes and lasted for months, and changes and resolutions
were offered for years. The minutes of a discussion of a party and
dance, an unusual event, included such details as the owner's pledge
that "If he makes good at the Bar, he may either lower the price of
the hall or give it to us entirely free of charge," and the credit given
Mrs. Palka "for getting the musicians at $2.00 a man instead of
$3.00 as they had first requested." The women looked after their
own, resolving that the club purchase goods and services from members whenever possible, setting up a benefit for one of the men
whose arms were amputated in an accident, or arranging a bunco
party for a female Polish Democrat whose brother was being ordained. Every meeting ended with a bunco game or coffee and cake.
In the forties, they sponsored cigarette drives for servicemen and
raised money for charities. And like the men, they retained their
cultural ties to Poland. Appeals to vote often stressed the need to
help Polish candidates, and when Mrs. H. Struzynas talked on "the
place of a women in politics and her duty," the minutes emphasized
that "she also spoke in her beautiful Polish" and "received a storm
of applause."[35]

Since there was lavish attention to the ritual of meetings, it followed that internal regulation was an important order of business.
When athletic teams were organized, only members could play. Re-
crimination over charity baskets at Christmas led to audits. Resolutions were passed to ban gossip from the meetings, any member
who carried news out of a meeting was to be expelled, and for a time
there was a secret committee to investigate new members. This
committee was proposed by a man and lasted only a short while.
The discussion about a gift for John Kluczynski was typical. Mrs.
Vera Detloff (wife of precinct captain and park supervisor Joseph)
suggested that, instead of flowers, the women offer a more practical
gift, like a gladstone bag. Miss Wanda Meyers suggested that the
bag be purchased wholesale, and the motion passed. Miss Meyers
then informed the members that she could purchase the bag at "better than 50% discount." Unfortunately, the next motion was by Miss
Kubaszak, who "said that she could secure a better discount than
Miss Meyers." Mrs. Detloff, clearly a diplomat, suggested that the
two women obtain prices before a decision would be made. Miss
Frejmark then moved that Mrs. Kluczynski (mother of John and
grande dame of the club) "accompany the ladies who are making the
purchase." The minutes' report on her response was brief and
pungent: "Mrs. Kluczynski refused to participate."[36]

Involved with their own world and pleased with the freedom the club offered, the women acted independently and brooked little interference. Although males usually attended the auxiliary's business sessions, the women sometimes rebelled: Miss Frejmark once moved to nominate a sergeant at arms to "keep all the men away during our meetings." The members complained when the men loaned out their bunco tables without permission and they balked at helping with the club's rent when the men neglected to pay their membership dues. Prior to a New Year's Eve party in 1932, Joseph Palka of the men's club asked for and received a list of the women who had volunteered to help at the party. Apparently the men's purpose was to assess the attractiveness of the women who would be present, and they were disappointed. When word of this reached members of the women's club they called Miss Frejmark, who had released the list, to account. They absolved her when she explained that she had no idea of the reason for Mr. Palka's request, but Mrs. Paluch felt that "It was very unkind of the men to take such an attitude." She was sure that "The women will make their appearance as presentable when they are dressed in white uniforms as any of the other young ladies." Mr. Palka protested that all the men were satisfied with the list, and after a few more conciliatory remarks everyone dropped the matter.[37]

Politics played a much smaller role in the women's club than in the men's. In this area, the females accepted male domination, but they set their own standards. Most of their political activities centered on speeches exhorting the women to register, vote, and attend mass meetings. On one occasion they offered to contribute to Representative Kluczynski's campaign, but he declined because he was running unopposed. At another meeting, the chair discussed rumors that some of the members were voting for O'Grady instead of McDermott (in 1933, McDermott's first race for alderman). In the men's club, this would have been heresy, and would have been dealt with severely. Mrs. Detloff merely asked that "If there were any, to please change and vote for Mr. McDermott."[38]

In much the same way as the parent ward claimed Visitation parish as its own, the Poles of the Fourteenth Ward organization claimed St. John of God as the heart of their segmented group. According to Thomas Kluczynski, "St. John of God was where the [Polish] leaders of the Fourteenth Ward Democratic Organization attended." John Kluczynski went there, as did his supporters, in part because they came from the area around the church. The club met at 48th Street and Throop Avenue in those days: St. John of God was the nearest Polish parish and its pastor, Father Louis Grudzinski, was a leading Polish nationalist. The pastor always stayed in the background, but Father Edward Plawinski recalled that he "held strong feelings on the need for more Polish representation and on the Irish domination of the ward." The Back of the Yards Neighborhood Council later listed the Regular Polish Democratic Club as one of St. John of God's societies, and St. John of God was very helpful to the Poles of the Fourteenth Ward. Father Grudzinski supported the club by announcing its raffles and fund-raising efforts from the pulpit. He opened the church hall to their Thanksgiving dinners, for their bingo and other games of chance, for the installation of their officers, and he released his school's hall for their mass meetings during campaigns. In return, the club's members contributed regularly to the church. When, under financial stress, the club voted to stop purchasing tickets to the functions of other organizations and to stop advertising in their programs, it exempted the Polish daily papers, the Regular Democratic Organization of the Fourteenth Ward, and St. John of God parish. The church, therefore, had the same relationship to the Fourteenth Ward Regular Polish Democratic Club that every church had to the associations in its neighborhood: social center, meeting place, and focal point of local activities. Martha Palka recalled the banquets and dinners at the St. John of God hall and said, "It was always the same people and you had a good time."[39]

The main purpose of the Polish Democratic Club, despite all the social activities, was politics. The club worked for more local representation for Poles—more city jobs, more precinct captains, and more Polish candidates for office. To achieve this goal, the members worked zealously for the regular organization by helping to plan mass meetings, providing speakers for Polish gatherings, and generally getting out the vote by endorsing Democratic candidates and making an honorary member of any Pole running for office on that party's ticket. Kluczynski often spoke, explaining the issues and asking Poles to vote the straight Democratic ticket. Club members vied with each other in expressions of support for the Democrats and denunciations of the Republicans. At the meeting on 13 September 1940, for example, the discussion began when Mr. J. Kaczanowski "pointed out that any Pole voting for Willkie [the Republican candidate for the presidency] is voting against himself and his nationality and his religion and . . . it was our duty to vote for Pres. Roosevelt." Mr. Burdzinski went on: "Roosevelt is the liberation of the working man and the poor man. Where would our

banks and building and loans be today without Roosevelt?" Not to
be outdone, Mr. Bogaczyk claimed that "Willkie is worst than Hitler
and asks the members to make sure they are properly registered."
Mr. Lewandowski summed it up: "The Germans always vote
against the Poles and we should vote against their kind." From a
Democratic presidential campaign, the members had derived a holy
crusade against Teutonic domination, not an unlikely connection in
those days.[40]

The club's constitution specifically defined one of its purposes as
"to strive to secure nominations for elective office for Polish Americans . . . on the Democratic ticket." And while the members generally agreed to support Irish candidates and considered the ward's
leaders their backers and friends, their resentment continued to fes-
ter. Their feeling was that, "They're all good alderman for the
Irish." Some Poles had jobs, of course, but it always seemed to be
the little jobs, and Stanley K. compared it to throwing a bone to a
dog. As of 1939, no Pole appeared on the cards or literature of the
Regular Democratic Organization of the Fourteenth Ward. To obtain more power, the Poles needed one of their own in higher office:
they especially wanted a Polish alderman. In 1939, when John
Kluczynski advanced from state representative to state senator, the
club discussed trying to elect another Polish representative—"and
in due time a Polish alderman will be elected with the support of the
regular Democratic organization." According to Walter S. Kozubowski, the Poles experienced "a great deal of aggravation . . . and
a great deal of discussion. . . . There were some really heated de-
bates." It was John Kluczynski's job to handle this resentment, but
in the early 1940s his ability to do so waned. At the meeting on 9
January 1942, the club's members rejected Joseph Palka's suggestion that they endorse all the Democratic candidates. Ted
Piasecki argued that it was too early to make such an endorsement
since they did not know who the candidates were: "We should not
endorse any ticket blindly." He also suggested that a letter be sent
to John Kluczynski, asking him to attend meetings more often.[41]

A more direct challenge occurred soon after. In 1942, James
McDermott decided to step down as alderman following his election
to the County Board of Tax Appeals. As early as 13 February, the
members of the Fourteenth Ward's Polish Democratic Club passed
a resolution asking its executive committee to try to get a Pole
slated for alderman. A month later, no action had been taken. Mr.
Burdzinski suggested that, since two Poles were running for the
Illinois House of Representatives from the Fourth District, mem-

bers should vote for either one. Mr. Skrentny contested this suggestion and asked that the Poles vote solidly for their countryman who was the regular Democratic candidate, and Ed Majewski said he could not understand why Burdzinski wanted them to vote for anyone not part of the regular organization. The Club endorsed the entire Democratic ticket. The quest for a Polish alderman did not die however. According to Martha Palka, Joseph Palka's wife, the precinct captains in the club were upset about the quality of the patronage jobs available to them. In October, they formed a committee to lobby for a Polish alderman. On 9 October 1942, Palka, a party stalwart who was usually the first to ask them to endorse the ticket, "informed the members that he threw his hat in the ring for the office of alderman and told Judge Sullivan that he would like to get the endorsement of the Regular organizations."[42]

A group of Poles, including Father Louis Grudzinski, went to Judge Sullivan's house to ask him to back Palka. They argued, "Don't you think it's time we had a Polish alderman?" Sullivan replied, "Well, I don't see nothing wrong with it"; he felt it was "possible." When asked directly if he would support Joseph Palka, he told them, "I'll be with whoever the precinct captains nominate, and I'll be with him heart and soul. If they nominate Palka I'll be with him a hundred percent, financially and every other way." He then called a meeting and chose five men to screen applications and select a captain. There were three contenders: Dan O'Brien, Palka, and Clarence Wagner. Both Sullivan and McDermott wanted Wagner, a precinct captain, a lawyer with a good record, personable, bright, "dependable," and a good politician, Irish on his mother's side (his full name was Clarence Patrick Wagner), and a member of Visitation parish. There was no contest: Sullivan told the committee of five whom he wanted and they turned in Wagner's name.[43]

The Polish club was outraged. At the meeting on 8 January 1943, Burdzinski asked about the progress of the committee working for Palka's nomination. Mr. Postanowicz, chair of the committee, told them that he had expected to hear by Christmas, but that no word had come, and that Wagner was the new candidate. He felt that his delegation had been "ignored." Mr. Frankowski moved to endorse Joseph Palka for the office of alderman of the Fourteenth Ward and the members approved. Seven Polish societies also endorsed Palka, and the local Polish National Alliance offered to hold a bingo party to raise funds. Mr. Kalicki suggested that they change the name of the club and take certain pictures off the wall, but this suggestion was dropped. After some debate, the members voted $500 for Pal-

ka's campaign. He thanked them and declared that he intended to
stay with the race. Having launched their insurrection, the members adjourned.[44]

A short, rotund man of forty-one, Joseph Palka was a precinct
captain in 1943. Besides working in politics, he and his brother
Frank operated a cigar factory in Joe's home. They sold mostly to
taverns, Frank handling the manufacturing side and Joe the business end. Joe visited his customers every Monday to drum up business and take orders, which supported his political aspirations
because he could meet and befriend many people. When the Vol-
stead Act became law, sales fell and he asked Judge Sullivan for a
job, arguing that he had always obtained positions for others and
that now he needed work. The judge agreed and made Joe a license
inspector, checking retail stores. In 1933, he became bailiff in the
office of the municipal court clerk, a job he still held when he decided to run for alderman.[45]

The Fourteenth Ward's regular Democratic organization reacted
swiftly and efficiently. Sullivan and McDermott had no intention of
turning power over to the Poles. They spent lavishly; McDermott
later told Palka, "Of all the men running up against our men, nobody broke our till like you did." They also tried to split the vote.
The field of candidates, besides Wagner and Palka, was increased to
include Jozef Pash, a Slovak, and Thomas Tomaskiewicz, another
Pole. Residents told investigators that Tomaskiewicz, a laborer at
Swift & Company, was put on the ballot to siphon off Polish votes
from Palka. But the organization's most powerful weapon was its
control of the precinct captains. Sullivan summoned them all and
told them they had to beat Palka: they were either going to support
Wagner or they were out of a job. Some, like John H., rationalized
the situation: "We had too many Polish fellows who had jobs with
the city who would have lost if they had gone with Palka." Others,
including Stanley K., focussed on their personal problems: "If your
job is on the line and all the pressure comes. . . . You just got to
back off, that's all." These precinct captains then went out and
fought for Wagner, becoming the chief instruments of Palka's defeat. Edward M., a Polish precinct captain, encountered some problems that year and had to work harder. He told voters that Palka
wasn't qualified, that he didn't have a good enough background, and
that Wagner was a polished, educated professional. The man had a
job to do and he did it well; Wagner won in his precinct.[46]

Palka was opposed even at home. Upon hearing of his nomination, his wife told him, "Joe, don't you run for no alderman." She
realized it was wrong for him, and throughout the campaign she

repeated, "I hope you lose." And in the election on 23 February 1943, her husband did lose, mostly because, as Konstanty G. put it, "He didn't have no power." The vote was 11,794 for Wagner, 3,696 for Palka, 440 for Tomaskiewicz, and 240 for Pash.[47]

Palka did everything he could to reingratiate himself. At a meeting on 5 March 1943, he promised his cooperation and said he would ask his supporters to do the same. Other members urged everyone to "forget bygones," but they all pointed out that they should always work with the regular organization. At the meeting on 19 March, the president read the club's by-laws, "impressing on their minds that this organization is 100 percent regular Democratic at all times." Palka explained that he ran only because the leaders of the Polish societies would not let him withdraw and forced him to continue. Finally, the meeting voted to send Alderman Wagner a message of congratulations and to obtain a copy of his picture for the wall. Palka had forfeited his city job to run for office, and it was a year before the ward leaders restored it. The Polish revolt was over.[48]

Politics, which drew its strength from the city's legal structure and the Democratic Party's control of patronage, was a major source of power in Back of the Yards. Its control was concentrated in the hands of a small group, a clique like any other in the area. The Visitation circle made all the decisions, from choosing candidates to dispensing the jobs and favors, the fuel that ran the ward organization. The voters benefited because city officials responded to their needs, which was far from likely under a different type of administration. Government was accessible, as people who were frozen out of the bureaucracy found that the city's services were made available in their neighborhood in a humane, practical way. It would have been easy for the citizens to neglect their rights and to allow the city to ignore them if a request meant a trip downtown to confront a stony-faced clerk. Instead, encouraged by local politicians who shared their values and standards, the residents felt free to seek their share of the city's benefits. Politics was, therefore, a force in building and stabilizing the neighborhood.

But the price the residents paid for their political benefits was high. They released control of a structure strong enough to challenge, or at least place pressure on, the packers. The ward leaders had no interest in contesting the packers; moreover, they promoted the neighborhood's ethnic and national divisions as a way of staying in power. At no time did they teach anyone to unite or how to gain or use power, since that might have fostered political opposition. It would take a very different kind of organization, with a unique structure, to attain independence and achieve unity.

8

Spheres of Power: The University of Chicago Settlement House

Class at the University of Chicago Settlement House
Chicago Historical Society

Some institutions stood apart from the world of meat-packers and workers, as well as from politics and the churches, drawing their power from sources that had little to do with the stockyards and the ward. As such, they had separate, independent spheres of power. They existed within the segmented neighborhood but outside of its dominant pattern, and therefore effected little change. One, the University of Chicago Settlement House, played a major role in the area and became part of the story of Back of the Yards, but it never developed the kind of independent community leadership that could have helped the residents to become autonomous. Its most important contribution was to provide help and leadership to the Mexican immigrants.

In 1894, the Department of Economics of the University of Chicago, after surveying various areas in the city, chose to locate a settlement house in Back of the Yards. That year, Mary McDowell moved to Gross Avenue, just off Ashland Avenue, and inaugurated the University of Chicago Settlement House, and in 1906 she moved to a new building on the same block. This remained the permanent site until the Settlement House's demise nearly sixty years later. In commemoration of the institution's founder and most important resident, the city changed the name of the street to McDowell Avenue.[1]

Neither Miss McDowell nor the Department of Economics knew anything about a zone of transition or a system of quandrants. The economics faculty felt that the site was centrally located, and the Settlement House's head resident saw that this was a bad part of the neighborhood. Leo S., another resident at the Settlement House, explained what made this spot attractive to reformers: "It was a rough neighborhood . . . and that is the reason a settlement house is placed in any neighborhood, because it was . . . rough." The institution started, therefore, and remained right in the heart of Quadrant I, the most difficult, the most transient area in Back of the Yards (see map 2).[2]

The Settlement House and its workers did what they could for the neighborhood. By the 1930s, the site contained 45,000 square feet, much of it in a central, four-story brick building. The facilities included a boxing room, five club rooms, a game room, junior and senior girls' rooms, a library, manual-training and sewing sections, an area for music appreciation, a nursery, showers, and two play lots, one on the roof. There were two large gymnasiums, one each for boys and girls, and a visiting-nurse program. Residents, on call twenty-four hours a day, dealt with all age groups—three-year-olds in the nursery, elementary school youngsters, preteens, teenagers,

young married people, adults, and senior citizens. There were naturalization classes and, whenever possible, interpreters to help settle
disputes. The Settlement House gave away baskets at Christmas
and served as a home base for social workers investigating conditions for general or specific relief. People came for advice, for help
in getting children out of jail, and especially to use the showers.[3]

Most of the attention went to the children, for several reasons.
The Progressive Era mentality of residents viewed youth as the
hope of the future, the critical challenge to a constantly improving
democracy. Children had to be taught right from wrong and taught
how to think so that they could understand and improve the world
around them. They needed education, nutrition, and a middle-class
home life so they could take their rightful place in society. Having
children at the Settlement House also guaranteed the presence of
parents, and youth services became a recruiting tool. The Mothers'
Club was the most active organization for many years. Service to
youngsters began at the nursery-school level; the house had facilities for three-to-five-year-olds and there was always a nurse on the
premises. Older boys attended classes in woodworking and manual
training, girls had classes in cooking and sewing, and both were
offered instruction in arts and crafts. Boy Scout and Girl Scout
troops met there. In the backyard, many children were assigned
their own small plots of land and taught to work the soil. Once a
week there was a movie, shown on the roof in summer, or a show
produced by the youngsters. There were dances, hosted by one or
another of the various clubs and teams affiliated with the Settlement House, and the dance hall became neutral territory when rival
gangs attended a "dress-up affair."[4]

These affiliated clubs and teams were the most important part of
the youth programs. A great deal of athletic activity went on at the
Settlement House, providing welcome release and entertainment
for the area's youngsters. There were, as we observed earlier,
many social and athletic clubs (SACs) in the neighborhood; on the
SAC circuit, the most prominent team from the house on Gross Avenue was the Settlement Feds. The residents also had outreach programs to channel juvenile delinquents into more acceptable
activities. They "would form clubs out of gangs," according to Leo
S., which meant that they helped a club choose a name and provided
a set of rules and a place to meet. After that, the residents exercised
minimal supervision, merely helping the club's members to develop
a program of activities using the facilities at the Settlement House.
Thanks to these kinds of programs, many, like Raymond K. felt

that, "It was the greatest thing in the world. . . . It did a lot of good for a lot of kids. . . . They turned them around."[5]

The Settlement House also stressed brotherhood. Mary McDowell taught that "all are brothers and all are citizens," and that "the things that are common to all are stronger than the things that are different to all." Leo S. felt that "The Settlement House was able to break down the ethnic walls" so that members of different nationalities could "become friends." His wife, Enid, recalled that old women, Polish and Mexican, would "teach each other some of the art forms" native to their respective countries. Through meetings like these, some barriers did fall, at least within the confines of the Settlement.[6]

Many people, however, did not visit the Settlement House, which really had a very limited effect on the neighborhood. Monsignor Edward Plawinski, for example, felt that "she [Mary McDowell] didn't do anything." Many important institutions in the community were opposed to it. Politicians shied away from this reforming center in Back of the Yards and had little to do with it. The Roman Catholic church was vehement: "It was well known that the Settlement House was a no-no as far as the Catholic people were concerned." Father Joseph Kelly, of St. Rose of Lima, remembered no connection whatsoever between his church and the Settlement House in the years he lived in Back of the Yards, despite the fact that St. Rose was the nearest church. The church had its reasons for this attitude, some practical, some cultural. The Settlement House was viewed as competition, and as a Protestant establishment. Miss McDowell attended Community Methodist Church on 50th Street, and she held teas. The Catholics seemed to view her activities not only as Protestant but even left-wing. There was "a general sense," according to Leo S., "that this was a radical operation . . . and that it tended to dilute and minimize church organization."[7]

Moreover, the Settlement House's funds were of alien origin. They came from Hyde Park, the home of the University of Chicago, which was snobbish, condescending, middle-class, and Protestant, or from the very rich, the bankers and business leaders in faraway North Shore suburbs like Evanston and Winnetka—worlds apart from the residents of Back of the Yards. Worst of all, some of the money came from the Swift and Armour clans themselves, the hated overlords of the packing plants. These companies had no influence over the institution's policies, but their presence on the list of donators was a powerful weapon for the Settlement House's opponents. Even the Settlement House's residents were outsiders. They had none of the social guarantees that went along with being part of a local group, and stood outside the nationalistic system because they were not ethnics, but WASPs. Thus, the system of characterization that provided predictability to the local world failed in their case. Everyone knew that the Mulligans drank too much and that the Goldbergs were canny in business, but who were the Joneses and the Smiths? Not the kind of people those in Back of the Yards knew about. And the Settlement House workers were, in fact, from different backgrounds than their immigrant clients. There is no study of social workers in Back of the Yards, but Allen Davis, in *Spearheads for Reform*, found that, nationally, settlement-house workers were young (in their twenties), raised in the city (but, it is safe to assume, in middle-class neighborhoods), single, native-born, of English or Scotch-Irish heritage, Protestant, and educated (90 percent had some college and 80 percent had a Bachelor's degree). Back of the Yards, in comparison, was a working-class neighborhood, most of whose residents were born on a European farm or were the children of such immigrants, was overwhelmingly Roman Catholic, and considered a grade school diploma a fine achievement. A final problem was that residents did not really need the services of the Settlement House. Religious and social organizations were already doing most of the job. The Settlement House was redundant and offered few novel attractions. This was one of the reasons the priests opposed Miss McDowell's work; it was competition, and it was competition from outsiders who did not understand or really care for the people of the Back of the Yards.[8]

These differences led to misperceptions and failed understandings. During Prohibition, Miss McDowell openly stated that one positive result of bad alcohol was that the habitual drunkards would kill themselves off, leaving the neighborhood in far better condition. She spoke bitterly, and from experience with drunkards; but her statement was a far cry from Father Kelly's story about Chip and his false teeth, recounted in chapter 4. The most damaging of all the problems was the suspicion of insincerity. Back of the Yards residents were quick to note any hesitation, any sense of superiority. Leo S. said that clients "would soon get away from those who tended to patronize them. . . . They made that differentiation quickly. . . . They separated out the workers." Many Settlement House workers were dedicated, many did enter into the daily world of the neighborhood; there were some, however, who could not bridge the gap, and these never did accept or become part of the community west of the stockyards.[9]

The strongest clerical opposition came from the Polish priests, since it was their people who were most affected by Miss McDowell's efforts. When she set up shop on Gross Avenue, her immediate audience was Eastern European and especially Polish. Father Louis Grudzinski of St. John of God, the most nationalistic of the area's three Polish pastors, took the lead in attacking the Settlement House. Monsignor Edward Plawinski, assistant pastor at that church from 1940 to 1948, learned well the Settlement House's shortcomings. His description was long and vituperative. Nobody went to the Settlement House during its half-century history. Miss McDowell "duped" her backers because "she didn't do anything. . . . It was a soft bed for her. . . . It was a good job." The Settlement House was "never effective. . . . She never went down to the grass roots." The only people he ever saw there were a few University of Chicago social workers and students "that were studying to gain a degree in social work. They would come in and . . . spend a couple of weeks over there, write a thesis on the poor people in the Back of the Yards." His pastor, Father Grudzinski, "did more for the people of the Back of the Yards than she ever did."[10]

Father Grudzinski was a man of strong feelings who eschewed harsh words for rigorous action. He never discussed the Settlement House in the pulpit; instead, he built a competing institution next door. Thus, ironically, one of Mary McDowell's greatest impacts on the neighborhood was the impetus she gave to Catholic priests to build the Guardian Angel Day Nursery and Home for Working Girls. In 1912, he enlisted the aid of Father Stanislaus Cholewinski of St. Joseph and Father Frances Karabasz of Sacred Heart, the other Polish churches, to build a social-service center on Gross Avenue: "He did it to take effect . . . away from the Settlement House." By 1915, they had assembled the money, bought lots, and began construction of the Guardian Angel Day Nursery and Home for Working Girls at the corner of 46th Street and Gross Avenue, just a few doors from the Settlement House. The new center launched a wide range of activities. It held classes in arts and crafts and in naturalization in the evenings; it had a visiting nurse, a lawyer, and a social worker, and it rented out a hall especially for weddings. Father Grudzinski soon bought out the other two priests' interests.[11]

The Guardian Angel's most important services were the nursery, the rooms for young girls, and the clinic. Working mothers dropped their youngsters off on their way to work, anywhere from 6:00 to 9:00 A.M. Parents were supposed to pick up their offspring at 5:30 P.M., but sometimes they came as late as 8 P.M. because of overtime in the yards. The nursery had games and toys, athletic equipment, and the nuns played with the children and gave them lessons. The parents left lunch for the children, but the center also provided hot soup and fruit. As many as twenty-five infants and eighty-five children attended this nursery school and, in the summer, there were often as many as one hundred and fifty. The original purpose of the home for girls was to take care of young female Polish immigrants. These were girls fresh off the boat who had not yet made safe connections in the neighborhood. There was "much fear" in Father Grudzinski's mind that these women "would be lost" and that they might get involved with "white slavers." Most of these live-in boarders were sixteen-to-twenty-years old, but occasionally the nuns gave temporary shelter to children abandoned by their parents. They even raised one two-year-old girl. The young women for whom the home was intended lived in upstairs dormitories, divided into large rooms each of which had ten to twelve beds, dressers, and chairs, each set of furniture enclosed by white pull curtains similar to those in hospitals. For a fee, the sisters provided three meals a day (if the tenant could not return home for lunch they set out bread and cold cuts so she could make sandwiches), plus laundry service. An average of thirty-eight women stayed there daily.[12]

The free clinic in the basement was equipped with four consultation rooms, an X-ray machine and a pharmacy. The only charge was for medicine, at cost. From the first, two of the three doctors were women, including the supervising physician, Dr. Stella Napieralski, a Polish immigrant. During the First World War, Dr. Napieralski had ministered to wounded Polish soldiers. Her sister, living in the United States, met Father Grudzinski through the Polish Roman Catholic Union and told him about her distinguished relative. He wrote the doctor and persuaded her to set up and run the clinic, which she did with special generosity. Sister Mary D. declared that Dr. Napieralski was "a wonderful person. . . . She really took care of those people." In the early years, more than fifteen hundred people were treated each year; by the thirties the figure had risen to twenty-five hundred; and by 1945, it exceeded forty-three hundred.[13]

The workers at the Settlement House realized the problems they faced and the barriers erected against them, and accepted the challenge: problems were "a given . . . it was understood. This was a set of conditions that were typical of setting up a settlement house." Anyone who volunteered expected to face obstacles. As Leo S. observed, "Of course, you had to be a fighter. . . . You weren't selected for it unless you had some very strong fighting mettle." And these gladiators did win victories. Many people received care at the Settlement House, and the nursery and gyms and clubs and dances improved the lives of quite a few. But the help was limited. It paled before the assistance of the church, the lodge, and the segmented and nationalistic groups. Facing the church's opposition—even Leo S. admitted that "you could not move if the church was in opposition"—and placed outside the segmented system, the Settlement House could accomplish little within the world of the immigrants back of the yards. Standing on the outside, they tried to break down walls and heal the socially ill, but they never reached the heart of the neighborhood's enclaves. For this reason, they could not help those people to build a democratic, stable society.[14]

With one significant exception. The Settlement House became a major factor in the life of the Mexican community in Back of the Yards. The Mexicans first arrived during the First World War, and more came in the 1920s, though their numbers were small compared to the European immigrant groups; only five hundred Mexicans arrived in 1921 and 1922. These people, and their countrymen who reached Back of the Yards in later years, started life in the central plateaus of Mexico; in particular, in the states of Jalisco, Guanajuato, Zacatecas, and Michoacan. They migrated mainly for economic reasons. Workers in Mexico toiled at agricultural labor, earning wages that were meager compared to what they could earn in the United States. In 1910, about 90 percent of Mexico's people were farm workers who, on the average, earned 25¢ for a sunup-to-sundown day in the fields. John Sanchez's father had "to work the land seven days a week in order to eke out an existence. He was unable to attend school . . . because he was needed on the farm." Moreover, the Mexican Revolution drove Mexicans across the border to escape the chaos in many parts of their country. There were fewer bandits north of the Rio Grande, no impressment into Villa's hordes, and less fear that armed men would ride in to loot their homes.[15]

The journey north to Chicago was a long one. There were three routes. The first was special transport from cities in South Texas such as San Antonio, arranged by the steel and rail companies. The second was to move north by working at odd jobs, especially track maintenance, along the way. The third was to work as seasonal laborers in the vegetable fields of the Midwest, especially Wisconsin, Minnesota, and Michigan; when the work gave out, the ex-farmers eventually made their way to Chicago. John Sanchez's father worked in the fruit and beet fields of Michigan, Ohio, and Wisconsin

during the harvest. After that, he worked on the railroads, saved
his money, brought his wife north, and rented an apartment in
downtown Chicago. Shortly after, he found a job in the yards and
moved there.[16]

The Mexicans entered the packing plants gradually. In 1920,
Swift & Company employed 97 Mexicans; within a few years this
figure rose to 217, 400 were employed at Armour, and 94 more at
Wilson & Company. Most of these jobs were made available to Mexicans during the 1921 strike, when the packers hired anyone they
could find. Later, the Mexicans became an accepted, or rather, a
tolerated presence; by 1928; 5.7 percent of both Swift's and Armour's employees came from south of the border, and by the end of
the decade three thousand Mexicans lived in Back of the Yards.
Their work was usually unskilled, they received few promotions,
and their wages reflected their status. They earned more than they
would have on the railroads and less than steelworkers—the other
two major possibilities open to Mexicans in Chicago in the 1920s.
They were, on the whole, young: 60 percent were under thirty and
90 percent were under forty. Many were unmarried and one-third of
the married men had left their wives at home.[17]

The Mexicans lived in poor conditions. Prejudice from Europeans
forced them into a small section of the neighborhood, and they
wound up in the most dilapidated structures despite the fact that
they paid more rent. Overcrowding was one solution to the high
rents, and it was easier for single young men to put up with. In one
apartment, seventeen lodgers shared five bedrooms with the two
adults who leased the space. Their system of boarding followed the
pattern established by the European immigrants. To get a place to
live, one went to a relative or had someone vouch for one. There was
little furniture. Chairs were a luxury and people sat on the floor or
on old boxes. Like the Europeans, however, the Mexican women
kept their quarters clean, and many maintained small gardens behind their rented homes. The Mexicans, too, saved their money. By
1928, Peoples Bank at 47th Street and Ashland Avenue had one
thousand Mexican depositors; Depositors State Bank, across the
street, had another one-hundred-and-fifty.[18]

There were many similarities between the experience of the immigrant Mexicans and immigrant Europeans. The Mexicans lived
segmented and apart, just like the other nationalities. Father
Joseph Kelly described them as an "isolated small community"; for
that matter he could have been describing any ethnic cluster in the
neighborhood. Their group was based in Quadrant I, the foremost

zone of transition, and later in Quadrant II (see map 2). The sixteen Mexican businesses in the neighborhood in 1928 were all north of 47th Street. Each of the different components of this small society found outlets for its needs and energies within this area. The youth organized storefront associations such as the Club Anahuac at 47th Street and Loomis Avenue, a SAC with thirty-five members in 1928. They were enthusiastic about sports—it was the one area in which the Mexican youth could compete on relatively fair terms with anyone else—and teams like the Aztecas and Incas flourished. Adults had their own diversions. The women stopped to talk on their way to their ethnic stores, as always, and there were several Mexican food stores, including *La Reforma* and *La Tienda Colorado* ("the red brick store"), between 45th and 46th streets on Ashland Avenue. Men met at sporting events and at taverns. By the 1930s, segmentation had advanced sufficiently that several such institutions became strictly Mexican businesses. Each had its own distinctive reputation. *La Paloma* was notorious for frequent outbursts of violence; the South of the Border also had a "dubious" reputation; the Monte Carlo was stable and quiet; and the most family-oriented establishment was Chominsky's at 45th and Justine streets, run by an Argentinian and Polish couple. One male social center that was uniquely Mexican was the pool hall. It was a combination information center, hiring agency, job and housing referral service, and bank. Newcomers went there to meet members of the community and to seek advice about finding needed services. Other nationalities played pool, but only the Mexicans used this game room for so many community functions.[19]

Like the earlier immigrant groups, the Mexicans built their own network. Many workers, including John Sanchez's father, started at the yards through the intercession of a friend or a relative. Women helped one another, and entire families joined together in the struggle for survival. Children left school to earn money for the household. The system of mutual support maintained the Mexican cluster, just as it did all the others in the neighborhood. But there were also great differences between the Mexican and the European experience.

Some were matters of degree. All immigrant groups experienced prejudice—from the larger society, from earlier ethnic arrivals like the Irish, and from old European opponents—but for the Mexicans it was worse. European immigrant groups may not have liked each other, but they could at least identify their enemies; the names of countries like Germany or Bohemia or Poland were recognizable,

and so were the languages. The Mexicans were unknown and unusual. Their dark complexion, a contrast to the paleness of the
Slavs, made them easy targets for bigotry. Father Vito Mikolaitis
claimed that "the prejudice against them (the Mexicans) was quite,
quite bitter," and Mexican Richard P. reported simply that "There
was feeling against us."[20]

Following tradition in Back of the Yards, the Europeans assigned epithets and characteristics to the new group. The Mexicans
became "spics" or "greasers." They were thieves and carried
knives. The Europeans tried to keep them inside their tiny enclave
and generally avoided all contact with them. Some places, like the
parks, were off limits, and there were other boundaries that Mexicans could not trespass, especially at night. Mexicans who went
swimming at the parks in the 1930s endured dunkings and received
warnings not to come back. Dating between a European and a Mexican was also out of the question. If a youngster dated a European of
a different national origin, the parents would express concern and
try to change the child's mind, but if the companion was a Mexican,
the consequence would be a direct order to break off the relationship. The most brutal expression of prejudice, however, was the
constant fighting. John Sanchez remembered the physical battles at
school, and Richard P. learned that "when the case came to be a
fight, the Europeans would work together and isolate the Mexicans." Encarnacion Chico, who came to Back of the Yards in the
1920s as part of the first wave of Mexican immigrants, remembered
those early days as "pretty rough. . . . Practically every Saturday,
if you didn't kill one or two Mexicans you sent them to hospital." Mr.
Chico and his friends learned to avoid alleys, the most likely place to
get beaten up: as a Mexican walked by the entrance, an arm would
sneak out to pull him in, and the rest was bruises.[21]

The Mexicans fought back, and not just in the alleys. They found
their own labels for their ethnic enemies and bad traits to endow
them with. Since the police were prejudiced—as Mr. Chico explained, "When a Mexican do something in those days, he not even
reach into the house when a policeman catch him, but when the guys
[Europeans] do something, never catch them"—all police became
"Polacks" to the Mexicans, (the same police were "turkey birds" to
the Poles). The Poles were supplied with obnoxious traits all their
own. They "knew nothing" and they had no pride: "The Poles always pretend they are Americans; they are ashamed to say they are
Poles. They say they are Germans or Americans." Thus, the Mexicans performed the same ritual of verbal defense on the Slavs that

the Slavs had turned on their predecessors, the Irish and the Germans.[22]

Another difference of degree was caused by the ties the Mexicans maintained with their homeland. Unlike the other immigrant groups back of the yards, the Mexicans could return to their country of origin with relative ease. This mitigated the pressure to recreate their native lives in a new country and to participate in the various new aspects of life in the United States. The Mexicans were as nationalistic as any European cluster and they held ethnic celebrations on traditional dates, but they never felt compelled to make the continuous public displays of nationalism that the Europeans did. The Mexicans also saw less reason to become U.S. citizens—an unfortunate circumstance because it nullified their power as voters and froze them out of the patronage system. Their small number of voters kept them from attaining even a single Mexican precinct captainship until the 1950s.[23]

Other major differences between the Mexicans and the Europeans in Back of the Yards involved their institutions. Though the Mexicans used the segmented group and the nationalistic enclave as a means of self-help, they never developed the same institutions or, when they did, established them over a much longer period of time. For many years, for example, the Mexicans made no move to build their own house of worship; instead, they attended services at St. Rose of Lima, the nearest church. In 1931, a group of Mexicans formed Our Lady of Guadalupe Society, named after the patron saint of Mexico, a fund-raising and church-service organization. Two women, Guadalupe Chavez and Cornelio Florez, made *urnas*, a picture of the saint atop a small drawer that had a slot for donations. Members of the society took these from house to house each week; at the end of the month, the leaders opened the drawer and doled out the money. This money paid for important religious services. One was carfare for a group of Cordi-Marion sisters, catechists who taught the children their lessons for communion once a week. At the first class, held at Mr. Chico's house, there were so many students that some had to move out of the house and sit in the backyard. (The landlord objected and the school had to move.) More money went to pay the carfare of the priest who came to say Mass on Sunday. The executive committee allocated funds to rent storefronts for a chapel and a school, first on Gross Avenue, then Justine Street, and finally, by 1940, on Ashland Avenue and 43rd Street. There were still problems: the altar was a converted icebox, a leaky roof dripped constantly, and visiting priests from St. Francis objected to the whole arrangement, particularly its location right in the middle of Whiskey Row.[24]

The resident Mexicans did what they could to improve the situation. One member of the congregation painted holy pictures on the improvised altar and others supplied altar cloths, seats, kneeling benches, and altar railings. A St. Vincent DePaul Society was organized to make sure all tasks found a worker: while the men constructed and installed fixtures, the women washed the walls and benches and the children ran errands.[25]

By this time the congregation was actively seeking a church of its own, *la capilla* ("the chapel"). On Sunday, after Mass, the men moved the benches against the wall and the Mothers' Committee and the St. Vincent DePaul Society cooked Mexican food to sell at a fund-raising dance that evening. Things proceeded slowly, however, until the early 1940s, when Father James Tort arrived. A member of the Claretian order, Father Tort had founded the St. Jude Police League to give spiritual assistance to officers—a connection that later became helpful to Mexicans in trouble with the law. He stopped in Back of the Yards sometime about 1942, returned to say Mass that Sunday; and immediately made obtaining a new church for this Mexican community an important project of his own.[26]

Father Tort was Spanish, a Catalonian, short, tough, a "grumpy, irrascible, straight-shooting man." He was also "a mover," according to Matthew Rodriguez, "a man dedicated to the Mexican community." One of his tactics in dealing with the archdiocese was to complete a project and then ask for permission. Richard P. recalled him as "stern, but a heart of gold." Father Tort would walk into a parishioner's home without knocking, so that "the next thing we'd know he is right in the middle of the room." The priest would say "That's right! I don't want you to invite me because then you'll prepare. . . . I want to see you as you really are." He scolded Richard's father when the older man missed services: "You got to go to church. Look at all these beautiful children." He was a determined man: "He never give up. . . . Whatever he want to do, he'll do." John Sanchez said that Tort had "a one-track mind. That track was to build that church." In his first sermon in Back of the Yards, he upbraided the congregation for being so slow to obtain a church, a speech Encarnacion Chico recalled almost forty years later. Father Tort yelled at him and the others: "What's a matter with you guys? . . . Over ten years. . . . You fellows don't do nothing, you're sleeping." Mr. Chico said of this session, still with a sense of shock and awe, "Right in the church, that's the way he talking." But Tort did more than talk. He stepped up the level of fund-raising activities, fought for support from the archdiocese, and advocated a new church on his regular visits in the neighborhood. Under his direction, the parishioners held bazaars and carnivals, often on Mexican saints' days, thus combining religion, entertainment, fund-raising, and nationalism.[27]

In 1944, these efforts began to bear fruit. Father Tort bought four storefronts at Ashland Avenue and 45th Street on March 5th, and construction began shortly. On 30 December 1945, Cardinal Stritch dedicated the chapel, but he changed its name, to the amazement of the parishioners. They wanted their church to bear the title of the patron saint of Mexico, Our Lady of Guadalupe. Unfortunately there was already a church in the diocese with that name, so His Eminence named it Immaculate Heart of Mary Vicariate.[28]

As impressive as these efforts to found a new church were, there remained the long delay before Father Tort's arrival, which would have been unthinkable to the European immigrants. Mark Reisler, in *By The Sweat of Their Brow*, a study of Mexicans in Chicago, offered some reasons. Compared to the colorful, festive ceremonies of rural Mexico, the churches in the United States seemed pale and cold, neither familiar nor welcoming. Moreover, the neighborhood was dominated by European ethnic groups who did not greet the Hispanics with open arms. Even so, there must have been other significant differences between the Europeans' and the Mexicans' attitudes toward the church. How else explain why the Eastern Europeans, also facing the problem of a church that was tightly controlled by an Irish and German hierarchy that did not welcome Slavs, nevertheless supported new churches and constantly demanded more national parishes, whereas the Mexicans in Back of the Yards waited a quarter-century to start a church—twice as long as the Poles? Thus, the Mexicans, less separated from their homeland, apparently had less need to create national institutions. There were other differences as well. The Mexican children attended public, not Catholic, schools. They received religious instruction after hours, but not the training in nationalism that the earlier groups received in their church schools. And, without the church as an anchor, there were fewer lodges and benefit societies, and none that lasted very long. In one listing of twenty-one organizations in the three major Mexican neighborhoods in Chicago in 1928, only one was in Back of the Yards, and that was a SAC.[29]

Into this gap stepped other organizations. The most important one, one that filled many of the the roles of the church, was the

University of Chicago Settlement House. Almost immediately after
their arrival, the Mexicans gravitated toward the Settlement House
and by the late 1930s, they were the largest group using its facilities. It "was a very important part of our lives," John Sanchez said,
and Richard P. added, "I practically lived there. . . . They had such
terrific programs." Leo S., a resident of the Settlement House, recalled that the Mexicans helped "on any given occasion," and Enid
S., his wife, remembered that "They overextended themselves to
us."[30]

Mexicans turned to the Settlement House for many reasons. It
was conveniently located: both the Mexican community and Miss
McDowell's home were in Quadrant I, although the Hispanics
spilled over into Quadrant II. Second, the Settlement House provided services that the Mexicans badly needed. Other ethnic groups
had their churches, but until 1945 there was none for the Mexicans;
even then, the church was slow to undertake welfare work while it
built its resources. The Settlement House offered the Mexicans athletic activities—gyms, games, teams—and dances, music, art, English lessons, citizenship classes, crafts for men and homemaking
classes for women, and movies on the roof, all when the city's facilities were dangerous places for the Mexicans to visit. Most Mexican
groups used the meeting rooms there, even radical political leagues
like the *Partido Nacional Revolucionario*, active in the mid-1930s.
The Mothers' Club, which began as a class in handicrafts, evolved
into a well-known activist organization renamed the Mexican Wom-
en's English Club in 1939. The members of the Boys' Club persuaded their fathers to form a Mexican Fathers' Club. Residents of
the Settlement House also worked with police and social agencies to
obtain fair play for the Mexicans. Most important, perhaps, for people with few places to hold meetings, the Settlement House had a
hall. Before 1945, when Immaculate Heart of Mary Vicariate
opened, weddings took place at St. Francis church, several miles
north, but the receptions were held either at home or at the hall on
Gross Avenue.[31]

The Settlement House was the only place in all of Back of the
Yards that accepted the Hispanics, even the illegal aliens. There
they could relax, away from the packers and free from their neighbor's prejudice. "The atmosphere in the Settlement House brooked
no hostility of any kind because of national origin," Leo S. explained. And there was less institutional opposition to the Mexicans'
use of the building than there was to the Europeans' visits to it. The
politicians resented the social workers, but the Mexicans had little

contact with the ward's officials. Latino priests, like their European counterparts, disliked this seemingly Protestant, radical institution, and they condemned it even more openly than the European priests. However, the Mexican church did not carry much weight until 1945, and then delayed in creating the network of ties that would have added strength to the priest's words. The Settlement House competed successfully with the Mexican church because the preachers offered so little and the reformers so much. One loyal parishioner of Immaculate Heart of Mary explained that he went to the Settlement House because "the Mexican church offered no alternative." In return, the Mexican patrons trusted and respected the Settlement House's residents. They accepted even the absent-minded academic residents: "As long as on the whole they were reasonable human beings whose heart was in the right place, we accepted their aberrations," said one son of Mexican immigrants about these people of a different nationality and class. Thus, the University of Chicago Settlement House became part of the core of the Mexican community rather than an outside influence. It was a place where the Mexicans could go in peace and act with freedom. This was a special relationship cherished by both sides. As John Sanchez summed it up: "The Settlement House, we believed in."[32]

9

The Back of the Yards Neighborhood Council

Early Meeting of Back of the Yards Neighborhood Council at
Davis Square Park. *Standing at left:* Ambrose Ondrak.
Courtesy of Back of the Yards Neighborhood Council

he people of the Back of the Yards had created small worlds
of stability and democracy within their families, associations,
and parishes. They had discovered a way to create private
areas of freedom and, within them, gained some control over
their lives and formed a secure social environment. In these
ways, their solution functioned well. But it also perpetuated cleavages and disharmony. The walls of nationalism were high and the
possibility of collective action had receded by the time the Great
Depression struck.

In 1929, when the community faced a calamity of unprecedented
magnitude, the consequences of these divisions became clear. The
enclaves did not have the resources to meet the challenge. Not the
churches, not the ward organization, not the University of Chicago
Settlement House had the knowledge or strength to save the neighborhood's people. Unity was required, a unified approach to the
federal government and other organizations that commanded billions of dollars, plus the power that went with that kind of money.
But to move in this direction meant endangering the system that
had worked so well. It took the Great Depression to persuade the
people in Back of the Yards that they needed to transcend their
segmented bonds.

The Great Depression hit hard back of the yards, as it did everywhere in the United States. Unemployment was devastating. Underemployment, as we observed earlier, was endemic in Back of the
Yards, but the 1930s made that terrible problem seem relatively
mild in comparison. Large numbers of workers stayed out of work
for years. In 1930, unemployment in Chicago rose to 10 percent of
the workforce, but it was 12-to-14 percent in the meat-packing industry. The foreign-born were hit hardest. At first, they were
merely "laid off," presumably until conditions improved. The weeks
turned into months and the months into years before hope disappeared and the dreadful meaning of *layoff* became fully apparent.
By far the highest rates of unemployment were suffered by men in
the prime of their career, those thirty-five to forty-four-years old.
Thus, more than anyone else it was the breadwinner, the head of
the family, who was out of work. This situation was typical of industrial communities across the United States. By April 1930, 15 percent of Philadelphia's work force was unemployed; in Buffalo, 26
percent. The Ford Motor Company, the largest employer in Detroit, employed 128,142 persons in March 1929 and had only 37,000
employees, many of them on part time, in August 1931.[1]

The economic catastrophe hurt businesses as well as workers.

Small and medium-sized stores closed for lack of customers. Some establishments, especially the corner groceries, bakeries and butcher shops that extended credit to their patrons, ran out of funds and closed. The number of Lithuanian stores, factories, and workshops in Chicago decreased by half during the Depression, and the Lithuanian Alliance of America was forced to evict countrymen who defaulted on their mortgages. For the first time since its development in Back of the Yards, the segmented and nationalist systems failed, their resources exhausted. How could a small clique aid its members when not just one or two but many of its breadwinners faced hunger? To make matters worse, people pulled even further back into their small circles. There was already too little for the family or the clique; nothing remained for outsiders. Monsignor Plawinski remarked that the national sin of the Poles was "jealousy," that "they couldn't see that, through the good office of one, the others would be helped too."[2]

At the beginning of 1932, the banks, which held in trust the savings of thousands of residents, began to close. The four major banks that served the neighborhood had all locked their doors by July. People sat in front of the entrances, crying and begging them to reopen. Some of the money was eventually returned, but nowhere near the original sums, and the repayment took a long while. The largest, People's Bank at 47th Street and Ashland Avenue, owed its customers just over three million dollars when it shut down on June 20th. Depositor's Bank had closed earlier, on January 18th, owing one thousand customers almost two-and-a-half million dollars, and two years later it had still made no restitution. The bank took five years to return about one-fifth of the hard-earned money and seven years to return a third, at which time state banking officials estimated that the bank would eventually repay about 40 percent of the money.[3]

It was a "terrible" time, a "real tough time." "The Depression hit everybody." People scrimped and went without. According to Ted. P., "They survived—but it was unbelievable the way they did." Families paid their rent first, then they bought food and, if anything was left, "incidentals" like shoes. They ate just enough to keep from starving; as Konstanty G. recalled, "You eat what you get." What you got was a lot of starch—bread, potatoes, stale bread dampened with water and covered with sugar or mustard—and sauerkraut. Stanley Z.'s family bought a dozen cakes for a dollar and lived on that and coffee for a week. Women and children prowled the railroad tracks for pieces of coal that fell off the trains, and even made off with loose boards. At 6:00 P.M. in many households, like Ted P.'s, "the last lump of coal went in. That was it, no more." If, God forbid, you had to get up at night to use the toilet, "you could see your breath." A notice in the *Town of Lake Journal* on 20 July 1939 offered a reward for the return of stolen clothing. The contraband consisted of two polo shirts, three pants, and a dress. The paper added, redundantly, that "The family is in straitened circumstances."[4]

Some funds came from private charities. The churches tried to help. In Back of the Yards, one pastor created a special fund for the needy of his parish and distributed thousands of dollars to the families of unemployed workers. Other pastors employed a registered nurse to give free medical assistance. At the Guardian Angel Day Care Center, St. John of God set up a soup kitchen and the nuns made sandwiches. The Catholic Charities of Chicago increased its budget from $435,784 in 1930 to $1,755,500 in 1931, but even a fourfold increase in charity was far too little. The archdiocese, in an editorial in its official organ *New World*, observed that "Charity cannot and should not be expected to meet the terrific strain. . . . It was never meant to aid the majority." The University of Chicago Settlement House reported helping an average of sixty-eight families a month between December 1931 and December 1932. In that thirteen-month period, the Settlement House expended $11,000, an average of $11.70 a month per family. Unable, like the other private institutions, to handle a debacle, it raised too little money for too few.[5]

Unemployment rose to 20 percent in the mid-1930s and stayed there. One out of five were out of work, and of these, fully 74 percent were experienced workers. Mary M.'s husband was out of work a full year. She herself was employed only two days a week and earned $14 every two weeks. Each month they put one check aside for rent and they lived on the other. As late as 14 July 1938, the *Town of Lake Journal* wrote that unemployment was "still our biggest problem."[6]

By far the greatest assistance came from the federal government's New Deal, which began in 1933. One of its programs, the National Youth Administration (NYA), assisted high-school students; in 1936, 252 young people back of the yards were paid for work in this program (see table 3).[7]

Even so, the available relief barely permitted families to survive. A family of five received about $50 a month and their "undernourished children" had "shoes so worn they'd barely stay on the

Table 3. Expenditures of the National Youth Administration in Back of the Yards, 1936

Location	No. of Students	Amount
Tilden H.S.	181	$1,336
Lindbloom H.S.	71	427
Total	252	$1,763

Source: Town of Lake Journal, 21 January 1937, p. 1.

youngsters' feet." Parents told "despairing tales"; they didn't "know where the next meal is going to come from." In September 1939, this monthly allotment was reduced 20 percent. That month, 5.6 percent of the Back of the Yards' population was on relief, a total of 5,211 cases and 14,441 persons, at a cost to the government of $116,000.[8]

But relief often meant surplus food rather than cash. Armour bought drought-stricken cattle, cooked and canned the meat, and sold it to the government for relief allocations. Mary Z. and others received "dry stuff"—prunes, raisins, smoked hard meat, flour, rice, potatoes—nothing fresh. Sometimes coal was provided, but the truckers always dumped it on the sidewalk, creating an eyesore and exposing one's difficulties to the neighbors.[9]

Some people refused to accept even the meager help offered by the government. The spirit of self-help, of independence, persisted even amidst famine. In 1940, when 20 percent of the workers in Back of the Yards were unemployed, slightly more than 4.2 percent accepted public-welfare jobs; 15.5 percent, almost four times as many as were on work relief, were still seeking private jobs. People "hated" to accept public aid. Paul J.'s father told him he would rather "chew on a penny." Phyllis H., too poor to buy milk, finally and reluctantly accepted the deliveryman's advice to apply for an allocation of milk; even then, her husband refused, and in the end consented only for the sake of the children. They "felt like heels."[10]

The residents were of course aware of the work available in the agencies of the New Deal. Road gangs hired by the Works Progress Administration (WPA), often one or two hundred men, improved and paved streets throughout the area. Between July 1935, when the agency began its operations, and October 1938, the WPA rehabilitated forty-nine miles of streets in Back of the Yards. In Cornell Square Park, the agency built ten tennis courts and a baseball backstop; in Davis Square Park, four tennis courts. Cornell Square

Park also served as headquarters for the federally funded adult-education classes that were held in the parks.[11]

Slowly the people back of the yards began to look toward the future. The first symptoms of change were new approaches to community service and organization. New and different people, with different perceptions of the area's problems and with novel solutions, began to appear. Leaders themselves, but younger and more acculturated than the old ethnic guardians, they understood the community's social patterns and traditions, the importance of its ethnic organizations, and the people's resentment against the packers—and they tried to use their understanding to get people to work together.

The most important of these new leaders was Joseph Meegan, who became director of Davis Square Park in 1937. Meegan was Irish, the son of an immigrant who had worked fourteen hours a day in the yards for a dollar's pay and who later became janitor at St. Cecilia Church, where he served for forty-four years. Joseph and his three brothers gravitated to the park that became their second home. They went to play, and Joseph showered at nearby Fuller Park twice a week. He received a Bachelor's degree from DePaul University, became a school teacher in 1932, and in 1936 took and passed the examination for park district director. On 17 March 1937, the South Park Board transferred him to Davis Square Park, familiar territory because his uncle Pat owned a tavern on Whiskey Point.[12]

Meegan quickly took control of Davis Square and the surrounding area. His staff scrubbed the facilities every other day. Drunks, purveyors of illegal whiskey, and other undesirables made their exit. In 1938, Meegan called on the Department of Agriculture's office in Chicago to set up a lunch program with surplus government food. He convinced the finest hotels in Chicago, like the Palmer House, to donate outdated china and flatware. On Halloween, fifteen hundred children enjoyed a free party in the park, and there were seven more celebrations at Christmas. Meegan talked the community's merchants into giving money, on the grounds that wholesome recreation would decrease vandalism and delinquency, and he organized a chorus of seventy-five voices to sing Christmas carols in front of every donor's establishment.[13]

The neighborhood was quick to accept Meegan as a community leader. In March 1938, a former student at Holy Cross, the nearby Lithuanian church, wrote the *Town of Lake Journal* to express thanks to him for making Davis Square "the finest and cleanest park in the city," and added that "the director has been so nice." In June, the Davis Socials' Athletic Club sent the *Town of Lake Journal* an open letter to Joseph Meegan; it read, in part: "We are certainly proud to have a director who . . . understands our youngsters and in turn has their love, respect and admiration."[14]

Meegan was outraged by conditions in the neighborhood: the hungry youngsters who ate only one meal a day; the nonexistent dental programs; the parents treated for tuberculosis who returned home to damp, dingy houses where they contracted the disease again. In his first years as park director—1937, 1938, and 1939—he began to formulate some basic concepts of organization. He felt that welfare work was inadequate because it never attacked the roots, and that to be effective one "must always attack the cause and not the end products . . .you cannot deal effectively with one problem without getting involved in all the others which are related and contributing to that problem." For Meegan, this meant creating a democratic organization that used the residents' knowledge to identify their community's needs and then marshalled their energies to find solutions.[15]

Other people were also helping to lay the groundwork. Aaron Hurwitz, copublisher of the *Town of Lake Journal*, recognizing the potential usefulness of the extensive number of youth groups in the neighborhood, proposed a council of clubs in the pages of his paper in 1937. The *Journal* would provide space and publicity for the league, but the league was to elect its own officers and would be free of interference. The idea caught on quickly, and on 12 April 1937 the Council of Clubs held its first meeting. In the months to come, it sponsored softball tournaments and coordinated programs among various member clubs. Hurwitz viewed the council as "a sort of union of senior young people's clubs in the community" whose purpose was "to promote greater harmony and understanding between the various groups in the neighborhood, to work for cooperation. . . ." Joseph Meegan was elected as vice president at the first meeting and the *Journal* announced that "the next meeting will be held at Davis Square."[16]

A more extensive force working for unity in Back of the Yards was a new union for stockyards workers. On 24 October 1936, the fledging Congress of Industrial Organizations (CIO) established the Packinghouse Workers Organizing Committee (PWOC) under the leadership of Van Bittner, an experienced mining and steel organizer. The first target was Armour & Company, and the aggressive union quickly gained a foothold there. As important as the potential economic impact of the union was, its effect on morale was equally significant. People who were initially hesitant and fearful of retaliation from the packers began to turn out in large numbers. A meeting held on 5 May 1937 attracted a crowd of two thousand; another four hundred were turned away for lack of space. The workers began to agree with Sigmund Wlodarczyk, an organizer, that the union was "the only thing they had left. . . . You'd either die in there or try to get better working conditions."[17]

The feeling grew quickly. Victoria Starr, another PWOC worker, recalled "a certain momentum developed and a spirit . . . you had this going on in the yards. You had a certain excitement." Soon it became more like a fever. "Workers would come in and plump down their dollars and say 'I want to join the CIO'. . . . They came in droves." She told how, "You had the sense that people were ready, come hell or high water, to get together, to protect each other. . . . They had this feeling of solidarity." According to Herbert March, the director of District 1, PWOC, "the desire, the passion that workers had for the development of the dignity and strength that comes with an organization was something to behold."[18]

The idea of workers protecting each other was an old one; what the CIO helped residents adjust to was the idea of working together in a common cause. The union's leaders furthered this process by injecting themselves into many issues in the community and bringing a unifying influence to bear. Their reasons were partly ideological, a desire to help their members. March asserted that "the union . . . had a certain amount of social vision. It was attempting to affect the whole living standard of the community." They also had practical reasons: the support of the community was vital to the union's success. The chances of successful organizing were enormously increased if the community supported the union and its members. And when the local community opposed a project, it often collapsed. The union publicized meetings like the American Slav Congress, raised funds for Polish orphans, sent its officials to attend neighborhood conferences on housing, and sponsored the Packingtown Youth Committee. This was an organization for young unionists, formed to help other youths by improving their recreational facilities and helping them find jobs. The traditional path to employment, a father's recommendation, had been closed by the Depression, so many out-of-work youngsters were turning to petty crime as a way of releasing their frustration and picking up a little money. The lack of recreational facilities only exacerbated the problem. Sixty-six delegates from twenty-six different youth organizations attended the first meeting of the Packingtown Youth Committee, held on 23 February 1939 at the YMCA at 1607 West 51st Street. Among the resolutions passed was a call for increased WPA and, especially, NYA jobs in the neighborhood, and a recommendation that a railroad yard at 47th Street and Damen Avenue, a dangerous site where children roamed unsupervised, be purchased and turned into a recreational center.[19]

The meeting was the first that looked beyond the neighborhood for a solution to its problems: for the first time, the residents sought to bring pressure on the federal government rather than on the packers. Joseph Meegan attended this meeting. So did Saul Alinsky.[20]

Born on 30 January 1909 in Chicago, Saul David was the son of Benjamin Alinsky and Sara Tannenbaum, Orthodox Jews and Russian immigrants. He entered the University of Chicago in 1926 and, by the time he was graduated, had developed definite interests and distinctive traits of personality. He had become interested in analyzing and handling social problems, taken courses in sociology and criminology, and had begun to demonstrate the tough, streetwise style he used later as a community organizer. The University of Chicago awarded him a graduate fellowship in sociology, but he never completed the program.[21]

From 1931 to 1939, Alinsky worked at various jobs for the State of Illinois, first in the Institute for Juvenile Research (IJR) and then in the prison at Joliet as a penologist. In 1936, he returned to the IJR, where he worked with Clifford Shaw. Shaw was a founder of the Chicago Area Project, an attempt to deal with juvenile delinquency. The project, begun in 1932, was notable because it relied primarily on local groups and local leadership rather than on outside social-work agencies and because it was an attempt to attack conditions underlying the delinquency as well as the immediate problem. Alinsky helped set up committees in various neighborhoods, and in 1938 delivered a speech in which he stressed factors inherent in the community as creating neighborhood difficulties and said that organizing had to resolve "profound" issues. Michael Connolly, one of Alinsky's biographers, wrote that the organizing concepts that A-linsky espoused throughout his life "predate 1939." Although A-linsky despised and ridiculed social workers, his ideas were similar to the Chicago Area Project's. The closeness of their concepts, the years he spent with Shaw, and the fact that he delivered a paper related to his work with the IJR suggest that he was strongly influenced by these relatively early experiences. Given Alinsky's ego and his attitude towards academics, however, it was not surprising that he did not give them any credit.[22]

During this same period, Alinsky became fascinated with another type of social force that exerted a major influence on his life and work: the union movement, and particularly the rise of the Congress of Industrial Organizations. He met and became friendly with John L. Lewis, whom he later described as "an extraordinary individual and certainly one of the most outstanding figures of our time." He also learned the art of ridicule. Workers had become immobilized by fear—of the company, of the supervisors, and of losing their jobs. The union organizers countered this fear by making fun of the bosses, exposing them to scorn, and bringing them down to the level of ordinary human beings. As Herbert March said, "We didn't hesitate to expose, to ridicule, and to be very, very critical, even in the personal sense." The union showed the foremen up as poor workers and accused them of slowing down production by their petty actions. "Those were exciting days to be alive in," Alinsky later wrote.[23]

In the fall of 1938, Clifford Shaw sent Alinsky to Back of the Yards to investigate the possibility of organizing youth committees to combat juvenile delinquency. Alinsky liked the idea: Back of the Yards was a symbol of injustice, the setting for Upton Sinclair's *The Jungle,* and the scene of a major CIO organizing drive. It was not just another faceless slum. To Alinsky, a man of flair and style, it was an important assignment. At first he went to the University of Chicago Settlement House for ideas, but he soon began to spend most of his time walking around the community, as Upton Sinclair had done. Victoria Starr asked Alinsky to attend the first meeting of the Packingtown Youth Committee, since he was supposed to be an expert on youth problems; he declined, but then came in during the meeting and stood in the back, watching and listening.[24]

Alinsky approached Meegan at Davis Square Park. At first the park director was leery. He "was rather suspicious" because this might be just another foolish do-gooder. When Meegan discovered "that he didn't believe in the same philosophy" as other social workers, the two took to each other and soon became close friends. They began to talk about shared concerns and frustrations: "We talked about the problems of the area . . . the youth problems primarily. . . . We agreed that the kids were hungry and there were problems of health and housing and everything else." Moreover, Alinsky "didn't particularly like what he was doing and I didn't like what I was doing." Both men felt that they were not doing enough;

more action, direct action was needed. In conversations at Meegan's home, at restaurants, at taverns where they went for a beer, the two developed a common approach.[25]

In a recent interview, Joseph Meegan observed, "The Back of the Yards Council was the result of two people getting together." These simple words, however, described a remarkable combination: two men, both devoted to helping others, both geniuses at organizing; but with entirely different styles and working in very different arenas. Helen Meegan, Joseph's wife, said that Saul wanted the same things Joe did, but had no roots. This was true: Meegan was, according to his wife, "very parochial," part and parcel of Back of the Yards; Alinsky, on the other hand, had experience in many cities and environments, was beholden to none, and avoided identifying himself with any one place. Thus Meegan, the man of the community, stayed in Back of the Yards for the rest of his life, nurturing the organization they created, while Alinsky moved away, rarely to return, and in 1940 created the Industrial Areas Foundation (IAF) as a way of funding his organizing work around the country. His wider career and the national publicity he attracted allowed Alinsky to write books, train others, and eventually become the philosopher and mentor of the community organizing movement in the United States. (Heather Booth later said that "Alinsky is to community organizing as Freud is to psychoanalysis.") When Alinsky set up the IAF, however, he asked Meegan to join him. Mrs. Meegan was there, and she urged Joe to refuse, which he did. She turned to Alinsky, whom she "loved dearly," and said, "My God, Saul, you don't understand!" But Helen Meegan, a wise and perceptive woman, did know, instinctively, that Joe had to stay, and Saul go, that they needed different paths. In Back of the Yards in 1939, however, in Joe Meegan's words, "It was a joint effort."[26]

The two men quickly settled on a division of labor. Alinsky stayed in the background and worked with the union while Meegan dealt publicly with the community. Years later, Meegan joked that this made him the "fall guy," but the connections and abilities of the two men made the dichotomy a logical one.[27]

Alinsky's previous work with the CIO and friendship with John L. Lewis had led to acquaintanceships with the higher-ups in the PWOC. He knew Ralph Helstein, soon to be president, and Herbert March and Hank Johnson, respectively district director and assistant, in the Chicago area. Meegan knew some of the older Irish workers, but he had not met the leadership of the new union. And the union, for its part, was eager to join the effort to organize the community. Herb March, though a communist and atheist, realized the value of community support for a union organizing drive, especially when the employers were tough and anti-union companies like packers. When Alinsky approached him and others, he was received warmly.[28]

Alinsky's personality also made the division of responsibility a logical one. Despite his later reputation as a fearsome community worker, he was in fact a quiet, lonely man. Thomas Gaudette, a community organizer, claimed that his mentor was less an activist than an investigator, that he preferred to remain in the background as "the thinker." He was not a great speaker and had little flair for public work. Gaudette commented that "Saul was not a charismatic leader. Saul couldn't lead two people down the street." He "never obtruded," Father Joseph Kelly remarked. Similarly, Helen D., who remembered the organizer with great affection, discussed his bookish manner and said that "Saul didn't speak the language of our people."[29]

Still, some of the neighborhood people came to care deeply for Alinsky. His emotional commitment to them, his sincerity, won them over. Though he knew few clerics at first, he met priests and found friends through Meegan. The local religious figures both loved and hated his partner, Meegan recalled. At Friday lunch with the clergy, Alinsky not only ate meat, thus breaking Catholic law, but ordered ham, violating his own Jewish codes. The priests promised they would pray for him and he laughed, but he adored the attention. In return, he cared back, and in the case of Father Ambrose Ondrak of St. Michael, Alinsky "loved that man." But he could not make his caring clear to a larger public and so he stayed in the background. Aaron Hurwitz of the *Journal* described Alinsky as having an "excellent mind, but cold," and Meegan as having an "excellent mind, but warm." Furthermore, Alinsky's background in social work brought him into conflict with local society. He envisaged a coalition that went beyond the segmented, nationalistic system: he hoped to tear down the walls that separated the people back of the yards by building a new organization and absorbing the nationalistic groups into a larger whole.[30]

Meegan, observed Leslie Orear, editor of the Packinghouse Workers' paper, was "quite the opposite of Alinsky. He was the molasses and oil man." And being Irish like the politicians, he was an acceptable leader, albeit one on which the other ethnic groups had to keep an eye. Like a politician, he knew the entire neighborhood. Youth groups and social-athletic clubs knew him because of his work at Davis Square Park and business owners recognized the tall man because, for years, he had edited *Church Leaves*, the monthly bulletin of St. Rose of Lima, a job that included soliciting ads, especially from the larger shops on Ashland Avenue and 47th Street. By the time he approached them on behalf of the Back of the Yards Neighborhood Council, he was an old acquaintance.[31]

Besides his tie to St. Rose, where his wife also served as organist, Meegan worked with the Catholic Youth Organization's (CYO) summer projects, and Mrs. Meegan was a drama instructor at local institutions. Meegan saw, therefore, that the neighborhood's institutions could be used as building blocks for a wider community organization, and he never tried to eliminate them. Meegan also knew Bishop Bernard Sheil, and the two founders agreed that Meegan "was to talk to the Bishop about the possibility of forming an all-community organization that would embrace all the people that we have."[32]

Bishop Sheil was an extraordinary person in the Catholic Church in the United States. His early ambition was to be a major-league baseball pitcher but he turned instead to God and rose in the ranks; by 1939, he was auxiliary archbishop of the Archdiocese of Chicago. He lived "in a tradition of personal humility," according to one writer, and displayed a "remarkable . . . breadth of mind." Most of his wisdom and energy went to helping others less fortunate; Sheil founded the Catholic Youth Organization, for example, to provide children with badly needed recreation. Chicago's Catholics loved him. Even Herbert March said, "I think that his ambition was . . . to acquire prominence as a man who was widely known as a very, very fine person." He also "represented . . . a more forward-looking element in the Catholic Church." The bishop spoke out on social issues, particularly in support of workers' rights and against fear and intolerance. Herbert March once asked the bishop to write a pamphlet attacking racism. He did so, and it became the standard CIO piece on the subject in many parts of the country.[33]

Meegan had several connections to Bishop Sheil. His brother Peter, a monsignor, was Sheil's secretary. In addition, the park director and the cleric were of Irish descent, and their interest in young people dated back to Meegan's work with the CYO at Sherman Park and Davis Square Park. In 1938, Bishop Bernard Sheil was the commencement speaker at the CYO's summer school at Davis Square Park, a school cosponsored by St. Rose of Lima Church and the Chicago Park Board. Meegan and Sheil's paths also crossed in the NYA, the WPA, and Chicago Park District projects.[34]

18
Baseball Game on the Field at 47th Street and Damen Avenue.
Left to right, Judge Robert Dunne, Police Commissioner John
Prendergast, Father Edward Plawinski, Bishop Bernard Sheil
Courtesy of Joseph B. Meegan

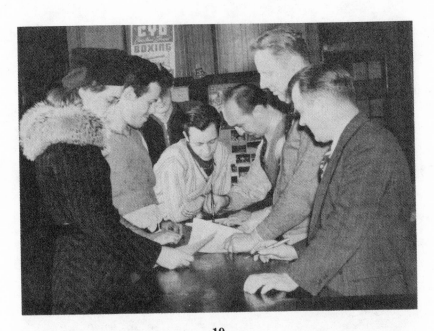

19

National Youth Administration Registration at Davis Square Park
Courtesy of Back of the Yards Neighborhood Council

20

Father Edward Plawinski, First President of Back of the Yards
Neighborhood Council
Courtesy of Back of the Yards Neighborhood Council

21

Celebration of Ambrose Ondrak's Elevation to Benedictine
Abbott. His Eminence Samuel Cardinal Stritch, *center front*,
is presenting the pectoral cross to Abbott Ambrose.
Second from left, Saul Alinsky (wearing tie); *sixth from left*,
Father Charles Florek of St. Michael Church
Courtesy of Back of the Yards Neighborhood Council

22
Joseph Meegan
Courtesy of Joseph B. Meegan

23
Joseph Palka, Photographed for His Unsuccessful
Aldermanic Campaign, 1944
Courtesy of Martha Palka

24
John Kluczynski
Chicago Historical Society ICHi-18554

25

The Hot Lunch Program at Davis Square Park.
Standing in rear, Father Joseph Kelly
Courtesy of Joseph B. Meegan

Sheil helped to organize the BYNC in several ways. He advised Meegan about receptive churches and priests and told him which ones to avoid. He urged some churches to join the fledging Council, others to forsake their bitter attitudes toward other nationalities and toward labor and, most of all, got them to give Meegan a hearing. Without Sheil, claimed Evelyn Ostrowski, "some of the churches would probably have kicked Alinsky and Joe both out of there." Even so, reactions to the Council varied. According to John H., some churches had to be coaxed into it and "kind of bribed." Father Grudzinski of St. John of God, for example, was lukewarm and remained, according to Monsignor Edward Plawinski, "very cautious. . . . He wanted to see what it's all about." At St. Joseph, Father Stanislaus Cholewinski, one of the most elderly of the local pastors, opposed the Council because Meegan was Irish and Cholewinski feared competition from nearby St. Rose of Lima. He "couldn't see the idea."[35]

Assisting Meegan was a group of young priests. Within the Chicago archdiocese in the 1930s a growing number of clergy were creating a "ferment within the church," according to Father Joseph Kelly. These men saw the need for reform, and began working for it. In Back of the Yards, they were all native-born and thus free of the immigrants' suspicions of other nationalities. Many had been classmates in seminary and had become good friends. Father Kelly, who was Irish, described Polish Father Plawinski as a "good guy. He wanted to help people." These young men served as assistant pastors in Back of the Yards, and viewed their pastors as "the end of an era." Priests like Kelly used to quip that the assistants were all Democrats; the pastors, all Republicans. It was this younger group that asked permission to work with the Back of the Yards Neighborhood Council, received it from their wary pastors, and allied themselves with Joseph Meegan, becoming the bulwark of his religious support. They included such outstanding BYNC leaders as Father Ambrose Ondrak of St. Michael, Father Joseph Kelly of St. Rose, Father Edward Plawinski of St. John of God, and a future president of the Council, Father Roman Berendt of Sacred Heart.[36]

The pieces began to fall into place. Meegan and Alinsky talked on the phone "for hours," then met in the evenings to discuss matters further. They decided that the Council had to have a democratic, local base and that it should not be governed by outside investigators and reformers. Membership was limited to organizations, such as parish clubs, SACs, or nationalistic lodges. Each organization would have one vote and send three representatives, elected by

popular vote, to meetings. The two leaders thus organized not the
national blocs, but the small groups, and thus the Council's structure resembled the earlier, segmented order. The democratic
nature of this new community forum was further highlighted by the
inclusion, once again, of women's and youth organizations.[37]

In March 1939, the Back of the Yards Neighborhood Council was
incorporated as a not-for-profit organization. Bishop Sheil made the
Council the official welcoming committee for a contingent of Irish
boxers who were coming to meet a CYO team, and some priests
began asking representatives of parish clubs to attend BYNC meetings. James T., a member of the St. Michael's Young Men's Club,
was asked by Father Ondrak to show up at the Council's first meeting on behalf of his club. Ondrak told him there was to be a meeting
of the neighborhood groups, and that it was a good thing to be interested in. James's appointment was approved by the club's membership. He was, so he said, "pretty active" at the time, and it was
logical for him to receive the appointment.[38]

Before the first meeting on 14 July 1939, Alinsky and Meegan
"sat down together" and wrote a declaration. This call to a Community Conference, to be held at Davis Square, read in part:

For fifty years we have waited for someone to offer a
solution—but nothing has happened. Today we know that we
ourselves must face and solve these problems. We know what
poor housing, disease, unemployment and juvenile
delinquency means; and we are sure that if a way out is to be
found, we can and must find it.

So we have stopped waiting. We churchmen, businessmen
and union men have formed the Back of the Yards
Neighborhood Council. The Council is inviting
representatives of all the neighborhood organizations,
church, business, social, fraternal, and labor to participate in
a conference on July 14th at the Davis Square Auditorium.
The purpose of the conference is to thoroughly discuss the
problems facing the community, and to form a program of
joint action which can effectively attack the evils of disease,
bad housing, crime and unemployment.

The purpose of the conference can perhaps be best
expressed through the statement of purpose of the
Neighborhood Council.

"This organization is founded for the purpose of uniting all
of the organizations within that community known as the

'Back of the Yards' in order to promote the welfare of all
residents of that community regardless of their race, color or
creed, so that they may all have the opportunity to find
health, happiness and security through the democratic way of
life."[39]

The meeting of 350 people, representing 76 organizations, began
with a benediction by Reverend Ambrose Ondrak. Bishop Sheil,
elected honorary chairman, was the main speaker. The participants
separated into four committees—health, child welfare, housing, and
unemployment—to discuss specific issues. After these conferences,
each committee presented a report, which was discussed, and resolutions, which were voted on. Among those passed was one calling
for the development of 47th Street and Damen Avenue as a recreational center. Throughout the meeting, chaired by Meegan, people
spoke openly and freely. Everyone seemed to realize that these
were neighborhood people working for the entire neighborhood.
Some learned for the first time that Sig Wlodarczyk of the PWOC
belonged to St. John of God's Holy Name Society. Bishop Sheil later
called it "one of the most vivid demonstrations of the democratic
process in action that I have ever witnessed" and Konstanty G. explained that, "if you had something on your mind, you go in a meeting and get up and spoken about it." The community now had a
forum where people could unite for common purposes.[40]

The Council had been founded, however, against a background of
violence. During the same time that Meegan and Alinsky had been
so busy, March and the PWOC were also hard at work. Their target
was Armour & Company, the toughest and harshest of the meat-
packers. Armour refused to permit elections (which the National
Labor Relations Board soon demanded) and declined to meet with
the union. The Packinghouse Workers' Organizing Committee began to consider a strike—reluctantly, because they were not yet
prepared for a major confrontation. Armour's gave them no choice.

The PWOC called a mass meeting at the Chicago Coliseum on 16
July, and John L. Lewis, the hulking leader of the CIO, was the
speaker. Bishop Sheil also agreed to appear, welcome news because
he was the first member of the Catholic hierarchy in the United
States to give his sanction to industrial unions. As Leslie Orear
said, "It made the whole CIO look good." But Sheil acted in the face
of criticism. Clergy and laymen alike urged him to withdraw. One
prominent Catholic threatened him with a reprisal from the Vat-
ican, screaming, "I'll see that you're thrown out of here." According

to Sheil's biographer, "John L. Lewis himself couldn't have thought up a better way of insuring the Bishop's presence at the meeting." And some went beyond verbal abuse. Sheil began to receive telephoned threats against his life that eventually came hourly. Shortly before the meeting, someone fired shots at the bishop through a restaurant window. When he appeared at the Coliseum, fifty policemen guarded him.[41]

If violence against a leader of the church seemed unusual, it was commonplace against the PWOC. Walter S. Kozubowski's father, a CIO organizer, had been assaulted: "He was coming home from work . . . and three or four fellows got him in an alley and they really did a number on him. They knocked some of his teeth out and he was kicked in the temple. . . . They really worked him over." The union hall, at 48th Street and Marshfield Avenue, was repeatedly attacked. Shots were fired through the windows and on 20 September 1938 a small bomb exploded in the doorway. Worse was to come. If Sheil's brief role called forth violence, Herbert March, director of the union, was viewed as "the key to the development of the union." On 1 December 1938, March was driving down Ashland Avenue to his home at 59th Street; at 51st Street, a car pulled up to his and gunmen fired nine shots. March jumped out of the car onto the sidewalk and escaped with a scraped face. After this, he began to carry a .45 automatic in his glove compartment. On July 13th, the day before the first meeting of the Back of the Yards Neighborhood Council and three days before the event at the Chicago Coliseum, three men drove up to him and fired a .38-caliber revolver. March twisted the wheel and slammed down the accelerator. He heard "the loud report of a pistol and bits of glass hit my face and I felt a sharp blow on my shoulder." The bullet entered his shoulder and lodged in his neck. By then he had driven the car over the curb and into a tree. March heard later that a thug working for company unions, angry and drunk because of the impending BYNC meeting, had gone looking for the CIO leader. "It was an amateurish job," he reported, "A professional would have knocked me over."[42]

The union had a prominent place at the Council's first meeting: Aaron Hurwitz recalled that the "stockyards was the first thing that the Council turned attention to." A resolution, supported by the clergy, called for Armour & Company to avert a strike and expressed solidarity with the union. At the meeting at the Chicago Coliseum two days later, Bishop Sheil told his audience that "the worker . . . has the strict right to receive from his labors such returns as will ensure him those necessary commodities. When returns fall below these requirements . . . an irrational condition is created and the natural rights of man are grievously violated." After the benediction, Sheil shook hands with John L. Lewis; the photograph was telegraphed across the country. The *Chicago News* declared that it was "unprecedented in the social history of Chicago" and Leslie Orear of the PWOC felt that "it was the maximum embrace." The next day, Armour granted the union recognition and a modest pay increase.[43]

The Back of the Yards Neighborhood Council was on its way. Its genius lay in its simultaneous acceptance of segmented and nationalistic separations and its development of a way to overcome the restrictions of those systems. Meegan assumed that the Poles would still resent the Lithuanians, that the Slovaks would still detest the Bohemians, and that the basic patterns of association would remain unaltered. The BYNC did not replace the nationalist groups and it never tried to: what it provided was a place where, once a month, everyone in the neighborhood could join together to try to wrest from outside authorities the resources they all needed. It provided an open forum, accepted by the community and all its parts as a way of helping everyone and as a necessary institution in the modern world of big government. This concept—that the Council would not challenge the private order of segmentation and nationalism, but instead create a public realm in which the individual pieces could join—was the secret of its success in building an independent and self-controlled community, and the proof of Alinsky's and Meegan's genius. Despite the fact that they functioned in an atmosphere of changing social patterns, they managed to create a body capable of bridging traditional antagonisms and old and new attitudes toward ethnicity. The BYNC's ability to attract both the immigrants and their native-born children to collective action thus guaranteed its continued existence for at least another generation.

10

Democracy Realized

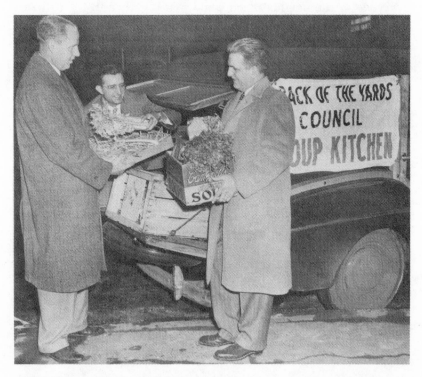

The Soup Kitchen during the 1946 Strike. *Left*, Joseph Meegan
Courtesy of Joseph B. Meegan

A s the established representative of the community, the Back of the Yards Neighborhood Council began working for control, stability, and freedom, articulating goals and realizing them. To do this, the Council not only placed pressure on powerful groups outside the neighborhood, but also dealt with powerful local institutions. During its founding years, the BYNC confronted both the meat-packers and the political system, and emerged victorious. Its power was based on the neighborhood's new sense of unity and on its leaders' skills.

Meetings were held every month. The delegates, as described by one participant, were "bright, lively people," more than willing to be part of the process of building a better community. Monsignor Edward Plawinski, the first Council president, said that "anybody was free to ask questions, debate whatever was on their agenda, and give [the] opinion of the group that they represented." The major topics, of course, were the intimate problems that made daily life so difficult. Delegates would "bring out certain . . . squabbles in the neighborhood," according to James T. of St. Michael's Young Men's Club. It was not uncommon to have members cite a block, or even a house or an owner that was a source of trouble.[1]

Various kinds of action could result from these citations. Delegates usually proposed remedies for the problems being debated and these were discussed. Final decisions were always made by majority vote of delegates. More frequently, however, a commitee was formed to look into the particular situation and return with a proposed form of action. Delegates would join whichever group interested them, and "everybody was on committees." The committees would also lead whatever activity was decided on, and it was not uncommon for groups to lobby at city or state agencies.[2]

A new generation of leaders emerged out of the Council meetings, people who understood the neighborhood's social structure intimately and whose main goal was the betterment of the residents' lives. Union organizers always played a large role in meetings, and Father Kelly felt that he and others "could always depend on the packinghouse workers" for support and leadership. He and other priests were also crucial to the Councils' success since they brought with them the parish's clubs and organizations. It was not surprising, therefore, that the Council's first president was a priest, Monsignor Edward Plawinski of St. John of God. Father Kelly believed that the delegates elected the Polish cleric—"a brilliant, talented man"—because of his skill and his willingness to give of his time, and because he represented the richest and most influential church in the neighborhood. Plawinski conducted investigations, served as the Council's public and press representative, and traveled on lobbying trips. One of his most important tasks was to serve as moderator at the monthly meetings; a difficult job, given the enthusiasm of the delegates. At first there were no time limitations, but Plawinski changed that because "they went on and on." He ended up by placing his wristwatch on the table in front of him and cueing each speaker when the allotted time was up.[3]

After these meetings, the delegates would report back to their constituency and receive instructions for the next session. Their method of submission varied from group to group. Sigmund Wlodarczyk gave regular reports to the union and James T. discussed Council business with any member of St. Michael's Club who was interested, but rarely assembled the full body to deliver a statement. Father Kelly held regular sessions about Council business with his pastor, Father William Ward. After every meeting, a dinner conversation at the rectory would be devoted to the Back of the Yards Council and the assembled priests would suggest ideas for Kelly to bring to the next meeting.[4]

The delegates also helped to expand the Council and to mobilize the yards' citizenry. Much of the discussion at the early meetings was about getting other groups to join. The delegates actively recruited new clubs, spread news about the Council's activities to the members of their own organizations, and arranged for their groups' participation. The delegates and their clubs' members also talked about the Council's programs to their friends and neighbors.

The Council also sought support from audiences outside the neighborhood, and Joseph Meegan and Saul Alinsky were expert promoters. On 16 October 1939, they held a meeting at Davis Square Park for 140 students of Chicago Teachers College. There the two men, joined by Herbert March and Father Ambrose Ondrak, explained the organization's purposes and goals and then the group joined a tour of the yards and the packing plants. Meegan also induced the publisher of the *Town of Lake Journal* to change its name to the *Back of the Yards Journal* and to accept a board of governors, appointed by the Council, with complete jurisdiction over the policy and character of the paper, thus becoming the Council's official organ.[5]

Before the first Council meetings, Joseph Meegan approached Aaron Hurwitz, the paper's publisher, and asked him if he wanted to become affiliated with the new organization. Hurwitz replied, "Oh, sure," but did not take the matter seriously and attended the first meeting with mixed feelings: "We didn't like anybody telling the newspaper what to do." But at the meeting he noticed the wide range of community leaders, many of whom had previously refused to cooperate with him; in particular, he noticed the priests, none of whom had ever provided material for the paper. The BYNC was obviously a superior place to gather news. After the meeting, Meegan cornered him and told him to change the name of the paper. Hurwitz said, "Okay, one of these days"; Meegan replied, "Not one of these days, now"; and Hurwitz agreed to make the change. Meegan and Alinsky, for their part, figured that if the newspaper carried the Council's name, they would gain recognition more quickly. Besides, they argued, Town of Lake was an old, outmoded name—there wasn't even any lake—and Back of the Yards was an accurate description of the neighborhood. Moreover, the new name created a greater sense of identity and uniqueness among the residents, promoting the feeling that they were.different from, and even better than, other neighborhoods.[6]

Funding for the BYNC was an early problem. At first, the Council's sole support came from local businesses and civic groups. At an early meeting, $1,000 was donated. As a going concern, however, the Council needed a steadier source of income, and it turned to the Community Fund, an association of charities. At that time, the packinghouses forced their workers to contribute to the Community Fund, a practice that made the companies look altruistic and the home of contented, well-paid employees. The union officials explained the Council's situation at a Community Fund budgeting session: as Herbert March, a participant, described the argument, "We were very pointed, we were young and blunt." They told the Fund's leaders: "Look. If our people see that you don't care anything for the Back of the Yards Council, they might donate less." The threat was pure bluff because the workers' contributions were mandatory, but the charity officials did not know this and the tactic worked. They voted $3,500 to the BYNC, the first of many contributions.[7]

Out of all this activity came a feeling of self-determination and self-esteem previously unknown in the neighborhood. The rationale of the Back of the Yards Council was that people could figure out their own solutions to problems. Meegan told a reporter, "we believe that no one, and I repeat no one, can possibly be as interested in our problems as ourselves . . . we believe that we are as intelligent as anyone else and can figure out the answers to our problems." Part of this dignity came from the newly found unity of this segmented neighborhood. The Council established the idea of treat-

ing "people as people when they came in," according to Monsignor
Edward Plawinski. He noted that, ". . . solidarity in the neighborhood was the important thing," especially if the Council was to
succeed in wresting resources from the government. "If you're
going to gain any power, if you're going to gain any leverage in the
City Council or anyplace . . . you have to present a united front."
Aaron Hurwitz of the *Journal* also noticed that the Council changed
things, that people started fighting for one another rather than with
one another. Before the Back of the Yards Council, said the publisher, "There was never any harmony." But "if you were a Council
member you were automatically a brother." He may have been
stretching the point for twenty-nine days of the month, but on the
thirtieth day, when the Council met, the statement was valid. The
Council had to challenge some of the nationalist boundaries to
achieve this unity, however. It sponsored "Americanism" dinners at
which it brought together citizens of different backgrounds. At the
hot-lunch program, the Polish and Lithuanian children refused to
eat with each other and stayed far away from Mexicans. Meegan
took a firm stand: "They ate together or they didn't eat."[8]

In the churches, also, barriers fell. The young priests argued that
"by joining and being concerned . . . there would be a profit for
everyone; everyone would grow." Each church began to draw support for its affairs from the entire community, not just its own parishioners. Father Ondrak of St. Michael went to lunch at St. Rose of
Lima, a major event at that time. When a local synagogue asked to
join the Council's hot-lunch program, Father Ondrak, a Slovak
priest, made the motion; Father Bernard Sokolowski, a Polish
priest, seconded it; and it passed overwhelmingly.[9]

To get support for the union, a newcomer, from traditional groups
in the local society, the Council explained to the neighborhood merchants that improvements in the standard of living meant that more
money would be spent in the neighborhood. When the Congress of
Industrial Organizations (CIO) held a picnic, shopkeepers placed
large ads in the program book. The *Back of the Yards Journal* ran
notices, "Store Owners! Your Help Is Needed." In response, the
union called a "sales week" and urged its members to shop in the local
stores, whose receipts increased 25 percent. Later, union representatives urged businesses to join the Chamber of Commerce. Moreover, the churches, hitherto opposed to the left-wing CIO, began to
accept the union. The closest link between the two was Sigmund
Wlodarczyk, a Pole with a fluent command of the language, a member of the Holy Name Society at St. John of God—and a labor orga-

nizer. "What's so strange about churches and unions working together? Why shouldn't they work together when the same men and women belong to both?" he asked. Wlodarczyk thought that the priests, who were concerned about the well-being of their flock, should respond to anyone willing to help improve living conditions, and the priests, agreeing, told their parishioners to vote for the CIO in union elections. Wlodarczyk would, according to his reports to Packinghouse Workers headquarters, "write the facts and they will put the religious angle themselves." He asked for, and received, backing from the pulpit during strikes and in support of labor legislation. The support was complete: "whatever we needed." And the union's leaders reciprocated: even Herbert March "found some very fine people in the Catholic Church."[10]

There were other efforts on behalf of the union. The president of the Packinghouse Workers Organizing Committee, Van Bittner, became the Council's honorary chairman, along with Bishop Sheil, at the first BYNC meeting, and Sigmund Wlodarczyk served as vice president for labor for many years. Meegan spoke to laborers as "a Catholic and an American citizen," and told them that "the Council supports . . . the PWOC [the Packinghouse Workers Organizing Committee]." In a paper delivered before the Central State Conference on Probation and Parole, he declared, "You can have all the innovations . . . all the frills and fads . . . but there are certain needs that must be met . . . .We look to the organized labor movement to combat many of these major destructive forces which impinge upon our community with such disastrous results." In support of the union, the Council convened town-hall meetings on the cost of living, discussed rising prices, and passed resolutions condemning the anti-union Taft-Hartley Act.[11]

The first social-service activity of the Back of the Yards Council was child welfare; Monsignor Plawinski called it "the main thrust." Meegan said, "We start with the family before anything else." It was also good strategy because it guaranteed the support of the parents. One of the first child-welfare projects was to bring to Back of the Yards an Infant Welfare Station, a charity run by Chicago's elite. It required pressure on an external agency and a decision by the Council to supplant the mother's traditional function with a more modern, bureaucratic, and scientific approach, but there was dire need of help. In 1937, the infant mortality rate in Back of the Yards was 44.0 deaths per 1,000 live births (compared to 23.7 per 1,000 in Hyde Park, the University of Chicago's neighborhood.) In June 1939, even before its first official meeting, the Council began lobbying for a station which would assure "to the babies in Back of the Yards" the right to live. On 14 December 1939 the station opened to parents and children under six. At first, the reaction to the new health service was hesitant. Parents, themselves unaccustomed to medical personnel, were wary of the idea. But Father Ondrak endorsed the clinic, thus delivering the sanction of the church. "I personally advocate the use of this welfare station to mothers," he told the *Back of the Yards Journal* in December. A Most Healthy Baby Contest promoted the new service by exploiting the mothers' pride in their children. The doctors from the Infant Welfare Station judged each contestant, diagnosed maladies, and promised a prize the next year if a child was treated. The number of families visiting the clinic rose considerably.[12]

The largest single project undertaken by the Back of the Yards Neighborhood Council was the free-lunch program which Joseph Meegan began when he was director of Davis Square Park and before the Council was organized. By late 1939, a thousand to fifteen-hundred children were having lunch at Davis Square Park daily. It was the first time that a federal program to distribute surplus food was used by a nonpublic organization and it was the prime example of the Council's ability to obtain from outside agencies the kind of assistance that the community so badly needed. The Council made sure, however, to portray the program as a supplement to a diet severely limited by the packinghouse workers' wages, not as a challenge to the mother's responsibility to cook for and feed her children.[13]

The Council expanded its role as a community advocate by teaching other institutions—both public and parochial schools—to inaugurate similar programs and launched a publicity campaign to help persuade them. "Thousands of dollars are spent on school equipment," the Council proclaimed, "but we cannot expect an undernourished body to do the best kind of school work." It arranged for the same hot-lunch programs in the schools' lunchrooms and auditoriums; by the end of 1941, fifty schools—not only in Back of the Yards but throughout Chicago—were participating. The standard meal included a main dish, raw or cooked vegetables, bread, milk, and dessert. The benefits were almost immediate. In October 1941, for example, when the program was instituted at St. Martini Evangelical Lutheran Church, 62 percent of the children were underweight. Within three months, that figure had declined to 45 percent, and 95 percent of the students had gained weight. By 1945, thirty-five hundred children were being fed through this program, directly under Council auspices. During the early 1940s, other cities heard about the program and launched their own version. The Council was thus the national pioneer of hot-lunch programs.[14]

In 1943, the federal government, fighting an overseas war on two fronts, withdrew its grants of surplus foods. Shortly thereafter, the Lanham bill, which provided for funds to continue the lunch and milk programs, was passed by the House of Representatives, but the section providing food for youngsters was defeated. Meegan and Father Plawinski flew to Washington to lobby in the Senate, where the program could be restored. They found that most senators failed to realize what had been done: Senators Lucas and Brooks of Illinois pledged cooperation and members of the Senate committee arranged for Meegan to testify. Alone, the BYNC and the Chicago Board of Education were carrying the fight for a program that fed 5,301,554 children in 73,001 schools throughout the United States. For this purpose, the Council mobilized its entire constituency. Meegan spoke of children learning to "eat democracy." Children throughout Chicago wrote twenty-three thousand letters to the senators. Ruth Borkie of St. Augustine pleaded that "many of us would go without milk." One student wrote, "Since we've started drinking milk in school, I've gained seven pounds. I promise I will be little trouble in the future and will repay the trouble caused. Please don't take the milk away—Raymond Gell." The Senate responded to their call and passed the Lanham Act, assuring the children of 7½¢ for a meal.[15]

The next move was on the state level. Senator Brooks told a delegation from the yards that the appropriation still depended on getting matching funds from Springfield. Only two weeks remained in the state legislature's session and most representatives were "apathetic." The Council organized a lobbying effort: calls came into Springfield from church, labor, and ethnic groups—and schoolchildren again wrote. One new state senator from Chicago, Richard J. Daley, "acted immediately." He pushed the necessary legislation through in record time. During the final vote, when the legislators were locked in a fourteen-hour session, Meegan sent in ham sandwiches and milk. Seventy-seven of the eighty members present voted aye. The state senator from Chicago who saw the bill through the state legislature went on to become the mayor of Chicago and a lifelong friend of the Back of the Yards Council.[16]

The program to feed youth continued. Chicago's schools charged students 1¢ for a half-pint of milk but the Council found a dairy which charged a penny less so their milk was free. In December

1943, the Back of the Yards Council served 161,430 meals, almost as many as the Archdiocese of Chicago. By the end of 1944, seventeen schools and 17,000 children ate hot lunches and drank free milk through the good offices of the Back of the Yards Neighborhood Council.[17]

In 1946, H.R. 3370, the Flannigan bill, was drafted to create a permanent appropriation for the program, but Congress was engaged in cutting the postwar budget. August Andresen, a Republican representative from Minnesota, questioned the need for federal standards of nutrition. The congressman didn't want the federal government telling juveniles what to eat: "If they told me I had to eat fish, or kohlrabi, I certainly wouldn't do it." Joseph Meegan testified: "Why, the standards we use now are . . . for Type A lunch, for example, you get a main course of two ounces of meat or fish or one egg or two ounces of cheese. What else is there to eat but meat or fish, eggs or cheese?" Andresen did not reply, but Congress did. The bill passed and President Truman signed the National School Lunch Act into law in June 1946; by 1948 the Council was cosponsoring lunch programs in ninety-nine schools. This was one of the Council's greatest triumphs. It proved the organization's ability to win lasting assistance from the federal government and it demonstrated the Council's ability to accept, understand, and manipulate the expanding structure of that government.[18]

The Council also combated juvenile delinquency. Meegan approached many of the rougher youth groups, and gave each $50 to spend as it pleased. The gangs, flabbergasted by being trusted, used the money for constructive purposes. Some took the younger children on a picnic, others bought athletic uniforms or baskets for the poor, and eventually they all organized a softball league. But the Council had a more formal method of dealing with juvenile delinquency. If police or merchants apprehended a young lawbreaker, they would call the Back of the Yards Council instead of taking him to the station. The Council then arranged a conference with the child, the parents, the priest, educators, union officials, and police or probation officers—representatives of all the community's resources. If the mother had to work to help support the family, the union officials found better work for the father, so that she could stay home and supervise the children. When more stringent measures were required, the Council arranged placement in special facilities, often run by holy orders such as the Franciscans. The Council did not attempt to usurp the family's responsibility for its children, but supported it by bringing all the neighborhood's assets to bear on the problem. It was the first program of its kind in the nation.[19]

The Council sought recreational and employment opportunities for youngsters as well. Exploration had its benefits, but it was also dangerous. In 1939, the BYNC bought the open ground at 47th Street and Damen Avenue on which they had resolved to erect a playground. They paid the railroads $1 for it, and the Chicago Recreational Commission agreed to buy the equipment. At a Community Fund budget meeting, a charity official questioned the absence of funds for a night watchman, citing thefts at public parks. One of the BYNC delegates explained the difference between the city and a democratic community: "Yeah, but those parks belong to the public'" he said. "This is ours. We're not going to steal our own stuff."[20]

Early on, in 1939, the Council replaced its previously haphazard search for jobs for youths with a systematic approach. Turning again to a government agency, the National Youth Administration paid $14 to $29 a month for fifty-six hours of work. The Council received permission to have applicants register at their headquarters at Davis Square Park, and sent the forms, plus letters of recommendation, downtown. By the end of November, more than one hundred and fifty boys and girls had found employment this way, and eventually three thousand obtained assistance.

The Council found jobs for youths in the neighborhood as well. Its officers surveyed local employers and found that they preferred hiring local people, so the Council became their employment agency, especially for busy periods like Christmas when more help was required. Young people of sixteen or older needed only a recommendation from a church or a member organization of the Council, and a social-security card. Hundreds were hired.[21]

The Back of the Yards Council sponsored many other projects for youth. To combat vitamin deficiencies, it launched a massive publicity campaign, using pulpit, union hall, and social club meetings, to convince parents to buy and serve orange juice. Patrol boys in fourteen local schools stayed dry in raincoats purchased by the BYNC. When a tavern owner sold wine to students at Seward School, Council officials, with the cooperation of the police and the courts, shut the tavern down. Three hundred children went to summer camp. Basketball and softball tournaments were held. When a dental survey discovered that 95 percent of the schoolchildren had cavities—99 percent in one school alone—the BYNC induced local dentists to perform free examinations in all the schools, notifying the parents if their offspring required treatment.[22]

One of the most important items on the Council's agenda was housing. In 1941, the Back of the Yards Council gave all the school-children in the neighborhood a questionnaire about housing violations and asked them to return it to Council headquarters. As a result, 3,610 houses with defects were reported to the Health Department and the Building Department. The following year, seventeen students from Chicago Teachers College gave the children lessons in how to fill out the forms. The program stopped during the Second World War, but resumed in 1945, when thirty women from the social service school at St. Xavier College surveyed the area and turned up 1,320 violations. They also tabulated a study done by neighborhood students, which resulted in a comprehensive evaluation of the community's housing. This was also turned over to the city, and this time recalcitrant owners found their names and addresses printed in the *Back of the Yards Journal*.[23]

The Back of the Yards Council worked to keep homes clean as well as safe. From 1945 on, it supplied garbage cans to residents, offering two thousand 55-gallon drums, worth about ten dollars each, for 75¢. In 1946, it purchased a portable exterminator and lent it out to residents. There were also health programs. In 1945, the BYNC began to support a local cancer society, providing speakers, films, and educational literature to various groups. In 1944, it helped to obtain a new post office and, in 1945, its outer offices, which contained a one-hundred-volume library, remained open on Monday and Friday evenings for the residents of the community. In 1946, the Council established an office to which families could come with any problem—broken streetlights, juvenile delinquency, or alcoholism. The Council's social worker and juvenile specialists handled some cases themselves and acted as a clearing bureau for others, arranging aid from all over the city.[24]

The Council also operated a credit union under the supervision of Father Bernard Sokolowski of Sacred Heart. Its purpose, editorialized the *Journal*, was to "save our families from those who profiteer on our people's financial troubles" and to assist them "efficiently and economically to stabilize their budget." Thirty-five members founded the credit union in 1945 and, by 1948, there were eighty-four. This gave the Council access to the residents' personal finances, hitherto sacrosanct territory; the Council now had a legitimate right to advise and assist families with their budgeting so that they could better meet their needs.[25]

The Council also experimented with new sources of funding. In May 1940, thirty-six social-athletic clubs sponsored a Jungle Jamboree; tickets cost 40¢ and the members of the clubs handled all the arrangements. In Setpember 1940, the Council held a fair at the field at 47th Street and Damen Avenue. It lasted eleven nights, each night honoring a different segment of the community: Friday was for labor, Saturday for youth, Monday for nationalities, and so forth. As many as ten thousand visitors came each night. Youthful clergy handled the money. "Perspiring young priests, sometimes stripped down to a T-shirt and black clerical trousers" carried it to safe places to await shipment to the bank. The division of labor at the fair was decided by the Council delegates. Father Joseph Kelly felt that the planning went smoothly because of the experience of the participants: "these people were all trained in carnival work; they did it in their parishes." It was a strictly local endeavor, organized and managed by the people of the neighborhood. The Council also strengthened its own organization. On 8 June 1945, an affiliate, the Back of the Yards Businessman's Association, held its first meeting. This group coordinated the activities of the commercial, industrial, and financial sectors of Back of the Yards. Bishop Sheil and the Reverend Herman Brauer of St. Martini's Evangelical Lutheran Church spoke at the first meeting, as did Sigmund Wlodarcyzk. The Businessman's Association sponsored sales, parades, and festivals, and it promoted good business practices such as remodeling sales space and keeping storefronts neat.[26]

There were, however, powerful groups in Back of the Yards that resented the Council's influence. Joseph Meegan had been warned by the Chicago Park District that he would have to choose between "social service work and park activities." A little later, toward the end of 1943, Robert Dunham, president of the Chicago Park District, had also "intimated" that the Council might have to leave Davis Square Park, but a delegation of clergy met with him and reached an amicable settlement. The Thursday after Christmas, however, Council headquarters received notice that the hot-lunch programs had to go. On 1 January 1944, Dunham instructed the Back of the Yards Neighborhood Council to vacate Davis Square Park and ordered Meegan, its executive secretary, transferred to Ogden Park, at 67th Street and Racine Avenue. According to Dunham, there should be equal access to the parks. If the Back of the Yards Council could use the park, why not other private agencies? Its monopoly might deter others from using public facilities. The facts, however, were that private clubs, such as yachting organizations, had long used park facilities without threat of eviction. The public's use of Davis Square Park had grown, not diminished; attendance in 1942 was 942,950, the highest of any site in the South Section of the Park District.[27]

The real reasons behind the move were more complex. Dunham was treasurer of the Cook County Democratic Party, whose leaders had always been wary of the BYNC, a competitor and possible opponent. The politicians "resented the power that he [Meegan] had . . . they were worried about their own power base." Monsignor Edward Plawinski claimed that the Democrats resented the Council because they handed out favors that had been the exclusive province of ward committeemen. By 1944, the politicians decided that, in Back of the Yards, "the people are getting out of line." But there were other, more direct reasons for the attack as well.[28]

Both the Council and the Chicago Board of Education ran hot-lunch and milk programs. The federal government subscribed 2¢ and the state 1¢ toward the cost of the half-pint of milk. A combine of five dairies charged the city 4¢—one of the highest rates in the state—and so Chicago had a "penny milk program." Other agencies paid from 2¢ to 2¾¢ a bottle. One anonymous executive explained that he could sell milk in a competitive market at 3¢ a bottle, but that he preferred the higher profits and the closed structure. The BYNC, which bought its milk from a different company, paid 3¢, the amount of the federal and state subsidies, and distributed its milk free of charge. A delegation from the dairy combine offered Meegan a kickback of ¼¢ a bottle if he bought from that group, but he refused. Shortly after, Dunham transferred Meegan and evicted the Council from Davis Square Park. It was well known that Dunham, as treasurer of the Democratic Party, received large political contributions from the dairies: "The Cook County Democrats expect us to kick in substantially, and we do."[29]

The Council retaliated by focusing on the closing of the hot-lunch program. Parents wrote letters to the papers. Fred Kaufman, about to be inducted into the army, informed the *Chicago Sun* that "I told Mr. Meegan I was leaving my children in his hands. Now he is gone and so are the children's lunches." As a result Kaufman's wife had to give up her job in the stockyards to take care of the children. The Council also appointed a Board of Strategy composed of three priests, a minister, and Saul Alinsky, who had returned from his travels. On 2 January 1944, the neighborhood churches conducted special children's Masses to pray for the retention of the Council and Meegan. The youngsters also wrote to the papers. Twelve-year-old Edward Landis wrote that he went home for lunch when the park facilities closed, "but Mamma was at work and there wasn't anything to eat." Eleanor Jurgovan pleaded: "I would like you to keep Mr. Joseph Meegan in Davis Square Park. He done a lot for people and service man. He give the poor people free lunch and milk. . . . Everyone love him."[30]

Mayor Edward Kelly tried to stay clear, claiming that "this question is one for the Park District to decide." His efforts were futile, and within a week he nullified two of his subordinate's orders. On 8 January 1944, the mayor "rescinded" the order to the Council to leave Davis Square Park, and observed that the Council had "done much good work . . . trying to build up the younger generation," but he kept Meegan's transfer in effect. The head of the BYNC then asked for a sixty-day leave of absence, and at a meeting with the strategy board on 7 January, the mayor agreed to the leave of absence.[31]

A week later, the conflict erupted again. The Park District refused to grant his leave and Meegan resigned on 15 January. The BYNC immediately voted him a salary and, the next day, announced that it would move to new headquarters at 4600 South Ashland Avenue. Children, parents, priests, and park workers carried out cooking equipment and stored it till new lunch facilities were opened at Holy Cross church. At the same time, the warfare continued, unabated. Dunham claimed that the Council did not really represent the neighborhood and that it exaggerated its membership. The lunch program was no longer needed because of higher wartime wages. He also sent several men to the park who asked embarrassing questions of the children at the lunchroom.

And then the Park District's head attacked Bishop Sheil. Dunham claimed, according to an article in the *Chicago Tribune* on 20 February 1944, that Sheil had promised to take care of moving the Council out of the park and terminating Meegan's local activities. This was a foolish, unpopular move. Sheil spoke to the press "as a Bishop of the Roman Catholic Church. . . . Mr. Dunham's statement that I made any promise . . . is false in its entirety. . . . The balance of his sly innuendos and his sinister charge . . . are entirely without basis in fact." Dunham feebly replied that he had "respect" for the church and that Sheil had a "failing memory," but in March the church again responded when Cardinal Stritch presented the Back of the Yards Council with a check for $500 and a note expressing "my earnest hope that the Council's good work will prosper and increase."[32]

Support for the Back of the Yards Council came from many directions. Soldiers, alerted by the Chicago papers and the *Back of the*

Yards Journal, wrote the papers to complain. Corporal Frank Gier-
tuga wrote: "Since I am a soldier and a gentleman I can't put into
words the contempt I have for the activities of the park district."
The federal government, particularly the executive branch, also began to investigate, in part because of the upcoming election. Officials in Washington did not like the image of the local Democratic
Party aligned against the people, the children, and the church. The
Department of Agriculture, in its broadcasts, praised the Council
for founding the lunch program and gave Meegan broadcasting time
to explain the project. The newspapers also helped. Marshall Field
III, a close friend of Alinsky's and the Council's, threw the resources of the *Chicago Sun* behind the BYNC, opening up space in
the paper's columns and assigning reporter Justin McCarthy to
work exclusively in the neighborhood. McCarthy "practically lived
with the people on the Council," according to Monsignor Plawinski.
In late February, the Field papers and others published the story of
the milk scandal behind the conflict. Mayor Kelly, vacationing in
Miami, asked that the press clippings, rather than his subordinate's
reports, be sent to him.[33]

On 11 March 1944, Dunham met the Council's representatives at
Bishop Sheil's Catholic Youth Organization office. At the three-hour
meeting, arranged by aldermen from wards in or adjacent to Back
of the Yards, Dunham offered the use of Davis Square Park, the
Council refused, and a gentleman's agreement to remain silent ended the matter. Dunham told the press that "The purposes of the
Council are laudable . . . organizations such as the Council . . . perform a valuable function in the community"; Monsignor Plawinski
said, "From the point of view of the Council the present controversy
is ended." Five hours later, Dunham claimed he had been misin-
terpreted: "Nothing that I said can be interpreted as an apology
. . . for our actions in this controversy. We are not retreating one
step from the position we originally took." The Council leaders,
maintaining the agreement, refused to comment.[34]

At this point Dunham made a fatal move. To prove his impar-
tiality, he asked the Infant Welfare Society, a private organization,
to remove its stations from the parks also. The six stations, some in
existence for thirty-three years, had handled 16,648 cases in 1943.
The public response was immediate and outraged. The society leaders who funded this charity, notably Phillip Armour, protested, and
so did mothers. The newspapers revealed that private groups sponsored 60 percent of all the activities in the parks, and reported that
no action seemed imminent against three yacht clubs, three archery

clubs, and a badminton group. The Back of the Yards Council offered to house the Infant Welfare Station in its headquarters but Dunham dropped the whole matter. The *Chicago Sun* declared, "thus, as in all previous battles, the 'little people' of the stockyards district, through their organization, the Back of the Yards Neighborhood Council, have won again." The victory—achieved by a coalition of the church, the union, the neighborhood clubs, and the residents; and supported by the press and the federal government—gave the Council citywide legitimacy and the status of a powerful force.[35]

But there was one more struggle ahead. In 1946, after years of static wages and rapidly rising prices, the United Packinghouse Workers of America (UPWA), CIO, decided to strike. Men like Walter Seraukas, a stockyards laborer and parishioner at Holy Cross, still earned only $17 for a thirty-six hour workweek, though the government estimated that the cost of living had increased 33 percent and that prices of essential products had risen 43.5 percent. The UPWA asked for a raise of 25¢ an hour; the company's best offer was 7½¢. The union's members authorized the action by a twenty-to-one margin in a National Labor Relations Board election, and the strike began at 12:01 A.M. on 16 January 1946. The picket lines that first night included such notables from the BYNC as Joseph Meegan and Saul Alinsky, as well as Isabelle Gross of the YWCA, the Reverend Herman Brauer of St. Martini's, Father Edward Plawinski, and Father Amrose Ondrak.[36]

The Council's leaders mapped out a program of support, starting with a donation of $1,000; by the successful end of the strike—only twelve days later—this cash contribution reached $8,000 and the Council had collected $1,600 more from merchants and residents. The Council operated a strike kitchen at the Guardian Angel Day Care Center, and some of the food was donated. Other services provided by the Council included providing temporary relief payments, making social workers available to striking families, and organizing entertainment. It induced local stores and landlords to extend credit for the duration of the strike, printers to make signs which the Council placed in stores, persuaded priests to preach sermons supporting the strikers, and issued statements to the press, such as Meegan's comment, "It is our people. It is our cause. It is our fight." An editorial in the *Back of the Yards Journal* on 24 January, four days before the strike ended, read: "It took a long time before the members of a community could identify their economic interests with one another." At this time, however, "the 185 businesses, church, labor and social organizations of the Back of the Yards Neighborhood Council have openly allied themselves with the stockyards workers out on strike."[37]

Other community institutions responded to the emergency. The Guardian Angel Day Care Center, besides running soup kitchens, took care of children while their parents picketed. Peter Barskis, president of the Back of the Yards Businessman's Association, offered full support. Leo Rose, owner of a local furniture and clothing store, donated $100 and suspended payment of bills. "If the strike lasts two weeks, we won't accept a payment for five weeks," he asserted. "We sell to workers, not the packing companies. Where do you suppose we stand?" Bakeries sent sweet breads, buns, whipped cream cakes, and 140 dozen rolls to strike headquarters. Cherry Brand Meat Packers, a small local outfit, sent 500 hot dogs. Dr. Mace Gazda was on call to treat the injured. Community and business support for a labor union was nothing new; their contributions in 1946 closely paralleled those they had made in the earlier strike of 1921 to 1922. The Council simply revived a network of support created decades earlier to continue to build a strong and prosperous neighborhood.

The strike succeeded. President Truman, acting under the War Labor Disputes Act, ordered the seizure of the packing plants. The workers returned to their jobs with a pay increase of 16¢ an hour, despite the packers' objections. Stanley Piontek, president of Local #28, UPWA, wrote to Joseph Meegan that, "It is the sincere and firm position that the Back of the Yards Council . . . made it possible for our Union to win the fight against such a powerful adversary as the packers. . . . It is difficult to express in mere words the appreciation of our Local Union and the workers in general but we wish [you] to know that we are grateful."[38]

The Council had proven itself amid smoke and fire. By the end of the forties, the Back of the Yards' own organization had met and overcome all the other bases of power in the community and had become a recognized force in Chicago. It had demonstrated the legitimacy of its right to represent the people of the stockyards district, both locally and nationally. The importance of the Council's performance in the 1940s, therefore, lay not so much in its victories but instead in the basis it established for widespread community self-control and rejuvenation in the fifties and sixties. The founding years were just that: a period of early successes and running fights that established the strength, leadership, and popular support of the community's chosen representative.

The Council's status and legitimacy was most publicly confirmed on 17 June 1948 when forty-six spotlights flashed on to inaugurate the ten-acre field at 47th Street and Damen Avenue, first conceived of in 1939 by the Packingtown Youth Committee, a forerunner of the Council, and developed by the Council over the years. The softball game, part of the opening celebration, was played by two notable teams. On one team, composed of Council leaders and friends, Bishop Sheil pitched, Abbott Ondrak received, and Police Captain Thomas Lyons of the 17th District served as left fielder. The opposing team was composed of radio and newspaper celebrities augmented by such officials as Judge Joseph Hermes of the Circuit Court and Alderman Clarence Wagner of the Fourteenth Ward. Evelyn Ostrowski remembered that "all those dignitaries enjoyed coming down to that game, and really wanted to be included." The Back of the Yards Neighborhood Council had arrived.[39]

Conclusion:
Our Own Destiny

47th Street Looking West from Ashland Avenue
Courtesy of Back of the Yards Neighborhood Council

This work is a case study, and it does not describe all workers, all migrants, or all city dwellers. Nevertheless, Back of the Yards is an important neighborhood because its residents were typical of the Eastern European immigrant workers who lived in the United States' industrialized cities in the first half of the twentieth century. Their fears, their oppressors, their goals—security and freedom—and their methods of achieving them were all remarkably similar, although each community was a separate part of the nationwide scene. For this reason, one neighborhood in Chicago represented many of the forces transforming this country and the lives of its workers.

Back of the Yards was the prototypical working-class community of this country. Formed by giant corporations, the neighborhood breathed, ate, and slept according to the packers' dictates. The companies that controlled the wages and working conditions also shaped the industrial landscape to their own requirements. Rebellion seemed useless: for seventy years, all attempts to challenge this power failed dismally.

Yet the residents created their own private world within this industrial context. In their own spheres, youngsters, women, and men sought and found pockets of experience they could call their own—areas where they could assume control, make decisions, and establish order. Eventually they created an entire social structure, a stable set of relationships in those parts of their environment that the packers did not dominate.

This social structure and the training it provided were vital to the development of the community. Because the residents established the limits of their personal freedom, the lessons they learned in doing so became their own, part of their fundamental attitude towards life. When the time came to mobilize the people of Back of the Yards, their education in assertion and self-control was decades old.

The residents created their power and learned how to use it in familiar arenas. It was more common for a man to learn public speaking at a benefit society than at a union hall, since the benefit society was the more intimate and responsive setting. The men took over the taverns and built them into refuges where they could freely exchange emotional and material support, far from the packers' grip. The women, whose hearth was their personal domain, asserted themselves at home. Here they ruled unchallenged and reaffirmed Old-World skills and talents. The young found their freedom in exploring the neighborhood as they played, in the comeraderie of the social athletic club, and in their expanding right to

225

select their own mates. Within the church, a realm the companies ignored, people acted collectively and bolstered their social world and its myriad institutions.

The strongest form of self-control resulted from the establishment of a network of cliques, based on Old-World village associations. These small, segmented groups protected their members from fraud and created practical ways of dealing with strangers—that is, most of the other immigrant people in the neighborhood. Each clique also provided its members with a stable social environment and a support system of astounding resources. Most important, it taught its members how to discover and maintain their private spheres of freedom, how to control admission to their own small groups, and how to make and enforce rules of conduct. With such advantages, the pattern of cliques gained tremendous strength as the neighborhood grew and developed. Later, new leaders redefined this system on the basis of nationality, imposed centralized and remote controls, supplanted the local democratic elements, and restructured the basic units of the community.

The residents paid a terrible price for both of these social systems. They were first separated into small segmented groups and then into national enclaves, each resentful of the others and jealous of its own turf. Old and new antagonisms grew until they became insurmountable barriers to any united neighborhood action. Even the local churches accepted this state of affairs, thus limiting their influence on small groups within the neighborhood. While successful as a means of creating tiny worlds of freedom, both segmentation and nationalism made it impossible to exert any power on a large scale.

Other institutions with bases of strength outside the community also failed to aid residents in their quest for freedom. One potentially powerful force, the Democratic Party's ward organization, helped individual residents to gain benefits from government but made it impossible for them to gain and use power as a group. The University of Chicago Settlement House was also impotent. Its middle-class residents were culturally too distant from the workers and its services were largely redundant in view of those offered by the churches and the neighborhood's cliques.

It took a disaster—the Depression—and two brilliant men, Saul Alinsky and Joseph Meegan, to overcome the resistance of the nationalist groups and to harness the talents of the neighborhood. The enclaves' remarkable assets were insufficient to meet the problems created by the Depression that began in 1929. Only united pressure on outside agencies, particularly on the government, could obtain the kind of help that was needed. Saul Alinsky and Joseph Meegan understood these problems and the federal bureaucracy, and they founded the Back of the Yards Neighborhood Council as a way of uniting the community to overcome its problems and of organizing it to get external assistance. The Council provided a public forum where residents could unite to pursue joint goals while their private realm remained relatively undisturbed. Using the power created by this solidarity, the Council was able to deal with other forces in the neighborhood, particularly the packers and the political system.

The Council's recognition of the dual public and private arenas was the immediate reason for its success, the reason it was able to mobilize an entire community. But the accomplishment was based on a history of years of training in democratic exercise of power and control. When the people of the neighborhood filed in to join and manage the Council's diverse committees and programs, they used the experience they had gained from their participation in lodges, social-athletic clubs, and church societies. There, and in the taverns, homes, and schoolyards, they had acquired considerable expertise in identifying problems, setting priorities, and designing solutions. Alinsky and Meegan moved this expertise to a broader stage and aimed it at more powerful outside organizations.

The larger successes of the Council were achieved in the 1950s and 1960s. During these decades, the community organization stabilized the neighborhood and helped it grow and prosper. Under the Council's direction, it became one of the most oustanding sections of any metropolis.

Typical was the Council's work in conservation. In the early fifties, much of the local housing stock was run-down, and the neighborhood looked dilapidated. Illegal conversions created congested and inferior housing. Rooming houses that catered to truckers appeared. Many families, especially the younger ones, moved to the suburbs. Back of the Yards seemed to be a classic victim of urban blight.[1]

On 2 July 1953, the Back of the Yards Neighborhood Council held a meeting. In attendance were representatives of all the sections of the neighborhood—church, labor, business, industrial, social, fraternal, real-estate, banking, and savings-and-loan organizations. Meegan asked for cooperation, advised people to stay in the neighborhood and remodel their property, and urged the bankers to invest in the area. Committees were formed to promote upgraded housing and the bankers agreed to release funds. The results were

impressive. In the first year, local banks made 560 home-improve-
ment loans. One institution loaned $1 million and eventually doubled
this amount, all at rates 1 percent below standard. By 1963, another
bank had invested $3 million in similar projects.[2]

The neighborhood's residents also responded enthusiastically.
Ten months after the meeting, more than fifteen hundred families
had modernized their homes. On Marshfield Avenue, 155 homes
were remodeled, 17 on one block. Real-estate values jumped 30 percent in two years. Within ten years, by 1963, more than ten thousand houses, 90 percent of the entire housing stock of Back of the
Yards, had been upgraded. The Chicago Real Estate Board held a
Better Block Crusade Contest in 1959, and 143 of the 189 blocks that
were entered were in Back of the Yards. The neighborhood won
first and third prizes and half of all the citations awarded in the city.
In addition, and also owing largely to the Council's efforts, more
than four hundred vacant storefronts were converted to apartments; more than eight hundred homes were built between 1953 and
1972 (compared with less than a half-dozen between 1946 and 1953);
and in the late fifties the Council sponsored a housing development,
Destiny Manor, whose buildings tripled in value within ten years.
Real-estate agents who tried to panic property owners into selling
at low prices were stopped, and the virtues of the neighborhood
were publicized as part of the effort to stem the flight to suburbia.[3]

All of this happened when the neighborhood, by standard social
science criteria, should have died. During the fifties most of the
packers left Chicago, taking with them the jobs and the industries
that had created the community west of the Union Stockyards—the
result of decentralization of meat-packing and the increasing use of
truck, rather than train, transport. The removal should have signaled the death knell for Back of the Yards, a time of despair and
deterioration. Instead, the fifties and the sixties were boom decades, a period of renewal and growth. This success, this triumph
over potential disaster, was the greatest achievement in the Council's history, and it grew directly out of democratic utilization of
community resources.

In 1951, Adlai Stevenson wrote Joseph Meegan, the executive
secretary, that, "If I were asked to choose in all America a single
agency which I felt most admirably represented all that our democracy stands for . . . I would select the Back of the Yards Council."
Back of the Yards, through its formal representative, did practice
participatory democracy in an efficient and meaningful way, using

its residents' energies and skills to create a better community for all. Yet the fundamental notion of democracy—that individuals determine their "own destiny"—did not suddenly appear in Back of the Yards in 1939: it was as old as the neighborhood that had formed around the Union Stock-Yards many years before.[4]

Appendix

An oral history is a long and complex undertaking. Finding interviewees, for example, is a task in itself. The author discovered that writing or calling potential sources of information, unknown and without introduction, was futile. I learned to make sure that there was always someone to recommend me to the person I wished to interview. Sometimes a long, drawn-out series of referrals was required before I could reach the desired interviewee with the appropriate bona fides in hand. But most interviewees were more easily approached. The large number of senior citizens' clubs in the neighborhood helped immensely. The president of the club or, most often, the priest or spiritual advisor of a church-affiliated group, introduced me to the members. I then delivered a brief talk and collected names and telephone numbers. Whenever possible, the interviews were held in the subjects' home. Some took place in rectories and convents (very good; the setting legitimized the interview), others in meeting halls (too casual), and some even during bingo games (terrible; the game was more important than the interview). A few interviewees who were not seen in their homes objected to my cassette recorder, and I was forced to take notes.

The information I sought was always about the person's attitudes or actual activities and behavior. The feeling of Poles toward Lithuanians was an attitude hard to quantify but easy to remember. No one recalled exactly how much soap they used for the laundry, but the steps involved came back easily, memory the product of repeated action. At no point did I make a significant effort to obtain numbers—dates, amounts, population, statistics of any sort—from the interviews. Documentary evidence was used for this information

Initials have been used for the interviewees' last names to protect their privacy, except for persons who have been public figures. For ease of reference, I have separated the list of interviewees into categories—community organizers, clergy and religious, and members of national groups. All the interviewees were born in the United States unless otherwise noted. Church membership is given when known; *attended* means the interviewee attended a church or school as a youngster.

Community Organizers

Helen D.: Irish-Polish. Born and raised in Back of the Yards. Married an Italian. Employed by Back of the Yards Neighborhood Council.

Thomas Gaudette: Irish-French Canadian. Associate of Saul Alinsky; helped found Northwest Community Organization.

Aaron Hurwitz: Jewish. Publisher of the *Town of Lake Journal*, renamed *Back of the Yards Journal*.

Helen Meegan: Irish. Wife of Joseph Meegan.

Joseph Meegan: Irish. Director, Davis Square Park. Founded Back of the Yards Neighborhood Council with Saul Alinsky, and served as executive secretary from 1939 to 1982, later as consultant.

Bertram M.: Jewish. Friend of Saul Alinsky. Former alderman in Hyde Park's Fifth Ward.

Clergy and Religious

Father Joseph Kelly: Irish. Former associate pastor of St. Rose of Lima. Early member of Back of the Yards Neighborhood Council.

Father Vito Mikolaitis: Lithuanian. Parents born in Lithuania. Father worked in stockyards. Attended Holy Cross Church and school, served as its pastor from 1971 to 1981.

Monsignor Edward Plawinski: Polish. Assistant pastor of St. John of God from 1940 to 1948. Founding member and first president of Back of the Yards Neighborhood Council from 1940 to 1945.

Sister Mary D.: Polish. Came to Guardian Angel Nursery and Home for Young Girls in 1933 for recuperation; remained to work there.

Sister Mary A.: Slovak. In first class at St. Michael parish. Classmate of Charles Florek, who became pastor of St. Michael Church.

Sister Mary M.: Slovak. Born and raised in St. Michael parish.

Sister Mary V.: Slovak. Born in Podvilik, Slovakia; came to United States at three. Attended St. Michael Church and school; took full vows at Benedictine Convent. Worked for Armour & Company as a girl.

Members of National Groups
Bohemians

William B.: Attended SS. Cyril and Methodius Church. Undertaker. Proprietor of family business in Back of the Yards, founded by his father in 1907.

Blanche G.: Member of Community Methodist Church. Served as Republican election judge. Worked for Armour & Company.

Phyllis H.: Married a Slovak. Father was foreman in stockyards. Attended church and school at SS. Cyril and Methodius. Head of cafeteria at church school.

Stephen S.: Attended SS. Cyril and Methodius Church and school. Member and former president, St. Michael's Senior Citizen Club. President and member of Back of the Yards Senior Citizens Club.

Germans

Teresa A.: Member of St. Augustine Senior Citizens Club.

Catherine B.: Member of St. Augustine Senior Citizens Club.

Henry B.: Member of St. Augustine Senior Citizens Club.

Irene C.: Member of St. Augustine Senior Citizens Club.

Colette D.: Member of St. Augustine Senior Citizens Club.

Louise D.: Married Henry D. (Irish). Member of St. Augustine Senior Citizens Club.

Teresa G.: Member of St. Augustine Senior Citizens Club.

Anne J.: German-French. Member of Back of the Yards Senior Citizens Club.

Arthur K.: Member of St. Martini Evangelical Lutheran Church.

Eleanor K.: Member of St. Martini Evangelical Lutheran Church.

Loretta K.: Member of St. Augustine Senior Citizens Club.

Walter K.: Married Marie K. (Irish). Real-estate and insurance agent in Back of the Yards.

Stephanie K.: Member of St. Augustine Senior Citizens Club.

Elsie L.: Member of Back of the Yards Senior Citizens Club.

Anna N.: Member of St. Augustine Senior Citizens Club.

Mary N.: Friend of Marie K. and Walter K.

Catherine P.: Member of St. Augustine Senior Citizens Club.

Cecelia P.: Member of St. Augustine Senior Citizens Club.

Elizabeth R.: Member of St. Augustine Senior Citizens Club.

Kitty S.: Attended St. Augustine. Member of Back of the Yards Senior Citizens Club.

Jewish

Leo M.: Polish. Co-owner of a department store in Back of the Yards.

Marvin P.: Member of Kesher Israel Synagogue on Marshfield Avenue between 47th and 48th streets. Attended Seward School and Lindbloom High School. Owner of hardware store in Back of the Yards.

Aaron S.: Member of Kesher Israel Synagogue. Attended Hamline School. Father owned dry-goods store.

Lithuanians

Angeline D.: Attended Holy Cross Church and school.

Ida K.: Born in Lithuania; came to Back of the Yards at nine. Aunt of Joan O. Attended Holy Cross Church and school.

Joan O.: Niece of Ida K. Attended Holy Cross Church and school, and Lindbloom High School.

Mexicans

Encarnacion Chico: Came to Back of the Yards in 1929. Founding member of Our Lady of Guadalupe Society and of Immaculate Heart of Mary Vicariate. Worked at Armour & Company, then at Swift & Company.

Richard P.: Member of Immaculate Heart of Mary Vicariate. Attended Hamline School.

Matthew Rodriguez: Mexican-Polish. Attended Sacred Heart school; was altar boy at Immaculate Heart of Mary Vicariate. Became Deputy Superintendent, Bureau of Technical Services, Chicago Police Department.

John Sanchez: Attended Seward School. Became Regional Programs Coordinator, Bureau of Mental Health, Department of Health, Chicago. Former president of the Back of the Yards Neighborhood Council.

Poles

Konstanty G.: Born in Dabrowa, Poland; came to the United States at seventeen. Member of Sacred Heart Church and St. Joseph Church. Member and former precinct captain of Fourteenth Ward Polish Democratic Club. Worked in stockyards.

Anne H.: Married Charles H. (Slovak). Attended Sacred Heart Church and school.

Anthony K.: Married Josephine K. Attended St. John of God Church and school. Worked at Swift & Company.

Josephine K.: Married Anthony K. Attended St. John of God Church and school.

Bruno K.: Father worked in stockyards and then bought a corner grocery. Dentist.

Lottie K.: Attended St. John of God Church and school. Worked as sausage linker at Libby, McNeil & Libby.

Raymond K.: Attended Tilden High School.

Anthony L.: Attended St. John of God Church and school; member of their Holy Name Society.

Genevieve N.: First married an Irish man, then a Slovak. Attended St. Joseph Church and school, and Hedges School. Worked at Libby, McNeil & Libby.

Evelyn Ostrowski: Married Ted Ostrowski. Father millwright for Wilson & Company. Attended Sacred Heart Church and school, St. Joseph High School, St. Xavier College, and Loyola University. Wrote Masters in Social Work thesis on the Back of the Yards Neighborhood Council. Served as election judge. Became the Council's first social worker.

Ted Ostrowski: Married Evelyn Ostrowski. Attended St. Joseph Church and school.

Ann P.: Attended Sacred Heart Church and school and served in many of their women's clubs.

Louis P.: Attended St. John of God Church and school. Member and president of St. Valentine Club #331, Polish Roman Catholic Union of America, that met there.

Ted P.: Father owned a corner grocery. Attended St. John of God Church and school. Worked in yards.

Joan S.: Member of Back of the Yards Senior Citizens Club. Worked in stockyards.

Reginald S.: Former organist, St. John of God. Attended founding meeting of Back of the Yards Neighborhood Council as a church delegate.

Wanda S.: Member of Back of the Yards Senior Citizens Club.

Anthony W.: Attended St. Joseph Church and school. Worked as a stationary engineer.

Stanley Z.: Born in Poland, came to the United States at age of one. Attended Sacred Heart Church.

Rusins

Joseph G.: Born in Ruthenia; came to the United States at two. Mother worked at Libby, McNeil & Libby. Attended St. Mary Byzantine Rite Church.

Catherine I.: Born in Ruthenia of peasant family; came to United States at sixteen. Member of St. Mary Byzantine Rite Church. Worked in pork trimming department of Armour & Company.

Ella V.: Member of St. Mary Byzantine Rite Church.

Slovaks

Elizabeth B.: Attended St. Michael Church.

John D.: Uncle of Frances W. Attended St. Michael Church. A founder of St. Michael's Young Mens Club.

Michael D.: Both parents members of sokol. Attended St. Michael Church and school, and Tilden High School. Member of St. Michael's Holy Name Society. Supreme physical director, Slovak Catholic Sokol.

George B.: Born in Slovakia, immigrated at eleven. Leading member and occasional president of Furdek Club. Officiated at many of the Catholic Slovak Days and served as president of one.

Charles H.: Husband of Anne H. (Pole). Attended St. Michael Church and school.

Paul J.: Attended St. Michael Church and school. Officer of St. Michael's Young Mens Club; member of choir and of St. Michael's Actor Guild. Barber.

Anna K.: Born in Slovakia. Wife of Joseph K. Attended St. Michael Church.

Joseph K.: Born in Slovakia. Husband of Anna K. Attended St. Michael Church.

Lillian K.: Attended St. Michael Church and school, and Hedges School.

Mary M.: Born in United States, but father brought family back to Slovakia when she was three. Returned to the United States at twelve. Attended St. Michael Church.

Sue N.: Attended St. Michael Church and school.

James T.: Attended St. Michael Church and school. Member of St. Michael's Young Mens Club. Attended founding meeting of Back of the Yards Neighborhood Council as his club's delegate. Worked at Armour & Company and in his father's tavern.

Joseph T.: Attended St. Michael Cnurch and school. Co-founder of Lemars Athletic Club.

Edward Tylka: Brother of Wendell Tylka and son of Wendell Tylka, founder of *Osadne Hlasy*.

Wendell Tylka: Brother of Edward Tylka and son of Wendell Tylka, founder of *Osadne Hlasy*.

Frances W.: Niece of John D. Attended St. Michael Church and school.

Mary Z.: Born in Slovakia. Husband was janitor of St. Michael Church. Attended St. Michael Church. Worked at Wilson & Company.

Miscellaneous Nationalities

Henry D.: Irish. Married Louise D. (German). Member of St. Augustine Senior Citizens Club.

Mary K.: Irish. Married Walter K. (German).

Edward L.: French. Attended St. Rose of Lima Church and school. Worked in stockyards and as dance teacher at the Trianon.

Stephanie M.: Ukranian. Father superintendent at small packing company. Member of Nativity of the Blessed Virgin Mary Church.

Mamie O.: Ukranian. Married a Russian. Member of Nativity of the Blessed Virgin Mary Church, later of St. Michael the Archangel Russian Orthodox Greek Catholic Church. Worked in yards.

Labor Organizers

Herbert March: Jewish. Organized the unemployed during the Depression. Former Director, District 1, (Chicago Region), Packinghouse Workers Organizing Committee (PWOC), and United Packinghouse Workers of America, CIO (UPWA). Advocated union support of Back of the Yards Neighborhood Council during its founding years.

Leslie Orear: Irish. Former Editor of *Packinghouse Worker*, official organ of the PWOC, and International Representative for the UPWA. Founder and president of Illinois Labor History Society.

Victoria Starr (also known as Stella Nowicki and Victoria Kramer): Croatian. Came to Back of the Yards in 1933. As union organizer, helped found Packingtown Youth Committee, predecessor to Back of the Yards Neighborhood Council. Worked in meat-packing plant.

Sigmund Wlodarczyk: Polish. Attended St. Joseph Church. Member of its Holy Name Society. Was organizer for PWOC and UPWA, secretary-treasurer of Armour Local #347, and served as liaison between Back of the Yards Neighborhood Council and the union. Worked at Armour & Company.

Politicians

John C.: Irish.

Tom D.: Irish. Attended Visitation parish. Fourteenth Ward precinct captain.

David Heffernan: Irish. Father was ward committeeman from old Thirtieth Ward (now Fourteenth). Neighbor of John McDermott, alderman and ward committeeman. Cook County deputy superintendent of schools and Chicago assistant superintendent of schools.

John H.: Polish. President of Fourteenth Ward Polish Democratic Club and precinct captain.

Thomas Kluczynski: Polish. Brother of John Kluczynski, founder of Fourteenth Ward Polish Democratic Club. Judge of Circuit Court of Cook County in the Criminal and Juvenile Departments and of the Appellate Supreme courts of Illinois.

Stanley K.: Polish. Attended St. Joseph Church and school; altar boy and member of its Holy Name Society. Precinct captain, member of the Fourteenth Ward Polish Democratic Club, and ward superintendent in charge of streets and sanitation.

Walter S. Kozubowski: Polish. Father worked for Armour & Company for 31 years and was a union organizer and member of Fourteenth Ward Polish Democratic Club. Precinct captain, president of Fourteenth Ward Polish Democratic Club, Illinois state representative, and Clerk of the City of Chicago.

Father John L.: Irish priest. Related to Fourteenth Ward political figure.

Edward M.: Polish. Attended St. John of God Church and school, and Tilden High School. Fourteenth Ward precinct captain.

Monsignor Ignatius M.: Irish priest. Related to Fourteenth Ward alderman.

Bruno N.: Polish. Attended St. John of God Church. Precinct captain.

Martha Palka: Polish. Married Joseph Palka. President of Women's Auxiliary, Fourteenth Ward Polish Democratic Club.

Others

Enid S.: Jewish. Married Leo S. Resident at University of Chicago Settlement House.

Leo S.: Jewish. Married Enid S. Resident at University of Chicago Settlement House; boys' director, program director, and assistant head resident. Executive director, Mayor's Commission on Youth Welfare.

Mary S.: Assistant principal, Fulton School.

Dr. Michael V.: Neighborhood doctor.

Notes

Introduction

1. Upton Sinclair, *The Autobiography of Upton Sinclair* (New York, 1962), p. 122; William Bloodworth, Jr., *Upton Sinclair* (Boston, 1977), p. 65; and Leon Harris, *Upton Sinclair: American Rebel* (New York, 1975), pp. 81–83.

2. Harris, *Upton Sinclair*, p. 67.

3. Bloodworth, *Upton Sinclair*, p. 67.

4. Sinclair, *Autobiography*, pp. 109, 112, 114; Harris, *Upton Sinclair*, pp. 70–71; and Bloodworth, *Upton Sinclair*, pp. 47–48.

5. Sinclair, *Autobiography*, pp. 109, 112, 114; and Harris, *Upton Sinclair*, pp. 70, 74.

6. Upton Sinclair, "What Life Means to Me," *Cosmopolitan*, October 1906, p. 594.

7. Sophonisba Breckenridge and Grace Abbott, "Housing Conditons in Chicago, Ill.: Back of the Yards," *American Journal of Sociology* 16 (January 1911): 433–48; Alice Miller, "Rents and Housing Conditions in the Stockyards District of Chicago" (Master's thesis, University of Chicago, 1932); Edith Abbott, *The Tenements of Chicago* (Chicago, 1936); and Clifford Shaw, *The Jack-Roller* (Chicago, 1930).

8. Robert Faris, *Chicago Sociology, 1920–1932* (San Francisco, 1967), p. 62.

9. Faris, *Chicago Sociology*, p. 59; and Robert Park and Ernest Burgess, *The City* (Chicago, 1967), pp. 77–79.

10. Park and Burgess, *City*, p. 24; and Harvey Zorbaugh, *The Gold Coast and the Slum* (Chicago, 1929), p. 251.

11. Ralph Turner, ed., *Robert E. Park on Social Control and Collective Behavior* (Chicago, 1967), p. 58; and Faris, *Chicago Sociology*, pp. 57–58.

12. Zorbaugh, *Gold Coast*, pp. 235–36, 182–84.

239

13. Barry Wellman and Barry Leighton, "Networks, Neighborhoods and Communities," *Urban Affairs Quarterly* 14 (March 1979): 368–72.

14. Charles Bowden and Lew Kreinberg, *Street Signs Chicago* (Chicago, 1981), pp. 12–13, 18, 32, 36, 40, 59, 75.

15. Wellman and Leighton, "Networks," p. 373–76.

16. E. P. Thompson, *The Making of the English Working Class* (New York, 1963), p. 11; and John Bodnar, Roger Simon, and Michael Weber, *Lives of Their Own* (Urbana, Ill., 1982), p. 3.

Some of the seminal works by American social historians that have influenced the author include: David Brody, *Steelworkers in America* (New York, 1960); Arthur Goren, *New York Jews and the Quest for Community* (New York, 1970); Victor Greene, *For God and Country* (Madison, 1975); Herbert Gutman, *Work, Culture and Society in Industrializing America* (New York, 1966); Oscar Handlin, *Boston's Immigrants* (Boston, 1941) and *The Uprooted* (New York, 1951); Marcus Hansen, *The Immigrant in American Society* (New York, 1940); Irving Howe, *World of Our Fathers* (New York, 1976); and Moses Rischin, *The Promised City* (New York, 1964).

17. George Hillery, "Definitions of Community: Areas of Agreement," *Rural Sociology* 20 (June 1955): 117–19; and Wellman and Leighton, "Networks," p. 365.

18. James Borchert, "Urban Neighborhood and Community: Informal Group Life," *Journal of Interdisciplinary History* 11 (Spring 1981): 620.

19. Bodnar, Simon, and Weber, *Lives of Their Own*, p. 3.

20. Department of Development and Planning, City of Chicago, *Historic City* (Chicago, 1976), p. 46.

21. U.S. Department of Commerce, Bureau of the Census. *Twelfth Census of the United States*, vol. 9, *Manufactures* iii (Washington, D.C., 1902), pp. 391–93, 407–10.

22. Ray Ginger, *Altgeld's America* (Chicago, 1958), pp. 8–9.

Chapter 1

1. Interviews with Stanley K. and Sister Mary D.

2. Benjamin Appel, *The People Talk* (New York, 1940), p. 169; Interviews with Ella V., Victoria Starr, Edward M., Dr. Michael V, Sue N., William B., Ann P., and Paul J.; and *Chicago Tribune*, 26 September 1954.

3. *Chicago Daily News*, 6 May 1922; Charles Bushnell "The Social Problem at the Chicago Stock Yards" (Ph.D. diss., University of Chicago, 1902), p. 30; St. Augustine, *Program and Chronological History* (Chicago, 1936), pp. 208, 221; *Back of the Yards Journal*, 21 November 1946; and Mary McDowell Papers, "From an Old Timer Back of the Yards," Chicago Historical Society, box 1, folder 3b, p. 1.

4. Louis Wirth and Margaret Furez, eds., *Local Community Fact Book, 1938* (Chicago, 1938), Community Area 61; Philip Hauser and Elizabeth Kitagawa, eds., *Local Community Fact Book for Chicago, 1950* (Chicago, 1953), p. 250; and *Town of Lake Journal*, 16 September 1937.

5. J. C. Kennedy et al., *Wages and Family Budgets in the Chicago Stock Yards District* (Chicago, 1914), p. 7; and Harper Leech and John Carroll, *Armour and His Times* (New York, 1938), p. 104.

6. Kennedy, *Wages and Family Budgets*, pp. 1–2; and *Chicago Daily News*, 20 December 1924.

7. Chicago Union Stockyards and Transit Company, *Chicago Union Stockyards* (Chicago, 1953), p. 16; and Janice Schaeffer, ed., "Back of the Yards," Report for the Medill School of Journalism, 1972, in personal files of Joseph Meegan.

8. Hauser and Kitagawa, *Fact Book, 1950*, p. 250; "Gustavus F. Swift Creates a Giant," press release, Swift & Company, 11 August 1980, p. 1; Mary McDowell Papers, "The Back of the Yards Area," box 1, folder 1, p. 1; Louise Wade, "Something More than Packers," *Chicago History* n.s. 2 (Fall–Winter 1973): 225–26; and City of Chicago, Commission on Historical and Cultural Landmarks, *Union Stock Yards Gate* (Chicago, 1967), pp. 2–4.

9. Edith Abbott and Sophonisba Breckenridge, "Women in Industry: The Chicago Stockyards," *Journal of Political Economy* 19 (October 1911): 633–34; Leech and Carroll, *Armour*, pp. 128–29; Robert Aduddell and Louis Cain, "Location and Collusion in the Meat Packing Industry," in Louis Cain and Paul Uselding, eds., *Business Enterprise and Economic Change* (Kent, Ohio, 1973), p. 95.

10. Abbott and Breckenridge, "Women in Industry," p. 634; and Leech and Carroll, *Armour*, p. 52.

11. Leech and Carroll, *Armour*, pp. 8–9; and Rudolf Clemen, *The American Livestock and Meat Industry* (New York, 1923), pp. 681–87.

12. Leech and Carroll, *Armour*, p. 47; and Floyd Bernard, "Study of Industrial Diseases of the Stockyards" (Master's thesis, University of Chicago, 1910), pp. 4–5.

13. Bernard, "Study of Industrial Diseases," p. 1; Albert Dilling and Langdon Pearse, *Report on Industrial Wastes from the Stockyards and Packingtown in Chicago* (Chicago, 1921), p. 52; Schaeffer, "Back of the Yards"; Theodore Purcell, *The Worker Speaks His Mind on Company and Union* (Cambridge; Mass., 1953), p. 20; and *Chicago Tribune*, 13 July 1959.

14. Back of the Yards Old Timers Club, *Back of the Yards, 1870 to 1890* (Chicago, 1938), pp. 5–6.

15. Reverend Msgr. Harry Koenig, *A History of the Parishes of the Archdiocese of Chicago* (Chicago, 1980); and Archdiocese of Chicago, *Diamond Jubilee* (Des Plaines, Ill., 1920), p. 487.

16. St. Augustine, *Program*, p. 19; Andrew Townsend, "The Germans of Chicago" (Ph.D. diss., University of Chicago, 1910), p. 11; Koenig, *History of Parishes of Chicago*, pp. 90–92; Archdiocese of Chicago, *Diamond Jubilee*, p. 473; St. Augustine, *Diamond Jubilee Book* (Chicago, 1954); St. Martini Evangelical Lutheran Church, *Diamond Jubilee* (Chicago, 1959), p. 14; and *Town of Lake Journal*, 14 September 1939.

17. Jacob Horak, "Assimilation of Czechs in Chicago" (Ph.D. diss., Uni-

versity of Chicago, 1920), p. 33; Archdiocese of Chicago, *Diamond Jubilee*, pp. 519–20; *Town of Lake Journal*, 12 October 1939; Koenig, *History of Parishes of Chicago*, pp. 219–20; SS. Cyril and Methodius, *Golden Jubilee of Very Reverend Thomas J. Bobal* (Chicago, 1940); Mary McDowell Papers, "The Foreign Born," p. 1, box 2, folder 12; and Community Methodist Church, *75th Anniversary* (Chicago, 1957), pp. 8–9.

18. Dominic Pacyga, "Back of the Yards," *Chicago History* 40 (24 June, 1981): 6; *Town of Lake Journal*, 14 September 1939; Hauser and Kitagawa, *Local Community Fact Book*, p. 250; Kennedy, *Wages and Family Budgets*, p. 5; Miller, "Rents and Housing Conditions," p. 19; and Breckenridge and Abbott, "Housing Conditions in Chicago," p. 465.

19. Koenig, *History of Parishes of Chicago*, pp. 515–19.

20. Ibid., pp. 496–98.

21. Ibid., pp. 870–72; and Sacred Heart, *Golden Jubilee* (Chicago, 1960), pp. 14–16.

22. Koenig, *History of Parishes of Chicago*, pp. 645–47, 363, 365; Mary Zahrobsky, "The Slovaks in Chicago" (Master's thesis, University of Chicago, 1924), pp. 34–37; Evangelical Lutheran Church of Dr. Martin Luther, "Brief History of the Founding" (Chicago, n.d.), p. 1; David Fainhauz, *Lithuanians in Multi-Ethnic Chicago* (Chicago, 1977), pp. 49–51; Holy Cross, *Golden Jubilee* (Chicago, 1954), pp. 101; 124, 137; Judith Krajewski, "Russian Americans," (1901), pp. 1, 5–6 (ms. provided by Father Cyril Lukashonek, St. Archangel Michael); St. Mary, *Golden Jubilee* (Chicago, 1955); "History of the Nativity of the Blessed Mary Parish in Chicago" (Chicago, n.d.), pp. 1–2; and University of Chicago Settlement House Papers, "Chronological List of Dates Important in the History of Back of the Yards," Chicago Historical Society, box 1, folder 1.

23. Interviews with Msgr. Edward Plawinski, Catherine I., and Mary M.

24. Interviews with Joseph G., Catherine I., Sister Mary V., and Anthony W.

25. Interviews with Joseph T., Joseph G., and William B.; and William Thomas and Florian Znaniecki, *The Polish Peasant in Europe and America* (Boston, 1918).

26. Ernest Burgess and Charles Newcomb, *Census Data of the City of Chicago, 1920* (Chicago, 1931), pp. 440–46, 448–52; U.S. Department of Commerce, Bureau of the Census, *Fourteenth Census of the United States*, vol. 9, *Manufactures* (Washington, D.C., 1923), p. 346; Juliuz Ozog, "A Study of Polish Home Ownership in Chicago" (Ph.D. diss., University of Chicago, 1942), p. 13; Miller, "Rents and Housing Conditions," p. 16; and Breckenridge and Abbott, "Housing Conditions," p. 440.

27. Burgess and Newcomb, *Census Data, 1920*, pp. 440–46, 448–52, 454–58; Miller, "Rents and Housing Conditions," p. 16; and Kennedy, *Wages and Family Budgets*, p. 5.

28. Miriam Rappe, "Mary McDowell," in Mary McDowell Papers, box 1, folder 1, p. 6; Fainhauz, *Lithuanians*, p. 97; and Shaw, *Jack-Roller*, p. 34.

29. Interviews with Anthony W., Genevieve N., Anthony K., Sister Mary D., Father Vito Mikolaitis, Ted P., and Joseph T.

30. Manuscript by Anthony W., describing local sounds, prepared for the author.

31. Breckenridge and Abbott, "Housing Conditions in Chicago," pp. 464–66; and Miller, "Rents and Housing Conditions," p. 12.

32. Dilling and Pearse, *Report on Industrial Wastes*, pp. 48–51, 213, 218; and Howard Wilson, *Mary McDowell, Neighbor* (Chicago, 1928), pp. 25, 157–58.

33. Schaeffer, "Back of the Yards"; Kenan Heise, *Is There Only One Chicago?* (Richmond, Va., 1973), p. 131; Gurney Breckenfeld, "Chicago: Back of the Yards," in Martin Millspaugh and Gurney Breckenfeld, eds., *The Human Side of Urban Renewal* (Baltimore, 1958), p. 205; Bernard, "Industrial Diseases," p. 10; A. M. Simons, *Packingtown* (Chicago, 1899), p. 10; and Interviews with Paul J., Anna K., Joseph G., Father Vito Mikolaitis, John D., Ella V., Joseph T., Charles H., Anthony W., Stanley K., Edward L., and Ted P.

34. Father Leo Kalmer, "Chronicle of St. Augustine Parish, 1879 to 1936," (Chicago, 1936), p. 39; Holy Cross, *Jubilee*, p. 152; Interviews with Arthur K., Eleanor K., and Bruno N.; and Chicago Transit Authority, *Historical Information, 1859–1965* (Chicago, 1966), p. 4.

35. *Back of the Yards Journal*, 18 February 1970; and Records of the Regular Democratic Organization of the Fourteenth Ward.

36. Interviews with Stanley K. and Joseph G.

37. Elizabeth Donnellan, "The Back of the Yards Neighborhood Council" (Master's in Social Work thesis, Loyola University, 1940), p. 51; and Interviews with Anne H., Genevieve N., Joseph G., Sue N., and Anthony W.

38. Arthur Todd, *The Chicago Recreation Survey, 1937* (Chicago, 1937), vol. 1, p. 235; Interviews with Anthony W., Sigmund Wlodarczyk, Richard P., Father Vito Mikolaitis, Enid S., John Sanchez, and Sister Mary D.; Donnellan, "Back of Yards Neighborhood Council," pp. 51–52; and Mary McDowell Papers, "Davis Square Field House," box 4, folder 20.

39. Louise Montgomery, *The American Girl in the Stockyards* (Chicago, 1913), p. 4.

40. Greene, *For God and Country*, pp. 14–17; Handlin, *Uprooted*, p. 19; Interview with Ted P.; and Joseph Wytrwal, *Behold! The Polish Americans* (Detroit, 1977), p. 4.

41. Greene, *For God and Country*, p. 53; and U.S. Senate, 64th Congress, 1st sess., Document 415, *Report of the Commission on Industrial Relations*, vol. 4 (Washington, D.C., 1916), p. 348.

42. Greene, *For God and Country*, p. 53; Dominic Pacyga, "Crisis and Community: The Back of the Yards, 1921," *Chicago History*, n.s., vol. 3, no. 6 (Fall 1977): 169–70; Edward Kantowicz, *Polish-American Politics in Chicago* (Chicago, 1975), p. 157; Burgess and Newcomb, *Census Data, 1920*, pp. 440–46, 448–52, 454–58; and Interview with James T.

43. Interviews with Anna K. and Ann P.

44. Interviews with Evelyn Ostrowski, Joseph K., Joseph G., Father Joseph Kelly, and James T.; and Zahrobsky, "Slovaks in Chicago," p. 39.

45. Breckenridge and Abbott, "Housing Conditions," pp. 441–43; Hauser and Kitagawa, *Local Community Fact Book*, p. 250; and Interview with Enid S.

46. Breckenridge and Abbott, "Housing Conditions," pp. 443–55, passim; Miller, "Rents and Housing Conditions," p. 28; and Thomas Philpott, *The Slum and the Ghetto* (New York, 1978), p. 343.

47. Interviews with Father Vito Mikolaitis, Charles H., Josephine K., Mary M., Msgr. Edward Plawinski, and Sue N.; Breckenridge and Abbott, "Housing Conditions," pp. 440, 457–59; Josephine Krisciunas, "Lithanians in Chicago" (Master's thesis, DePaul University, 1935), p. 15; Helen Zand, "Polish Family Folkways in the United States," *Polish-American Studies* 13 (July–December 1956): 78–79; John Modell and Tamara Hraven, "Urbanization and the Malleable Household," *Journal of Marriage and the Family* 35 (August 1973): 473–74, 477–78; and Carl Degler, *At Odds* (New York, 1980), pp. 393–94.

48. Interviews with Evelyn Ostrowski, Msgr. Edward Plawinski, Catherine B., Louis P., Stephen S., James T., John Sanchez, Encarnacion Chico, Ella V., Charles H., Angeline D., Genevieve N., Paul J., and Lillian K.; and Emily Balch, *Our Slavic Fellow Citizens* (New York, 1969), pp. 349–50.

49. Interviews with Phillis H., Ella V., Ann P., Charles H., Anthony W., and Stanley K.; Evelyn Zygmuntowicz, "Back of the Yards Neighborhood Council and Its Health and Welfare Services" (Master's in Social Work thesis, Loyola University, 1950, p. 15; Newcomb and Burgess, *Census Data, 1920*, pp. 440–46, 448–52, 454–58; and Carl Thompson, "Labor in the Packing Industry," *Journal of Political Economy* 15 (February 1907): 94–95.

50. Breckenridge and Abbott, "Housing Conditions," pp. 446–48; and Interviews with Stanley K. and Anthony W.

51. Howard Stein and Robert Hill, "Adaptive Modalities among Slavic-Americans: Some Issues in Cultural Continuity and Change," Paper presented at the Ninth Annual Conference on Social-Political History, State University of New York at Brockport, 1 October 1976, pp. 5–6.

52. Interviews with John D., Anthony W., Eleanor K., and Evelyn Ostrowski; Zygmuntowicz, "Back of the Yards Neighborhood Council," p. 15; Newcomb and Burgess, *Census Data, 1920*, pp. 440–46, 448–52, 454–58; and University of Chicago Settlement House Papers, "The Back of the Yards," box 1, folder 1, pp. 17, 39.

53. Interviews with Evelyn Ostrowski, Ted P., Father Joseph Kelly, Anthony W., Charles H., Anthony K., and Sue N.

54. Interviews with Ted P., Edward L., and Phyllis H.; and Kantowicz, *Polish-American Politics*, p. 23.

55. Interviews with Father Joseph Kelly, Charles H., Lillian K., Joseph T., Stanley K., Joseph G., Ella V., Stephen S., Bruno K., Ann P., Anthony W., Edward L., and Sister Mary D.

56. Interviews with Charles H. and Father Joseph Kelly; and Joseph Meegan, "The First 106 Days of Conservation in Back of the Yards" (1953), in Files of the Back of the Yards Neighborhood Council.

57. Bushnell, "Social Problem at Stock Yards," p. 61.

Chapter 2

1. Interviews with Anthony W., Sue N., Stanley K., Father Joseph Kelly, Angeline D., and Richard P.

2. Interviews with John Sanchez, Mary M., Sister Mary V., Genevieve N., and Paul J.

3. Bushnell, "Social Problem at Stock Yards," p. 38; Kalmer, "Chronicle of St. Augustine Parish," pp. 859–61; Zygmuntowicz, "Back of the Yards Neighborhood Council," p. 15; Fred Hoehler, Jr., "Community Action by the United Packinghouse Workers of America-CIO in the Back of the Yards Neighborhood of Chicago" (Master's thesis, University of Chicago, 1947), p. 11; and Interview with Joseph T.

4. Donnellan, "Back of the Yards Neighborhood Council," p. 52.

5. Johan Huizinga, *Homo Ludens* (London, 1949), pp. 1–27.

6. Interviews with Edward L., Richard P., Paul J., and Ted P.

7. Interviews with Anne H., Michael D., and Anthony W.

8. *Town of Lake Journal*, 14 September 1939; Kalmer, "Chronicle of St. Augustine Parish," p. 56; *Pfarbotte*, August–September 1934, p. 117., periodical in bound volumes in St. Augustine Church library, Chicago.

9. S. J. Kezys, *A Lithuanian Cemetery* (Chicago, 1976) pp. 212–14; Interviews with Angeline D., Joan O., and Ida K.

10. See Howe, *World of Our Fathers*, pp. 460–97, on the Yiddish theatre; Interviews with Anthony W., Stanley Z., and Konstanty G.; and *Town of Lake Journal*, 14 September 1939.

11. Interview with Ann P.

12. *Pfarbotte*, March 1940, p. 89, and February 1936, p. 57; Kalmer, "Chronicles of St. Augustine," p. 100; Program, *The Bells of Shannon*, provided by Edward LaPrise; *Town of Lake Journal*, 11 March 1937 and 18 February 1937; *Back of the Yards Journal*, 21 November 1939 and 14 December 1939; and Interviews with Father Vito Mikolaitis, Michael D., and Paul J.

13. U.S. Senate, 61st Congress, 2d sess., Document 633, *Reports of the Immigration Commission: Immigrants in Industries*, pt. 2, *Slaughtering and Meat Packing*, 1911, pp. 245–47.

14. Todd, *Chicago Recreation*, p. 230; Kalmer, "Chronicles of St. Augustine," pp. 883–94; *Town of Lake Journal*, 14 September 1939; Polish Day Association, *Poles in America* (Chicago, 1933), p. 215; Information provided by John Cichowski, librarian, Julius Slowacki Library; Julius

Slowacki Library, *Zloty Jubileusz* (Chicago, 1953, trans. Sister Mary Fulgenta), p. 1; and *Lietuva*, 23 August 1912, in the Chicago Foreign Language Press Survey, University of Chicago Library, Special Collections.

15. Interview with Stephen S.; Montgomery, *American Girl in the Stockyards*, pp. 5–6; and Timothy Smith, "Immigrant Social Aspirations and American Education, 1880–1939," *American Quarterly* 21 (Fall 1969): 523.

16. Interview with Msgr. Edward Plawinski; and Montgomery, *American Girl in Stockyards*, p. 7.

17. Interviews with Ann P., Paul J., Walter S. Kozubowski, Bruno K., and Genevieve N.

18. Interviews with Ann P., Paul J., Walter S. Kozubowski, Bruno K., and Genevieve N.

19. John Powers, *The Last Catholic in America* (New York, 1973), p. 11; Interviews with Anthony W., and Evelyn Ostrowski; Montgomery, *American Girl in the Stockyards*, pp. 5–6; and Interview with Msgr. Edward Plawinski.

20. Sacred Heart, *Golden Jubilee*, p. 35; and Interviews with Joseph T., and Phyllis H. According to Jay Dolan, the moral basis of education was also important to New York's Irish and German immigrants; see his *The Immigrant Church* (Baltimore, 1975), p. 101.

21. Holy Cross, *Golden Jubilee*, p. 114; Interview with Charles H.

22. Interviews with Ann P. and Msgr. Edward Plawinski.

23. Interviews with Catherine I. and Joseph G.

24. Sister Ellen Marie Kuznicki, "A Historical Perspective on the Polish-American Parochial School," *Polish-American Studies* 35 (Spring–Autumn 1978): 5; Interviews with Phyllis H. and Genevieve N.; Sister Mary Feliciana, *Fifty Years* (Chicago, 1960), pp. 2–3; Katherine Burton, *Lily and Sword and Crown* (Milwaukee, 1958), p. 93; Interviews with Edward L. and Evelyn Ostrowski; and James Sanders, *The Education of an Urban Minority* (New York, 1977), p. 48.

25. Interviews with James T., Sister Mary V., Frances W., Michael D., Louis P., and Catherine I.; Archdiocese of Chicago, *Diamond Jubilee*, p. 576.

26. Record Book of St. Joseph School, Fall 1913; and Interview with Sue N.

27. Interviews with Joseph T., Josephine K., Frances W., Father Vito Mikolaitis, Ted P., Angeline D., Anthony W., Stanley Z., and Charles H.

28. Interviews with Ted P. and Colette D.; Powers, *Last Catholic*, p. 19; and Interviews with Sue N. and Stanley K.

29. Archdiocese of Chicago, *Diamond Jubilee*, p. 573; Interviews with Father Vito Mikolaitis, James T., and Stephanie I.; and Anthony Kuzniewski, "Boot Straps and Book Learning," *Polish-American Studies* 32 (Autumn 1975). 6; and Holy Cross, *Golden Jubilee*, p. 114.

30. Sanders, *Education of Urban Minority*, p. 154; Fainhauz, *Lithuanians in Chicago* pp. 142–43; Kuznicki, "Historical Perspective," p. 9; and

Interviews with Ted Ostrowski, Sister Mary V., Evelyn Ostrowski, and Lillian K.

31. Interviews with Ted P., Anthony W., Sue N., Ann P., Phyllis H., Joseph T., Evelyn Ostrowski, Stanley K., Anthony K., Anne H., Joseph G., Stanley Z., and Anthony L.

32. *Pfarbotte*, September 1938, p. 281; and Interviews with Evelyn Ostrowski, Stanley K., Father Vito Mikolaitis, Anthony W., Raymond K., and Louis P.

33. Interviews with Lottie K., Father Vito Mikolaitis, Anne H., Lillian K., Anthony K., Anna K., Ted P., Richard P., Sigmund Wlodarczyk, James T., Anthony W., Joan O., Genevieve N., and Stanley K.

34. Interviews with Raymond K., Konstanty G., Louis P., Walter S. Kozubowski, and Lillian K.

35. Bushnell, "Social Problem in Stock Yards," p. 58; and Interviews with Mary S. and Genevieve N.

36. Interview with Mary S.

37. Montgomery, *American Girl in Stockyards*, pp. 12–13; and Helen Todd, "Why Children Work," *McClure's Magazine*, April 1913, p. 74.

38. Interviews with Walter S. Kozubowski, Charles H., Ted P., William B., and Joseph G.; Zygmuntowicz, "Back of Yards Neighborhood Council," p. 18; and Ernest Talbert, *Opportunities in School and Industry for Children of the Stockyards District* (Chicago, 1912), p. 22.

39. Talbert, *Opportunities in School and Industry*, pp. 23–24, 26, 31; Montgomery, *American Girl in Stockyards*, pp. 28–29, 31; John Commons, "Labor Conditions in Meat Packing and the Recent Strike," *Quarterly Journal of Economics* 19 (November 1904): 24–25; and Interview with Anne J.

40. Talbert, *Opportunities in School and Industry*, pp. 26, 29, 34; and Montgomery, *American Girl in Stockyards*, pp. 25–26, 37–39.

41. Interview with Msgr. Edward Plawinski; *Back of the Yards Journal*, 8 June 1944; Kalmer, "Chronicles of St. Augustine," pp. 499–501; St. Augustine, *Program and Chronological History*, pp. 125, 130; and Tilden High School, *Tekanhi*, June 1914, pp. 7–16, 22–28; The material on the history of schools is from listings of historical descriptions on file at the Central Reference Library, Board of Education, City of Chicago.

42. Tilden High School, *Tekhani*, June 1914, pp. 7, 39–46; Tilden High School, *Craftsman*, June 1920, pp. 71, 74–79; and Lindbloom High School, *Eagle*, June 1920, pp. 62–78.

43. *Town of Lake Journal*, 25 March 1937; Interviews with Charles H., Edward L., and Father Vito Mikolaitis.

44. Interviews with Joseph T., Frances W., Paul J., John Sanchez, Stanley K., Bruno N., John D., and Joseph G.

45. *Back of Yards Journal*, 21 November 1939.

46. Interviews with Charles H., Bruno N., and Anthony W.; and Joseph Hamzik, "The Schoenstadts Bring Nickelodeons to the Yards Area," *Back of the Yards Journal*, 8 July 1970, pp. 14, 17.

47. Interviews with Anthony W., Genevieve N., and Stanley K.

48. Interviews with Anthony W. and Stanley K.; Holy Cross File, *Sv. Kryziaus Parapijos, Piknikas*, 8 July 1923, Balzekas Museum, Chicago.

49. *Town of Lake Journal*, 2 February 1939.

50. Interview with Ted P.

51. *Town of Lake Journal*, 3 February 1938 and 26 October 1939; Interviews with Joseph G., Stephen S., Sister Mary V., Joseph T., Ted P., Anthony W., Stanley K., Edward L., Mamie O., Josephine K., Father Joseph Kelly, Anthony K., and Sigmund Wlodarczyk; and Nancy Banks, "The World's Most Beautiful Ballrooms," *Chicago History* 2, n.s., no. 4 (Fall–Winter 1973): 206–12.

52. Interviews with Stephen S., Father Joseph Kelly, Joseph T., Stanley K., Ted P., and Edward L.

53. Interviews with Joseph T. and Paul J.

54. Interviews with Lottie K., Michael D., Charles H., Joseph T., Anthony L., Sue N., Anthony W., Father Joseph Kelly, Ted P., Stanley K., Anne H., Frances W., and Josephine K.

55. Montgomery, *American Girl in Stockyards*, p. 59; and Interviews with Mamie O., Paul J., Stanley K., and Mary M.

56. Interviews with Evelyn Ostrowski, Lottie K., James T., Father Vito Mikolaitis, Mary M., and Ella V.

57. Interview with Mary Z.

58. Interviews with Genevieve N., Bruno N., Charles H., James T., Ann P., Mamie O., and Konstanty G.

59. *Pfarbotte*, May 1937, p. 155; and Interviews with Eleanor K., Arthur K., Joan O., John Sanchez, Richard P., Encarnacion Chico, Genevieve N., and Victoria Kramer.

60. Interviews with Anthony L., Ted P., Loretta K., Anna K., Elizabeth R., Catherine P., Cecilia P., Stephanie K., Mamie O., Edward L., Eleanor K., Arthur K., Sigmund Wlodarczyk, Joan O., Encarnacion Chico, Michael D., Joseph T., and Stanley K.

Chapter 3

1. *Pfarbotte*, November 1936, p. 301; Interviews with Ann P., Genevieve N., John Sanchez. Michael D., Anthony W., Mamie O., Father Joseph Kelly, Msgr. Edward Plawinski, and Anthony L.; and Wytrwal, *Behold! The Polish Americans*, pp. 294–95.

2. Interviews with Sue N., Edward L., Richard P., Sister Mary V., Ann P., Josephine K., Msgr. Edward Plawinski, Anthony W., Ted P., James T., Joseph G., Joseph T., and Genevieve N.; and Kennedy et al., *Wages and Family Budgets*, p. 75.

3. Interviews with Stanley K., Lottie K., Catherine I., Anthony W., Anthony L., Genevieve N., and Father Joseph Kelly; Ernest Poole, "A Mixing Bowl for Nations," *Everybody's Magazine*, October 1910, pp. 562–64; Helen Zand, "Polish American Weddings and Christenings," *Polish-*

American Studies 16 (January–June 1959): 25–27; Wytrwal, *Behold! The Polish Americans*, p. 296; and Interviews with Anthony W. and Catherine I.

4. Interviews with Stanley K., Anthony W., Sister Mary V., Anna K., Paul J., Ella V., Joseph G., Ida K., Angeline D., Stephanie M., Joseph T., Josephine K., Mary Z., Evelyn Ostrowski, and Phyllis H.

5. Kalmer, "Chronicle of St. Augustine Parish," p. 23; Interviews with Marie K. and Wanda S.; Leslie Tentler, *Wage-Earning Women* (New York, 1979), p. 178.

6. Interviews with Angeline D., Genevieve N., Angeline D., Evelyn Ostrowski, Mary M., and Catherine I.

7. Interviews with Joseph G., Genevieve N., Edward L., Ann P., Stanley K., Sue N., Loretta K., Anna K., Elizabeth R., Catherine P., Cecilia P., Stephanie K., Evelyn Ostrowski, Victoria Starr, Mamie O., Charles H., and Sigmund Wlodarczyk.

8. Interviews with Joseph T., Lottie K., Teresa A., Evelyn Ostrowski, Father Vito Mikolaitis, Frances W., Sue N., Anthony K., Joseph G., John Sanchez, Angeline D., and Ted P.

9. Interviews with Joseph T., Father Vito Mikolaitis, Evelyn Ostrowski, James T., Anthony L., Joseph G., Anne P., Genevieve N., and Ted P.

10. Father Vito Mikolaitis, Ted P., Angeline D., James T., Father Joseph Kelly, and Genevieve N.; and *Town of Lake Journal*, 28 January 1937.

11. Interview with Genevieve N.; and *Back of the Yards Journal*, 2 December 1939.

12. Interviews with Evelyn Ostrowski, Genevieve N., and Walter S. Kozubowski.

13. Simons, *Packingtown*, p. 9; Rappe, "Mary McDowell," p. 7; and Interviews with Sister Mary V., Sue N., Joan O., Sister Mary D., and John D.

14. Interviews with Helen D., Mary Z., Mary M., and Evelyn Ostrowski.

15. Interviews with Joseph G., Evelyn Ostrowski, Ann P., Anthony K., Mary M., Anthony W., Joseph T., Sue N., Genevieve N., Father Vito Mikolaitis, Stanley K., Lottie K., Anne H., Catherine I., Ella V., Josephine K., Charles H., and John Sanchez.

16. Interviews with Lottie K., Genevieve N., and Anne H.

17. Interviews with Evelyn Ostrowski, Sue N., Ella V., Anthony W., Genevieve N., Lillian K., Ann P., Mary M., and Phyllis H.

18. Interviews with Mary M., Lottie K., Genevieve N., Anna K., Anthony W., Mary Z., Sue N., Louise D., Catherine B., Ted P., and Evelyn Ostrowski.

19. Interviews with Anthony W., Sister Mary V., Stanley K., Josephine K., Ted P., Bruno K., Eleanor K., Arthur K.; and Dr. Michael V.

20. Interviews with Ted P., Father Vito Mikolaitis, Dr. Michael V., and Stanley K.
21. Interviews with Joseph T., Dr. Michael V., William B., Joseph G., Sue N., Father Vito Mikolaitis, Genevieve N., Paul J., and Sister Mary V.
22. Interviews with Sue N., Stanley K., Anthony W., Catherine I., Dr. Michael V., and Mary M.
23. Interviews with Joseph G., Ted P., Anne H., and Genevieve N.
24. Interviews with Anna K., Stanley K., Ted P., Michael D., Sue N., Anne H., Sister Mary V., James T., and Dr. Michael V.
25. Interviews with Stanley K., Anthony W., and Genevieve N.; and Zand, "Polish Family Folkways," p. 77.
26. Interviews with Anne J., Ella V., Josephine K., Lillian K., and Stephen S.; Stein and Hill, "Adaptive Modalities among Slavic-Americans," p. 6; and Degler, At Odds, p. 136.
27. Interviews with Loretta K., Anna K., Elizabeth R., Catherine P., Cecelia P., Stephanie K., Martha Palka, Eleanor K., Anthony L., Dr. Michael V., Lillian K., John Sanchez, Lottie K., Angeline D., Sue N., Frances W., and John D.; Zand, "Polish Family Folkways," p. 88; Louis Magierski, "Polish-American Activities in Chicago, 1919–1939" (Master's thesis, University of Illinois at Urbana, 1946), p. 21; and Degler, At Odds, p. 136.
28. Interview with Mary Z.
29. Interviews with Phyllis H., Wanda S., Louis D., Genevieve N., Ella V., Sue N., and Marie K.
30. Interviews with Anthony W., Lottie K., Paul J., Stephanie M., Frances W., and Ella V.
31. Interviews with Anthony W. and Joseph T.; and Mary McDowell Papers, "Stores and Businesses: District 61," box 2, folder 8.
32. Interviews with Martha Palka, Bruno K., Father Vito Mikolaitis, Leo M., Paul J., Anne H., Louis P., John H., Sister Mary V., Charles H., Mary M., and Ted P.; Back of the Yards Journal, 8 April 1981; and Clyde and Sally Griffen, "Small Business and Occupational Mobility in Mid-Nineteenth Century Poughkeepsie," in Stuart Bruchey, ed., Small Business in American Life (New York, 1980), pp. 138–40.
33. Interviews with Bruno K., Joan S., Father Joseph Kelly, Ella V., Stanley K., and Mary Z.; Program for St. Rose's Dramatic Club production of The Bells of Shannon, 18 and 19 May 1924, courtesy of Edward LaPrise; and Interview with Leo M.
34. Interviews with Paul J., Stanley K., Catherine I., Anne H., Ted P. and Joseph T.
35. Interviews with Anne H., Eleanor K., Anthony W., Angeline D., Lottie K., Arthur K., Martha Palka, Joseph T., Father Vito Mikolaitis, John D., Stanley K., Joan S., and John Sanchez.
36. Interviews with Phyllis H., Father Vito Mikolaitis, Anne H., Joseph G., Ted P., Walter S. Kozubowski, Stanley K., Bruno K., Ann P., Sister Mary V., Frances W., Genevieve N., and Sue N.

37. Interviews with Ted P., Bruno K., Ella V., Evelyn Ostrowski, Lillian K., Phyllis H., and Martha Palka.

38. Interviews with Evelyn Ostrowski, Joseph G., Father Vito Mikolaitis, and Ella V.

39. Interviews with Ella V., Ann P., Paul J., and Phyllis H.

40. Interviews with Msgr. Edward Plawinski and Ella V.

41. *Back of the Yards Journal*, 8 April 1981; St. Martini Evangelical Lutheran Church, *20th Anniversary*, p. 27; Interviews with Frances W., Sue N., and Paul J.; St. Augustine, *Program and Chronological History*, pp. 265–67; and Holy Cross, *Golden Jubilee* (Chicago, 1954), pp. 128, 129.

42. Holy Cross, *Golden Jubilee*, p. 131; St. Augustine, *Diamond Jubilee* (Chicago, 1954); Sacred Heart, *Golden Jubilee*, pp. 54–55; and St. Augustine, *Program and Chronological History*, pp. 266–67.

43. Holy Cross, *Golden Jubilee*, p. 129; St. Martini Evangelical Lutheran Church, *20th Anniversary*, p. 29; Interviews with Genevieve N., Marie K., Josephine K., and Mary M.; and *Pfarbotte*, January 1936, p. 8.

44. Norman Hayner, "The Effect of Prohibition in Packingtown" (Master's thesis, University of Chicago, 1921), p. 7; and Zand, "Polish Family Folkways," p. 84.

45. James T. Farrell, *Father and Son* (New York, 1940), p. 31.

46. Interview with Walter S. Kozubowski; and Abbott and Breckenridge, "Women in Industry," p. 650.

47. Ann Banks, ed., *First Person America* (New York, 1980), p. 53; Abbott and Breckenridge, "Women in Industry," pp. 635–37, 638, 640–43, and 653; Clemen, *American Livestock and Meat Industry*, pp. 689–92; and Interviews with Lottie K. and Ted P.

48. Kennedy, *Wages and Family Budgets*, pp. 11–13, 19–21; Abbott and Breckenridge, "Women in Industry," pp. 646–49; Elizabeth Humphreys, "Working Women in Chicago Factories and Department Stores, 1870–1895" (Master's thesis, University of Chicago, 1943), p. 25; and Interview with Charles H.

49. Abbot and Breckenridge, "Women in Industry," pp. 639–40; Banks, *First Person America*, pp. 57, 58, 63, 65; Bernard, "Study of Industrial Diseases," p. 20; and Interviews with Lottie K., Genevieve N., Sigmund Wlodarczyk, Blanche G., and Victoria Starr.

50. Interviews with Lottie K., Victoria Starr, and Genevieve N.; and Stella Nowicki, "Back of the Yards," in Alice Lynd and Staughton Lynd, eds., *Rank and File* (Boston, 1973), p. 79. Stella Nowicki was one of several names used by Victoria Starr, a union organizer.

51. Harry Rosenberg, "The Packing Industry and the Stockyards," p. 2, in Mary McDowell Papers, box 3, folder 15; Mary McDowell, "Story of a Woman's Labor Union," *Commons* 7 (January 1903): 1–3; and Alice Henry, *The Trade Union Woman* (New York, 1915), pp. 53–58.

52. David Brody, *The Butcher Workmen* (Cambridge, Mass., 1964), pp. 41–42; Abbott and Breckenridge, "Women in Industry," pp. 650–51; *National Provisioner*, 28 May 1904; and Degler, *At Odds*, p. 399.

Chapter 4

1. Wilson, *Mary McDowell, Neighbor,* p. 96; and Interviews with Konstanty G. and James T.

2. Commons, "Labor Conditions in Meatpacking," pp. 4, 6–8; and Clemen, *American Livestock and Meat Industry,* pp. 686–87.

3. Commons, "Labor Conditions in Meatpacking," pp. 4, 6–8; Samuel Naylor, "History of Labor Organization in the Slaughtering and Meat Packing Industry" (Master's thesis, University of Illinois, Urbana, 1935), pp. 7–8; and Kennedy et al., *Wages and Family Budgets,* pp. 6–7.

4. Interviews with Joseph T., Joseph G., and Lottie K.

5. Kennedy, *Wages and Family Budgets* pp. 9–10; Bushnell, "Social Problem at Chicago Stock Yards, p. 95.

6. Kennedy, *Wages and Family Budget,* pp. 10–19; and Commons, "Labor Conditions in Meatpacking," pp. 10–15.

7. Interviews with Victoria Kramer, Sigmund Wlodarczyk, and Herbert March; Naylor, "History of Labor Organization," pp. 6, 122; Commons, "Labor Conditions in Meatpacking," pp. 10–15; Kennedy, *Wages and Family Budgets,* pp. 10–19; Bushnell, "Social Problem at Chicago Stock Yards," p. 95; and Montgomery, *American Girl in Stockyards,* p. 4.

8. Tillie Olsen, *Yonnondio* (New York, 1974), pp. 144–45; and Interviews with Sigmund Wlodarczyk, Anthony L., Victoria Starr, Stanley Z., Blanche G., and Evelyn Ostrowski.

9. Interviews with Sigmund Wlodarczyk, Anthony L., Lottie K., Ted P., and Joseph T.; Bushnell, "Social Problem at Chicago Stock Yards," pp. 74, 75; Clemen, *American Livestock and Meat Industry,* p. 692; Humphreys, "Working Women in Chicago Factories," p. 25; and Donnellan, "Back of the Yards Neighborhood Council," p. 14.

10. Interviews with Joseph T. and Ted P.; Arthur Carver, *Personnel and Labor Problems in the Packing Industry* (Chicago, 1928), p. 161; Bushnell, "Social Problem at Chicago Stock Yards," p. 77; Frank P. Walsh Papers, Scrapbook no. 67, undated article, New York Public Library.

11. Bernard, "Industrial Diseases of the Stockyards," pp. 11–16; and Interview with James T.

12. Interview with Joseph T.; Carver, *Personnel and Labor Problems,* p. 165; Montgomery, *American Girl in Stockyards,* p. 29; Talbert, *Opportunities in School and Industry for Children,* pp. 62–63; and *National Provisioner,* 26 August 1911, p. 34.

13. Kantowicz, *Polish-American Politics in Chicago,* pp. 28–29.

14. Brody, *Butcher Workmen,* pp. 49–53; Purcell, *Worker Speaks His Mind,* pp. 45–46; and Commons, "Labor Conditions in Meat Packing," p. 31.

15. Brody, *Butcher Workmen,* pp. 53–55; Naylor, "History of Labor Organization," pp. 53–55; and "The Community Interest in the Stockyards Strike," *Commons* 19 (September 1904), pp. 402–406.

16. Brody, *Butcher Workmen,* pp. 55–58; Naylor, "History of Labor Organization," pp. 55–60; "Community Interest," p. 11.

17. U.S. Department of Labor, "Labor Award in Packing House Industries," *Monthly Labor Review* 6 (May 1918): 116, 123; and Zygmuntowicz, "Back of the Yards Neighborhood Council," p. 12.

18. Pacyga, "Crisis and Community," pp. 167–73.

19. Ibid., pp. 173–76; and *Dziennik Chicagoski*, 8, 9, 10, and 31 December 1921, 9, 10, 12, 18, and 19 January 1922, in Chicago Foreign Language Press Survey, University of Chicago Library, Special Collections.

20. Interviews with Stanley K. and Genevieve N.

21. Interviews with James T. and John D.

22. Interviews with Ted P., Joan O., Arthur K., Anthony W., Father Joseph Kelly, John Sanchez, Father Vito Mikolaitis, Sigmund Wlodarczyk, Angeline D., Anthony K., Encarnacion Chico, and Sue N.; Mary McDowell Papers, *Foreign Language Press Information*, box 2, folder 8; and Holy Cross, *Golden Jubilee*, p. 133.

23. Mary McDowell Papers, *Foreign Language Press Information*, box 2, folder 8; and Wirth and Furez, *Local Community Fact Book, 1938*.

24. Eugene Obidinski, "The Polish American Press," *Polish-American Studies* 34 (Autumn 1977): 43–46; Interview with Genevieve N.; and Morris Janowitz, *The Community Press in an Urban Setting* (Chicago, 1952), p. 2.

25. Interview with Aaron Hurwitz.

26. Files of the Back of the Yards Neighborhood Council, "List of Organizations," 20 October 1939.

27. Sanders, *Education of an Urban Minority*, p. 177; Sacred Heart, *Golden Jubilee*, p. 57; *Pfarbotte*, January 1937, p. 13; St. Augustine, *Program and Chronological History*, p. 285; Interviews with Stephen S., Anthony L., and Stanley K.; *Back of the Yards Journal*, 24 June 1981; St. Augustine, *Diamond Jubilee;* and St. John of God Holy Name Society, Minutes, 24 January 1941.

28. Interview with Lillian K.

29. Horak, "Assimilation of Czechs in Chicago," p. 66.

30. Howe, *World of Our Fathers*, p. 184; Interviews with Msgr. Edward Plawinski, Louis P., Paul J., and Walter S. Kozubowski; and Zand, "Polish Institutional Folkways in the United States," *Polish-American Studies* 14 (January–June 1957): 32.

31. Bushnell, "Social Problem at Chicago Stock Yards," p. 69; Todd, *Chicago Recreation Survey, 1937*, vol. 4, *Recreation by Community Areas in Chicago, District 61.*

32. Kantowicz, *Polish-American Politics*, p. 30; Krisciunas, "Lithuanians in Chicago," p. 63; Interviews with Charles H. and James T.; and U.S. Senate, 61st Congress, 2nd sess., Document 338, *Reports of the Immigration Commission: Immigrants in Cities*, vol. 1, 1911, p. 308.

33. Interviews with James T., Lottie K., Father Joseph Kelly, and Sigmund Wlodarczyk.

34. Miller, "Rents and Housing Conditions," p. 10; Interviews with Ted P., John D., Father Joseph Kelly, and Sigmund Wlodarczyk; Van Gordon Sauter, "Chicago's Not a Cow Town Anymore," *Chicago Tribune Maga-*

zine, 5 December 1971; Breckenridge and Abbott, "Housing Conditions in Chicago," p. 464; and Hayner, "Effect of Prohibition in Packingtown," p. 13.

35. Bushnell, "Social Problem at Chicago Stock Yards," pp. 76–77; Van Gordon Sauter, "Twilight at the Stockyards," *Chicago*, Winter 1968, p. 101; Interview with Joseph Meegan; and Hayner, "Effect of Prohibition in Packingtown," p. 12.

36. "The Community Interest in the Stockyards Strike," p. 405; Donnellan, "Back of Yards Neighborhood Council," pp. 14–15; Hayner, "Effect of Prohibition in Packingtown," p. 13; Zygmuntowicz, "Back of the Yards Neighborhood Council," pp. 13–14; Interviews with Bruno N., Msgr. Edward Plawinski, Charles H., Lottie K., Sister Mary V., and Sigmund Wlodarczyk; and Thompson, "Labor in the Packing Industry," pp. 807–808.

37. Abbott, *Tenements of Chicago*, p. 138; Interviews with James T., Joseph T., Stanley K., Charles H., and Dr. Michael V.; Breckenridge and Abbott, "Housing Conditions in Chicago," p. 164; and Dolan, *Immigrant Church*, pp. 31–32.

38. Interviews with Evelyn Ostrowski, Joseph T., Msgr. Edward Plawinski, Stephen S., Sister Mary V., Stephanie M., Angeline D., Sue N., Loretta K., Anna K., Elizabeth R., Catherine P., Cecelia P., Stephanie K., Charles H., Joseph Meegan, Louis P., James T., Stanley K., Dr. Michael V., and Anthony L.

39. Interviews with Father Joseph Kelly, Stanley Z., James T., Raymond K., Charles H., Bruno N., John Sanchez, and Anthony W.; and Borchert, "Urban Neighborhood and Community," p. 619.

40. Interviews with Catherine I., Lottie K., James T., Father Joseph Kelly, Martha Palka, Ted P., and Paul J.

41. Perry Duis, *The Saloon* (Urbana, Ill., 1983), p. 111.

42. Interviews with Father Joseph Kelly and James T.

43. Interview with Stephen S.; Douglas Bukowski, "William Dever and Prohibition," *Chicago History*, n.s. 7 (Summer 1978): 111; Mary McDowell Papers, "Prohibition Survey of the Stockyards Community," 1926, pp. 14–15, box 2, folder 7; and Hayner "Effect of Prohibition," pp. 16, 19–20, 26.

44. Interviews with Joseph T., Stephen S., and Father Vito Mikolaitis; and Hayner, "Effect of Prohibition," pp. 16–77, passim.

45. Hayner, "Effect of Prohibition," pp. 20–76, passim; and Interviews with John D., Louis P., Edward L., Father Vito Mikolaitis, Evelyn Ostrowski, and Anthony L.

46. Interviews with Evelyn Ostrowski, Msgr. Edward Plawinski, Bruno N., Michael D., and William B.

47. Interviews with William B., Anthony W., Evelyn Ostrowski, Bruno K., Bruno N., Stephen S., and Encarnacion Chico.

48. Interviews with William B., Arthur K., Eleanor K., Stephanie M., Anthony L., Genevieve N., and Father Vito Mikolaitis.

49. Interviews with Arthur K., Eleanor K., Ann P., Ella V., Genevieve N., William B., Mary Z., and Joseph T.

50. Interviews with William B., Ella V., Father Vito Mikolaitis. Joan O., Ida K., John D., John Sanchez, Angeline D., Michael D., and Msgr. Edward Plawinski.

51. Interviews with Joseph T., Evelyn Ostrowski, and Sue N.

52. Interviews with William B. and Joseph T.

53. Interviews with William B., Joseph T., and Anthony W.

54. Funeral costs from the 1913 account book of B. Funeral Home.

55. *Back of the Yards Journal*, 30 December 1970; and Interviews with Anthony W., William B., Arthur K., Eleanor K., Ted P., James T., John D., Charles H., and Joseph T.

56. Interviews with Edward L. and William B.; Kezys, *Lithuanian Cemetery*, pp. 205–11; Townsend, "Germans of Chicago," p. 117; material provided by Resurrection Cemetery; and *Dziennik Chicagoski*, 21 May 1904, Chicago Foreign Language Press Survey.

Chapter 5

1. Oscar Handlin, "The Social System," in Lloyd Rodwin, ed., *The Future Metropolis* (New York, 1961), p. 19.

2. C. J. Calhoun, "Community: Toward a Variable Conceptualization for Comparative Research," *Social History* 5 (January 1980): 109.

3. Algirdas Budreckis, ed., *The Lithuanians in America, 1751–1975* (Dobbs Ferry, N.Y., 1976), pp. 93–94; Montgomery, *American Girl in Stockyards*, p. 24; Handlin, *Uprooted*, p. 71; Grace Abbott, "The Employment Agency and the Immigrant Worker," *American Journal of Sociology* 14 (November 1908): 293–94; and "Employment Bureaus," *Dziennik Zwiazkowy*, 23 August 1910, and "Gullible Lithuanians," *Lieutuva*, 11 June 1915, both in Chicago Foreign Language Press Survey.

4. Will Herberg, *Protestant, Catholic, Jew* (Garden City, N.Y., 1955), pp. 11–12; Charles Shanabruch, *Chicago's Catholics* (Notre Dame, 1981), p. 47; Wytrwal, *Behold! The Polish Americans*, p. 98; and Interviews with Sister Mary M. and Sister Mary A.

5. Helen Lopata, "The Polish American Family," in Charles Mindel and Robert Habenstein, eds., *Ethnic Families in America* (New York, 1976), pp. 21–22.

6. Ozog, "A Study of Polish Home Ownership," p. 43; and Interview with Stanley K.

7. Balch, *Our Slavic Fellow Citizens*, p. 34.

8. Fabian Kemesis, "Cooperation among the Lithuanians in the United States of America" (Ph.D. diss., Catholic University of America, 1924), p. 43.

9. Hayner, "Effect of Prohibition," p. 7; and U.S. Senate, *Reports of the Immigration Commission: Immigrants in Cities*, vol. 1, pp. 332–33.

10. Elizabeth Bott, *Family and Social Structure* (London, 1957), p. 4; and Calhoun, "Community," p. 120.

11. Wellman and Leighton, "Neighborhoods, Networks, and Commu-

nities," p. 382; and Borchert, "Urban Neighborhood and Community," p. 622.

12. Interview with Walter S. Kozubowski, Raymond K., Bruno K., Stanley K., and Joseph G.

13. Interview with Mary Z.

14. Interviews with Walter S. Kozubowski, Raymond K., and Bruno K.

15. Interviews with Lillian K. and Kitty S.

16. Interview with Raymond K.

17. Interviews with Walter S. Kozubowski, William B., and Msgr. Edward Plawinski.

18. Interview with Evelyn Ostrowski, Joseph T., and Walter S. Kozubowski; *Chicago Sun*, 12 June 1945; Saul Alinsky, "A Departure in Community Organization," *Proceedings of the National Conference of Juvenile Agencies 36* (January 1940): 40; Dolan, *Immigrant Church*, p. 4; Marvin Schaefer, "The Catholic Church in Chicago: Its Growth and Administration" (Ph.D. diss., University of Chicago, 1929), p. 29; and Reverend Joseph Swastek, "The Contribution of the Catholic Church in Poland to the Catholic Church in the U.S.A.," *Polish-American Studies* 21 (June–July 1967): 22.

19. Reverend M. J. Madaj, "The Polish Immigrant and the Catholic Church in America," *Polish-American Studies* 6 (January–June 1949), 3–4; Holy Cross, *Golden Jubilee*, pp. 101–102; Zahrobsky, "Slovaks in Chicago," p. 39; Koenig, *History of the Parishes of Chicago*, p. 645; *Lietuva*, 7 March 1902, in Chicago Foreign Language Press Survey; Sacred Heart, *Golden Jubilee*, p. 14; Koenig, *History of Parishes in Chicago*, pp. 496, 870–72; St. John of God, *Golden Jubilee* (Chicago, 1957), p. 34; and Interview with Evelyn Ostrowski.

20. Interviews with Konstanty G., Louis P., John H., Walter S. Kozubowski, Msgr. Edward Plawinski, Bruno N., Mary M., Father Joseph Kelly, and Stanley K.

21. Interview with John H.

22. Koenig, *History of Parishes of Chicago*, p. 517; Greene, *For God and Country*, pp. 109–110; Joseph Parot, *Polish Catholics in Chicago, 1850–1920* (DeKalb, Ill., 1981), p. 119; *Dziennik Chicagoski*, 26 August 1895, in Chicago Foreign Language Press Survey; Interviews with Catherine I. and Joseph G.; and St. Mary, *75th Anniversary Book* (Chicago, 1978).

23. Interviews with Father Joseph Kelly, Anne H., Anthony L., Martha Palka, Msgr. Edward Plawinski, Mamie O., William B., Phyllis H., and Josephine K.

24. Interviews with Msgr. Edward Plawinski, Walter S. Kozubowski, Louis P., Stephen S., Anthony W., William B., and Leo M.; and Zahrobsky, "Slovaks in Chicago," p. 29.

25. Interviews with Anne J., James T., and Paul J.; and Greene, *For God and Country*, pp. 24–26.

26. James Farrell, *A World I Never Made* (New York, 1936), pp. 148–49.

27. St. Joseph, *Sacredotal Golden Jubilee of the Right Reverend Stanislaus Cholewinski*, p. 2 (trans. Sister Mary Fulgenta); SS. Cyril and Methodius, *Golden Jubilee of Very Reverend Thomas J. Bobal*, p. 1; Holy Cross, *Golden Jubilee*, p. 115; and Interviews with Joseph G. and Father Joseph Kelly.

28. Interviews with Konstanty G., Phyllis H., Anne K., Genevieve N., Ann P., Father Vito Mikolaitis, Stephanie M., and Anthony L.

29. Interviews with Genevieve N., Anne H., Anthony W., Stanley K., Sigmund Wlodarczyk, William B., Evelyn Ostrowski, Msgr. Edward Plawinski, Paul J., Sister Mary V., Mary Z., Genevieve N., Anna K., James T., Lillian K., and Michael D.

30. Alma Herbst, *The Negro in the Slaughtering and Meat Packing Industry in Chicago* (Boston, 1932), pp. 10, 99; *National Provisioner*, 1 January 1921–2 January 1922; and Mary Pidgeon, *The Employment of Women in Slaughtering and Meat Packing*, U.S. Department of Labor, Women's Bureau, *Bulletin 88* (Washington, D.C., 1932), p. 11.

31. U.S. Senate, *Reports of the Immigration Commission*, pt. 2, *Slaughtering and Meat Packing*, p. 229; Herbst, *Negro in Slaughtering*, pp. 143–44; U.S. Senate, *Report of Commission on Industrial Relations*, vol. 4, 1916, pp. 3504–08, 3521, 3463–64, and *Chicago Herald*, 16 April 1915.

32. Robert Doherty, *Society and Power* (Amherst, Mass., 1977), pp. 40–45.

33. Interviews with Sister Mary M. and George G.; and Slovak Catholic Sokol, *Pamatnica, 1967*.

34. *Town of Lake Journal*, 4 April 1939; Slovak Catholic Sokol, *Pamatnica, 1967*; Files of the Back of the Yards Neighborhood Council, *Narod Polski*, n.d.; material supplied by Prospect Federal Savings and Loan; Interview with Joseph G; material supplied by Hemlock Federal Savings and Loan; and *Lieutuva*, 3 January 1913, in Chicago Foreign Language Press Survey.

35. Prospect Federal Savings and Loan, *Charter*, 6 February 1951, p. 2.

36. Robert Wiebe, *The Segmented Society* (New York, 1975), p. 35.

Chapter 6

1. Karl Deutsch, *Nationalism and Social Communication* (Cambridge, 1953), pp. 95–97; and Eric Wolf, "Cultural Dissonance in the Italian Alps," *Comparative Studies in Society and History* 5 (1962): 1–14.

2. Anthony Smith, *The Ethnic Revival* (Cambridge, Mass., 1981), pp. 13, 19–20.

3. Vytautas Beliajus, *Ona* (Denver, 1977), p. 95; Helen Lopata, "The Functions of Voluntary Associations in an Ethnic Community: 'Polonia'" (Ph.D. diss., University of Chicago, 1954), p. 58; Balch, *Our Slavic Fellow Citizens*, pp. 19, 109–11, 448–49; Kemesis, "Cooperation among Lithuanians," p. 119; and Daniel Tanzone, *Fraternalism and the Slovak Immigrant* (Cleveland, 1978), p. 1.

4. Holy Cross, *Golden Jubilee*, pp. 115–16; and "Aleksandras

Skripkus," in Simon Suziedelis and Antanas Kucas, eds., *Encyclopedia Lithuanica*, vol. 5 (Boston, 1976), p. 211.

5. *Osadne Hlasy*, 21 January 1938 and 4 September 1936; Hrusovsky Frantisek, *Slovenski Rehole v Amerika* (Cleveland, 1955), pp. 13–18, (trans. Sister Mary Methodia); Josef Barton, "The Eastern Europeans," in John Higham, ed., *Ethnic Leadership in America* (Baltimore, 1978), p. 164; and Interviews with Sister Mary M. and Sister Mary A.

6. Shanabruch, *Chicago's Catholics*, pp. 37–40, 79–80.

7. Wytrwal, *Behold! The Polish Americans*, pp. 174, 178–79, 185–86.

8. Ibid, pp. 97, 150–51, 177, 194; and Parot, *Polish Catholics in Chicago*, pp. 180–81.

9. Frances Hodur, *The Confessions of Faith and the Eleven Great Principles of the Polish National Catholic Church*, (Chicago, 1975), pp. 31–32, 37–38. A Lithuanian national church was founded in 1906; see James Hennesey, *American Catholics* (New York, 1981), p. 209.

10. Koenig, *History of Parishes of Chicago*, pp. 363–64; *Dziennik Chicagoski*, 14 November 1895, Chicago Foreign Language Press Survey; discussion with Father Martin Wachna, pastor, Holy Family Polish National Catholic Church; and Holy Family Polish National Catholic Church, *Fortieth Anniversary*.

11. Shanabruch, *Chicago's Catholics*, pp. 162–231; Parot, *Polish Catholics in Chicago*, pp. 189, 191; and Edward Kantowicz, *Corporation Sole* (Notre Dame, 1983), pp. 13, 231.

12. Kantowicz, *Corporation Sole*, pp. 36, 154–55; and Shanabruch, *Chicago's Catholics*, pp. 164–210, passim.

13. Kantowicz, *Corporation Sole*, pp. 154–55, 77.

14. Wytrwal, *Behold! The Polish Americans*, p. 561; Kantowicz, *Polish-American Politics*, p. 174; Kantowicz, *Corporation Sole*, pp. 78–79; Parot, *Polish Catholics in Chicago*, pp. 197–200; and Edward Kantowicz, "Polish Chicago," in Melvin Holli and Peter Jones, eds., *The Ethnic Frontier* (Grand Rapids, Mich., 1977), p. 203.

15. Dolan, *Immigrant Church*, pp. 5, 6, 23, 67, 70.

16. Deutsch, *Nationalism and Social Communication*, p. 170; James J. Zientak Post #419, American Legion, *50th Anniversary Dinner Dance*, 27 May 1978; and *Osadne Hlasy*, 18 December 1931, 4 April and 10 April 1931, 29 September 1938 (trans. Sister Mary Methodia).

17. Interviews with George G. and Sister Mary M.; Frantisek, *Slovenski Rehole*, pp. 13–18, (trans. Sister Mary Methodia); *Osadne Hlasy*, 23 April 1937, 16 October 1931 (trans. Sister Mary Methodia); and *Siedmy Katolica Slovenska Dna u. Chicagu. Pamantnica* (Chicago, 1937, trans. Father Armand Gress).

18. *The New World*, 24 August 1923; *Dziennik Chicagoski*, 12 May 1894, in Chicago Foreign Language Press Survey; Mary McDowell Papers, "Chronology of Events"; St. John of God, *Golden Jubilee;* and Mary McDowell Papers, "The Primary Election," box 3, folder 19.

19. Mary McDowell Papers, "The Star of Victory," box 2, folder 12.

20. *Desiateho Katolica Slovenski Dna. Pamatnica, 1940* (trans. Sister Mary Methodia); and Interviews with Michael D., George G., Sister Mary M., and Sister Mary A.

21. *Dziennik Zwiazkowy,* 27 May 1917; *Lietuva,* 29 March 1912 and 14 November 1913; Record Books of the Association of Lithuanian Doctors of America, 1937; *Dziennik Chicagoski,* 11 June 1896, *Denni Hlastel,* 25 May 1901, and *Dziennik Zjednoczenia,* 26 April 1928, all from Chicago Foreign Language Press Survey; and St. John of God, *Golden Jubilee,* p. 36.

22. Turner, ed., *Robert E. Park on Social Control,* pp. 194–208.

23. Interview with George G.

24. Interviews with George G., Sister Mary A., and Sister Mary M.; and Slovak Catholic Sokol, *Pamatnica, 1967.*

25. *Osadne Hlasy,* 23 April 1937, 4 April 1930, 10 April 1931, 29 September 1933, 18 December 1931, and 4 September 1934 (trans. Sister Mary Methodia); Interviews with Sister Mary M., Sister Mary A., and George G.; *Lietuva,* 3 January 1913, Chicago Foreign Language Press Survey; and *Pamatnica 20. Vyrocia, Osadne Hlasy, 1928–1948,* (trans. Sister Mary Methodia).

26. *Osadne Hlasy,* 3 January 1930 (trans. Robert Slayton); *Osadne Hlasy,* 9 December 1932, 24 July 1931, 14 September 1934 and 29 May 1931 (trans. Sister Mary Methodia); *Osadne Hlasy,* 27 June 1930, Chicago Foreign Language Press Survey; and Interviews with George G. and Sister Mary M.

27. Interviews with George G., Sister Mary M., and Sister Mary A.; material from the files of Tylka Brothers Press.

28. Deutsch, *Nationalism and Social Communication,* p. 120; Catholic Slovak Sokol, *Pamatnica; Osadne Hlasy,* 30 March 1934, 13 January 1933, 2 March 1934, 20 November 1933, and 4 April 1930 (trans. Sister Mary Methodia); and *Osadne Hlasy,* 9 February 1934 and 18 December 1931, in Chicago Foreign Language Press Survey.

29. Park and Burgess, *City,* pp. 81–85; Interviews with George G., Wendell Tylka, and Edward Tylka; *Osadne Hlasy,* 23 April 1937 (trans. Sister Mary Methodia); *Osadne Hlasy* 20 February 1931, in Chicago Foreign Language Press Survey; *Osadne Hlasy, Pamatnica 20;* Interviews with Wendell Tylka and Edward Tylka; and *Osadne Hlasy, Pamatnica 20.*

30. *Dziennik Chicagoski,* 6 January 1928 and *Lietuva,* 23 November 1918, in Chicago Foreign Language Press Survey; and Fainhauz, "Lithuanians in Chicago," pp. 158–60.

31. U.S. Senate, *Report of the Commission on Industrial Relations,* vol. 4, p. 3515; Zygmuntowicz, "Back of the Yards Neighborhood Council," p. 8; Leech and Carroll, *Armour and His Times,* p. 232; Mark Reisler, *By the Sweat of Their Brow* (Westport, Conn., 1976), p. 105; and Interview with Ted P.

32. Lopata, "Functions of Voluntary Associations," pp. 128–31, 421–23.

33. Wyrtrwal, *Behold! The Polish Americans,* p. 266; and *Chicago Chronicle,* 20 February 1905, in Chicago Foreign Language Press Survey.

34. Interviews with Ann P., Msgr. Edward Plawinski, Evelyn Ostrowski, Mamie O., Paul J., Stanley K., Theresa G., Sue N., and Genevieve N.

35. Interviews with Msgr. Edward Plawinski, Stephen S., Anthony W., Colette D., Edward L., and Ann P.

36. Interview with Evelyn Ostrowski.

37. Interviews with Sigmund Wlodarczyk, Evelyn Ostrowski, Msgr. Edward Plawinski, Stephen S., and Herbert March; and Breckenfeld, "Chicago: Back of the Yards," pp. 183–84.

38. Interview with Msgr. Edward Plawinski.

Chapter 7

1. *Town of Lake Journal*, 21 April 1938; Interviews with Mary Z., Evelyn Ostrowski, Arthur K., Eleanor K., Bruno N. Catherine B., Martha Palka, and Ted P.; and John Allswang, *A House for All Peoples* (Lexington, 1971), p. 107.

2. Jane Addams, "Why the Ward Boss Rules," *Outlook* 58 (April 1898): 879; and Edward Kantowicz, *Polish-American Politics in Chicago*, p. 86.

3. David Heffernan, "Great Men Are Not 'Beautiful People,'" unpublished ms., pp. 2–4.

4. Simons, *Packingtown*, pp. 18–19; Records of the Fourteenth Ward Regular Democratic Organization; Interviews with Anthony W. and Edward L.; and *Back of the Yards Journal*, 10 June 1970.

5. Interviews with Msgr. Ignatius M., John C., Father John L., Martha Palka, and David Heffernan; and Records of the Fourteenth Ward Regular Democratic Organization.

6. Interview with Father John L. and John C.

7. Interviews with Martha Palka, Evelyn Ostrowski, John C., Msgr. Ignatius M., and Father John L.

8. Interviews with John C., Father John L., and David Heffernan.

9. Interviews with David Heffernan, John C., Father John L., and Thomas Kluczynski.

10. Interviews with Msgr. Ignatius M. and David Heffernan.

11. Interviews with Msgr. Ignatius M., Father John L., Tom D., Edward M., Stanley K., Ted P., and David Heffernan.

12. Interviews with Stanley K., Bruno N., David Heffernan, and Ted P.

13. Interviews with Thomas Kluczynski, David Heffernan, Raymond K., Louis P., John H., Walter S. Kozubowski, Bruno N., and Stanley K.

14. Interview with Louis P.; and Peter Yessne, *Quotations from Mayor Daley* (New York, 1969), p. 59.

15. Addams, "Why the Ward Boss Rules," p. 880; Interviews with William B., Encarnacion Chico, and Msgr. Ignatius M.; and St. Augustine Council #1419, Knights of Columbus, *Golden Jubilee* (Chicago, 1959), p. 55.

16. *Town of Lake Journal*, 15 July 1937, 30 June 1938, and 27 May, 2 December, 24 June, and 21 October 1937; and *Back of the Yards Journal*, 22 August 1946 and 19 July 1945.

17. Interviews with Thomas Kluczynski and Msgr. Ignatius M.; *Chicago News*, 19 August 1965; and *Chicago City Manual*, 1912, p. 50.

18. Interviews with Msgr. Ignatius M. and David Heffernan.

19. Interviews with Msgr. Ignatius M., John C., Father John L., and Thomas Kluczynski.

20. Interviews with Tom D., Edward M., Stanley K., John H., Victoria Starr, Father Joseph Kelly, and Bruno N.; and *Town of Lake Journal*, 16 February 1939.

21. Interviews with Thomas Kluczynski, Edward M., and Tom D.; and Sonya Forthal, *Cogwheels of Democracy* (New York, 1946), pp. 33–42.

22. Interviews with Edward M., Tom D., Stanley K., and Martha Palka.

23. Interviews with Stanley K. and Edward M.

24. Interviews with Walter S. Kozubowski, Marie K., Edward M., Stanley K., and Evelyn Ostrowski; and Forthal, *Cogwheels of Democracy*, p. 80.

25. Interview with Edward M., Martha Palka, Msgr. Ignatius M., Edward M., and Bruno N.

26. Interviews with Edward M., Tom D., and Martha Palka.

27. Interview with James T.; John White, "Lithuanians and the Democratic Party" (Ph.D. diss., University of Chicago, 1953), pp. 56, 64; *Town of Lake Journal*, 23 March 1939; and *Osadne Hlasy*, 30 March 1940 (trans. Sister Mary Methodia).

28. Interview with William B.

29. White, "Lithuanians," p. 64; Interview with Thomas Kluczynski; and *Town of Lake Journal*, 22 December 1938, and 26 January and 2 March 1939.

30. Interviews with Ann P., David Heffernan, Martha Palka, and Evelyn Ostrowski.

31. Files of the Regular Polish Democratic Club of the Fourteenth Ward, Incorporation Papers (1928) and *Constitution and By-Laws* (rev. 1956), p. 1; Interviews with Stanley K., Thomas Kluczynski, Martha Palka, Edward M., and Tom D.; *Town of Lake Journal*, 7 April 1938; and Files of the Regular Polish Democratic Club of the Fourteenth Ward. Women's Auxiliary, Minutes, 19 December 1954.

32. Interviews with Walter S. Kozubowski, Thomas Kluczynski, Bruno N., Stanley K., and Konstanty G.; Women's Auxiliary of the Regular Polish Democratic Club of the Fourteenth Ward, Minutes, 9 May 1941 and 5 December 1932; Regular Polish Democratic Club, Minutes, 15 November 1941, 2 April 1943, 14 February 1941, 12 September 1941, 26 January 1940, 11 November and 23 September 1938, 24 January 1947, and 8 May 1943; Regular Polish Democratic Club, Executive Committee, Minutes, 7 February and 7 March 1941; Arthur Thurner, "Polish Americans in Chicago Politics, 1890–1930," *Polish-American Studies* 28 (Spring 1971): 27.

33. Mary McDowell Papers, "Polish Democratic Club," box 3, folder 19.

34. Polish Democratic Club, Minutes, 23 September 1938, 8 December

1939; and Polish Democratic Club, Executive Committee, Minutes, 7 January 1943 and 9 April 1938.

35. Interviews with Walter S. Kozubowski and Martha Palka; Women's Auxiliary of Polish Democratic Club, Minutes, 18 March and 15 May 1935, 21 December 1936, 15 February 1937, 10 January 1938, 23 January 1933, 9 April, 23 May, 19 February, and 12 March 1934, 13 September 1943, 14 December 1942, and 15 October 1934.

36. Women's Auxiliary of Polish Democratic Club, Minutes, 18 December and 20 March 1933, 9 April 1934, 16 January 1933, 28 January 1932, 20 February and 8 March 1933, and 19 December 1932.

37. Ibid., 19 December 1932, 13 December 1940, 8 March and 20 March 1933, 28 December 1932.

38. Ibid., 9 April 1934, 16 March, 19 October and 30 March 1936, 14 March 1938, and 20 February 1933.

39. Interviews with Thomas Kluczynski, Martha Palka, Stanley K., and Msgr. Edward Plawinski; Back of the Yards Neighborhood Council, List of Organizations (1948), in the Files of the Back of the Yards Neighborhood Council; Polish Democratic Club, Minutes, 12 November 1943, 12 June 1940, 10 January 1941, 11 November 1938, 10 March 1941, 2 December 1938; Polish Democratic Club, Executive Committee, Minutes, 7 November 1941; Women's Auxiliary of Polish Democratic Club, Minutes, 9 January 1939, 12 December 1938; and Files of Polish Democratic Club, Letter from Father Louis Grudzinski to the Fourteenth Ward Polish Democratic Club (25 November 1941).

40. Interviews with Walter S. Kozubowski and Thomas Kluczynski; Polish Democratic Club, Minutes, 2 December and 14 October 1938, 10 April 1942, 11 October 1946, and 13 September 1940.

41. Polish Democratic Club, Constitution and By-Laws (rev. 1956), p. 3; Polish Democratic Club, Minutes, 10 February 1939, 9 February 1940; Polish Democratic Club, Executive Committee, Minutes, 19 May 1939; Files of Democratic Polish Club, Letter from James M. McDermott to Joseph Palka (8 August 1940), Letter from John J. Sullivan to Anthony Grabe (19 November 1948), Letter from James McDermott to the Polish Democratic Club (10 September 1948), and Resolution of the Polish Democratic Club Supporting Alderman James J. McDermott (12 December 1938); Interviews with Ted P., Stanley K., Tom D., and Walter S. Kozubowski; and Polish Democratic Club, Minutes, 9 January 1942.

42. *Chicago News*, 19 August 1965; Polish Democratic Club, Minutes, 13 February 1943; Interview with Martha Palka; and Polish Democratic Club, Minutes, 9 October 1942.

43. Interviews with John C., Tom D., and Thomas Kluczynski; and Polish Democratic Club, Minutes 11 December 1942.

44. Polish Democratic Club, Minutes, 8 January 1943.

45. Interviews with Martha Palka, John C., and Father John L.; and Citizens Association of Chicago, *Chicago Citizens Handbook for the Aldermanic Election* (Chicago, 1943), p. 11.

46. Interviews with Stanley K., Martha Palka, John C., and Father John L.; Citizens Association of Chicago, *Handbook*, p. 11; and Interviews with Bruno N., David Heffernan, Evelyn Ostrowski, Louis P., John H., Msgr. Ignatius M., Msgr. Edward Pawlinski, and Edward M.

47. Interviews with Martha Palka and Konstanty G.; and *Chicago Sun*, 24 February 1943.

48. Polish Democratic Club, Minutes, 5 March and 19 March 1943.

Chapter 8

1. Mary McDowell Papers, *The University of Chicago Settlement Handbook*, p. 1, box 1, folder 4.

2. Interviews with Leo S. and Ted P.; Mary McDowell Papers, *Handbook*, p. 1; and Rappe, "Mary McDowell," 1938, p. 1, in Mary McDowell Papers.

3. Todd, *Chicago Recreation Survey, 1937*, vol. 3, *Private Recreation*, p. 28; Interviews with Leo S., Enid S., Sister Mary V., Elsie L., Colette D., Theresa G., and Irene C.; Mary McDowell, "Story of a Women's Labor Union," pp. 1–3; U.S. Senate, *Report of the Commission on Industrial Relations*, vol. 4, 1916, p. 3461.

4. Interviews with Leo S., William B., Anne H., Angeline D., Ted P., Sister Mary V., and Anthony K.; William Blackburn, "Brief Report of the Origin, Program and Services of the University of Chicago Settlement House," 1928, p. 19, in Mary McDowell Papers, box 2, folder 7.

5. Interviews with John Sanchez, Joseph G., Bruno K., Sister Mary D., Stephanie M., Victoria Starr, Raymond K., John H., Stephen S., Konstanty G., and Walter S. Kozubowski.

6. Interviews with Leo S. and Enid S.

7. Mary McDowell, "Beginnings," 1918," p. 49, in Mary McDowell Papers, box 1, folder 3; Interviews with Father Joseph Kelly, Msgr. Edward Plawinski, Blanche G., and Leo S.; and Community Methodist Church, *75th Anniversary* (Chicago, 1957), p. 9.

8. Interviews with Leo S., Blanche G., and Msgr. Edward Plawinski; Community Methodist Church, *75th Anniversary*, p. 9; U.S. Senate, *Report on the Commission of Industrial Relations*, p. 3479; Allen Davis, *Spearheads for Reform* (New York, 1967), pp. 33–35; and Interview with Tom D.

9. Interview with Leo S.; Hayner, "Effect of Prohibition in Packingtown," pp. 31, 37.

10. Interview with Msgr. Edward Plawinski.

11. Sister Mary Ann Knawac, "Guardian Angel Day Care Center and Home for Girls," n.d., pp. 1–2; and Interviews with Msgr. Edward Plawinski, Ann P., Sister Mary D., Leo S., Bruno N., and Evelyn Ostrowski.

12. Interviews with Sister Mary D. and Msgr. Edward Plawinski; Magierski, "Polish-American Activities in Chicago," p. 34; Knawac, "Guardian Angel," p. 2; Interviews with Sister Mary D. and Msgr. Edward Plawinski;

Chicago Tribune, 6 April 1941; and *Back of the Yards Journal,* 22 August 1940.

13. Interviews with Msgr. Edward Plawinski and Sister Mary D.; Knawac, "Guardian Angel," p. 2; Leon Zglenicki, ed., *Poles of Chicago, 1837–1937* (Chicago, 1937), p. 116; Guardian Angel Day Care Center and Home for Girls, *Annual Service Reports.*

14. Interview with Leo S.

15. Interviews with Encarnacion Chico, John Sanchez, and Richard P.; Back of the Yards Old Timers Club, "Back of the Yards 1870 to 1890," p. 12; *Back of the Yards Journal,* 13 September 1945; Mary McDowell Papers, "Foreign Born," p. 2; Reisler, *By the Sweat of Their Brow,* pp. 14–17; and Paul Taylor, *Mexican Labor in the United States: Chicago and the Calumet Region* (Berkeley, 1932), pp. 48, 49.

16. Reisler, *By the Sweat of Their Brow,* p. 102–103; Interview with John Sanchez.

17. Anita Jones, "Conditions Surrounding Mexicans in Chicago" (Master's thesis, University of Chicago, 1923), pp. 39, 42; Elizabeth Hughes, *Living Conditions for Small-Wage Earners in Chicago* (Chicago, 1925), p. 56; and Louise Kerr, "The Chicano Experience in Chicago, 1920–1970" (Ph.D. diss., University of Illinois, Chicago Circle Campus, 1976), pp. 26, 28.

18. Miller, "Rents and Housing Conditions," pp. 21–23; Donnellan, "Back of the Yards Neighborhood Council," pp. 50–51; Abbott, *Tenements of Chicago,* pp. 136–37; Jones, "Conditions Surrounding Mexicans," pp. 43, 53; and Interview with Encarnacion Chico.

19. Interviews with Richard P., Encarnacion Chico, and Father Joseph Kelly; Jones, "Conditions Surrounding Mexicans," pp. 115, 118; M. R. Ibanez, "Report of the Mexican Work at the University of Chicago Settlement for the Years 1930–1931," pp. 2–3, in University of Chicago Settlement Papers, box 21, Chicago Historical Society; Kerr, "Chicano Experience," pp. 92–95; Interviews with John Sanchez, Matthew Rodriguez, and Encarnacion Chico; *Back of the Yards Journal,* 27 September 1945; material on use of pool halls by Mexicans from Father Joseph Peplansky, pastor, Immaculate Heart of Mary Vicariate; and Blackburn, "Brief Report on the University of Chicago Settlement House," p. 6.

20. Interview with John Sanchez; Kerr, "Chicano Experience," p. 37; and Interviews with Father Vito Mikolaitis and Richard P.

21. Interviews with Richard P., Genevieve N., Paul J., Marvin P., Encarnacion Chico, John Sanchez, and Father Vito Mikolaitis; Miller, "Rents and Housing Conditions," p. 22; Kerr, "Chicano Experience," p. 52; Mary McDowell Papers, "Foreign Born," p. 2; and Interview with Richard P.

22. Interview with Encarnacion Chico; Kerr, "Chicano Experience," pp. 28–29; and Interview with Martha Palka.

23. Interviews with John Sanchez and Richard P.; and Reisler, *By the Sweat of Their Brow,* pp. 110–11.

24. Interviews with Encarnacion Chico and Father Joseph Kelly; Im-

maculate Heart of Mary, *Souvenir and Dedication Program*, (Chicago, 1945); Interview with John Sanchez; *Back of the Yards Journal*, 28 November 1940; and *Catholic New World*, 14 March 1941.

25. *Back of the Yards Journal*, 28 November 1940; and *Catholic New World*, 14 March 1941.

26. Interview with Encarnacion Chico; and material provided by Immaculate Heart of Mary Vicariate.

27. Interviews with Matthew Rodriguez, John Sanchez, Richard P., and Encarnacion Chico; and *Back of the Yards Journal*, 18 September 1941.

28. Interview with Encarnacion Chico; and Koenig, *History of Parishes of Chicago*, pp. 444–46.

29. Reisler, *By the Sweat of Their Brow*, p. 108; Interview with John Sanchez; and Jones, "Conditions Surrounding Mexicans," pp. 115–17.

30. Interviews with Encarnacion Chico, John Sanchez, Msgr. Edward Plawinski, Raymond K., Leo S., Enid S., and Richard P.

31. Interviews with Encarnacion Chico, Richard P., John Sanchez, Leo S., and Matthew Rodriguez; and Kerr, "Chicano Experience," pp. 52–53, 84–86, 98, 103–14.

32. Interviews with John Sanchez, Matthew Rodriguez, and Leo S.

Chapter 9

1. U.S. Department of Commerce, Bureau of the Census, *Fifteenth Census of the United States, 1930: Unemployment* (Washington, D.C., 1931), vol. 1, pp. 294, 297–98, and vol. 2, pp. 126–27, 480–81, 645–46, 577–78; and Irving Bernstein, *The Lean Years* (Baltimore, 1960), pp. 255, 256.

2. Interview with Richard P.; Fainhauz, *Lithuanians in Chicago*, p. 120; Antanas Kucas, *Lithuanians in America*, trans. Joseph Boley (Boston, 1975), p. 95; and Interview with Msgr. Edward Plawinski.

3. Moody Investment Service, *Moody's Manual of Investments* (New York, 1934), pp. 557, 560; *Chicago Tribune*, 22 June 1932; and *Town of Lake Journal*, 29 August 1937, 10 February 1938, and 2 November 1939.

4. Interviews with Walter S. Kozubowski, Stanley K., Ted P., Konstanty G., Ann P., and Stanley Z.; and *Town of Lake Journal*, 20 July 1939.

5. Clorinne Brandenburg, "Chicago Relief and Services Statistics, 1928–1931" (Master's thesis, University of Chicago, 1932), p. 35; Zygmuntowicz, "Back of the Yards Neighborhood Council," p. 10; Interviews with Msgr. Edward Plawinski and Stanley Z.,; Sacred Heart, *Golden Jubilee*, p. 60; Koenig, *History of the Parishes of Chicago*, p. 95; Kantowicz, *Corporation Sole*, p. 206; and University of Chicago Settlement, *Statistical Report for Family Relief and Service*, Joint Emergency Relief Fund of Cook County, Inc., in Mary McDowell Papers, box 3, folder 18.

6. U.S. Department of Commerce, Bureau of the Census, *Sixteenth Census of the United States, 1940: Housing* (Washington, D.C., 1942), pp. 35, 307–14; *Town of Lake Journal*, 14 July 1938; and Interview with Mary M.

7. *Town of Lake Journal*, 22 January 1937.

8. *Town of Lake Journal*, 8 August 1939, 26 October 1939; and *Back of the Yards Journal*, 30 November 1939, 20 July 1944.

9. Interviews with Louis P., Mary Z., and Victoria Starr; and *Town of Lake Journal*, 5 October 1939.

10. U.S. Department of Commerce, *Sixteenth Census*, pp. 35, 307–14; and Interviews with Paul J. and Phyllis H.

11. *Town of Lake Journal*, 18 November 1939, 27 October 1938, 8 September and 2 August 1938; and Interview with Ted P.

12. John Bartlow Martin, "Certain Wise Men," *McCall's*, March 1949, p. 42; *Town of Lake Journal*, 19 August 1937; Helena Smith, "We Did It Ourselves," *Woman's Home Companion*, May 1946, p. 78; Edward Duff, "The Reluctant Hero," *Sign* 26 (February 1947): 8; and Interview with Joseph Meegan.

13. Personal files of Joseph Meegan, *Davis Square Park Christmas Program, 1937;* and Interview with Joseph Meegan.

14. *Town of Lake Journal*, 22 December 1937, 16 March 1938, 16 June 1938.

15. Betty Prevender, "Packinghouse Prophet," *Today*, April 1957, p. 4.

16. Interview with Aaron Hurwitz; *Town of Lake Journal*, 28 January 1937, 3 February 1937, 18 February 1937, 25 February 1937, 15 April 1937, 13 May 1937, 4 March 1937, 15 April 1937.

17. Barbara Newell, *Chicago and the Labor Movement* (Urbana, Ill., 1961), pp. 163–64; Interviews with Louis P., Walter S. Kozubowski, and Sigmund Wlodarczyk; and *Town of Lake Journal*, 13 May 1937.

18. Interviews with Victoria Starr and Herbert March; Stella Nowicki, "Back of the Yards," p. 87.

19. Interviews with Herbert March and Leslie Orear; United Packinghouse Worker of America Records, Wisconsin State Historical Society, Madison; Mary McDowell Settlement House Papers, Chicago Historical Society; *Town of Lake Journal*, 2 March 1939; Interviews with Msgr. Edward Plawinski, Sigmund Wlodarczyk, Victoria Starr, Herbert March, and Evelyn Ostrowski; and Roosevelt University Labor Oral History Project, Interview with Herbert March, pp. 69–71.

20. Michael Connolly, "An Historical Study of Change in Saul D. Alinsky's Community Organization Practice and Theory, 1939–1972" (Ph.D. diss., University of Minnesota, 1976), p. 20.

21. Material on Saul Alinsky, unless otherwise identified, was kindly provided by Sanford Horwitt, who is writing a biography of the organizer; Saul Alinsky, "My Contact with Problems of Personal and Social Organization," Paper written at University of Chicago, 1928, in Ernest Burgess Papers, University of Chicago Library, box 126, folder 10, pp. 3–5.

22. "Interview with Saul Alinsky," *Playboy*, March 1972; Connolly, *Historical Study of Change*, pp. 76–78; Walter Heitzman, "The Back of the Yards Neighborhood Council: A Study of the Community Organization Approach to Delinquency" (Master's thesis, University of Chicago, 1946), pp. 47–48; and Ernest Burgess, Joseph Lohman, and Clifford Shaw, "The Chi-

cago Area Project," in *Coping with Crime* [Proceedings of the National Probation Association] (New York, 1937), pp. 8–28.

23. Interviews with Thomas Gaudette and Herbert March; Saul Alinsky, *John L. Lewis* (New York, 1949), p. ix; and "Interview with Saul Alinsky," p. 70.

24. Interviews with Herbert March and Thomas Gaudette.

25. Connolly, "Historical Study of Changes," p. 34–35; Kathryn Close, "Back of the Yards," *Survey Graphic*, December 1940, p. 612; and Interviews with Thomas Gaudette, Victoria Starr, Joseph Meegan, and Helen Meegan.

26. Interviews with Joseph Meegan and Helen Meegan; and Harry Boyte, *The Backyard Revolution* (Philadelphia, 1980), p. 39.

27. Interview with Joseph Meegan.

28. Interviews with Joseph Meegan and Thomas Gaudette; and Hoehler, "Community Action by United Packinghouse Workers," p. 29.

29. Interviews with Herbert March, Joseph Meegan, Thomas Gaudette, Father Joseph Kelly, and Helen D.

30. Interviews with Joseph Meegan, Thomas Gaudette, and Aaron Hurwitz.

31. Interviews with Leslie Orear and Joseph Meegan.

32. Interviews with Joseph Meegan, Thomas Gaudette, and Sigmund Wlodarczyk.

33. Roger Treat, *Bishop Sheil and the CYO* (New York, 1951), pp. 22–29; Stephen Becker, *Marshall Field III* (New York, 1964), p. 353; Interviews with Herbert March and Sigmund Wlodarczyk; Roosevelt University Labor Oral History Project, Interview with Herbert March, p. 71; and Treat, *Bishop Sheil*, pp. 171–75.

34. Interviews with Sigmund Wlodarczyk and Joseph Meegan; *Town of Lake Journal*, 4 August 1938; and Kantowicz, *Corporation Sole*, p. 179.

35. Interviews with Evelyn Ostrowski, John H., Ted P., Thomas Gaudette, Reginald S., Msgr. Edward Plawinski, and Stanley K.

36. Interviews with Father Joseph Kelly, Father Vito Mikolaitis, and Msgr. Edward Plawinski; and Patrick Henry, "A Study of the Leadership of a 'People's Organization': The Back of the Yards Neighborhood Council" (Master's thesis, Loyola University, 1959), p. 17.

37. Interview with Joseph Meegan.

38. Files of the Back of the Yards Neighborhood Council, "The Back of the Yards Neighborhood Council"; *Town of Lake Journal*, 29 June 1939, 20 July 1939; and Interviews with James T. and Joseph Meegan.

39. Back of the Yards Neighborhood Council, "The Call to a Community Congress."

40. Interviews with James T. and Konstanty G.; Zygmuntowicz, "Back of the Yards Neighborhood Council," p. 29; and Becker, *Marshall Field III*, p. 357.

41. Interviews with Father Joseph Kelly and Leslie Orear; Treat, *Bishop Sheil*, pp. 167–69; Hoehler, "Community Action by the United

Packinghouse Workers," p. 44; *Chicago Times*, 16 July 1939; *Back of the Yards Journal*, 17 September 1969; Roosevelt University Labor Oral History Project, Interview with Herbert March, p. 82; Treat, *Bishop Sheil*, pp. 168–69; Kantowicz, *Corporation Sole*, p. 196; *Chicago Daily Record*, 18 July 1939, and Bishop Bernard Sheil Papers, Chicago Historical Society, box 1.

42. Interviews with Walter S. Kozubowski and Sigmund Wlodarczyk; *Town of Lake Journal*, 21 September 1938; *Chicago Times*, 16 July 1939; Interview with Herbert March; Appel, *People Talk*, p. 171; *Back of the Yards Journal*, 6 December 1945; Roosevelt University Labor Oral History Project, Interview with Herbert March, pp. 82–84; and *Chicago Herald*, 15 July 1939.

43. Interviews with Aaron Hurwitz, Herbert March, Sigmund Wlodarczyk, and Leslie Orear; Martin, "Certain Wise Men," p. 50; Files of the Back of the Yards Neighborhood Council, "Text of Invocation Delivered by the Most Reverend Bernard J. Sheil, D. D., U. G., Senior Auxiliary Bishop of Chicago and Founder of the C.Y.O. before the CIO Mass Meeting Held at the Coliseum on Sunday Night, 16 July 1939," p. 2; and *Chicago News*, 15 July 1939.

Chapter 10

1. Interviews with Msgr. Edward Plawinski, James T., Evelyn Ostrowski, and Helen D.

2. Interviews with Msgr. Edward Plawinski, Father Joseph Kelly, James T., Evelyn Ostrowski, and Sigmund Wlodarczyk.

3. Interviews with Father Joseph Kelly, Msgr. Edward Plawinski, Evelyn Ostrowski, Helen D., Sigmund Wlodarczyk, and James T.

4. Interviews with James T., Sigmund Wlodarczyk, Helen D., Father Joseph Kelly, and Msgr. Edward Plawinski.

5. *Town of Lake Journal*, 19 October 1939; Files of the Back of the Yards Neighborhood Council, "History of the Back of the Yards Neighborhood Council"; *Back of the Yards Journal*, 16 November 1939; and Interviews with Evelyn Ostrowski, Ella V., Joseph Meegan, Aaron Hurwitz, and Father Joseph Kelly.

6. Interviews with Aaron Hurwitz and Joseph Meegan.

7. Donnellan, "Back of the Yards Neighborhood Council," p. 93; Interviews with Herbert March and Sigmund Wlodarczyk; Hoehler, "Community Action by United Packinghouse Workers," p. 46; and *Back of the Yards Journal*, 22 February 1940.

8. Prevender, "Packinghouse Prophet," p. 4; Interviews with Msgr. Edward Plawinski, Aaron Hurwitz, and Reginald S.; Files of Back of Yards Neighborhood Council, List of Projects; and Martin, "Certain Wise Men," p. 50.

9. Interviews with Msgr. Edward Plawinski and Father Joseph Kelly; Files of Back of Yards Neighborhood Council, List of Projects; and Back of Yards Neighborhood Council, Minutes, 14 April 1943.

10. Interview with Herbert March; Close, "Back of the Yards," p. 612; Edward Skillin, Jr., "Back of the Stockyards" *Commonweal*, 29 November

1940, p. 145; *Back of the Yards Journal,* 5 June 1940; Interview with Sigmund Wlodarczyk; Edward Duff, "The Radicals and Their Reveille," *America,* 29 June 1946, p. 2 (reprint in Files of Back of Yards Neighborhood Council); United Packinghouse Workers of America Papers, Wisconsin State Historical Society, Madison, box 410, folders 11, 12.

11. Hoehler, "Community Action," p. 32; Skillin, "Back of Stockyards," p. 144; Duff, "Radicals," p. 4; Martin, "Certain Wise Men," p. 50; Donnellan, "Back of Yards Neighborhood Council," p. 106; Files of the Back of Yards Neighborhood Council, List of Projects.

12. Interviews with Msgr. Edward Plawinski and Joseph Meegan; Heitzman, "Back of the Yards Neighborhood Council," p. 50; *Back of the Yards Journal,* 30 November and 7 December 1939; and Smith, "We Did It Ourselves," p. 79.

13. *Town of Lake Journal,* 19 October 1939; *Chicago Tribune,* 9 June 1940; and Back of the Yards Neighborhood Council, "1941 Annual Report," p. 3.

14. Files of Back of Yards Neighborhood Council, List of Projects, "History of Back of Yards Neighborhood Council"; Back of Yards Neighborhood Council, "1941 Annual Report," pp. 1–4; *Chicago Tribune,* 25 January 1942; Duff, "Reluctant Hero," p. 8; and *Back of the Yards Journal,* 12 February and 5 March 1942.

15. Back of Yards Neighborhood Council, Minutes, 4 April 1943, p. 2, and 5 May 1943, p. 1; Files of Back of Yards Neighborhood Council, "History of the Back of Yards Neighborhood Council"; Herb Graffis, "Congressman Fathead Explains," *Chicago Times,* 18 April 1943; *Chicago Sun,* 3 May and 5 July 1943; and Herb Graffis, "Pressure Bloc Classics," *Chicago Times,* 12 May 1943.

16. Files of Back of Yards Neighborhood Council, Testimony before Senate Sub-Committee on Appropriations by Joseph Meegan, 26 June 1947; *Chicago Sun,* 5 July 1943; *Chicago Times,* 21 May 1943; and *Back of the Yards Journal,* 10 October 1946, 1 July 1981.

17. Back of Yards Neighborhood Council, Minutes, 6 October 1943; and *Back of the Yards Journal,* 26 October 1944.

18. Files of Back of Yards Neighborhood Council, "History of the Back of the Yards Neighborhood Council; and *Back of the Yards Journal,* 28 February 1946, 5 April 1945, 6 June 1946.

19. Donnellan, "Back of the Yards Neighborhood Council," pp. 94, 133; Close, "Back of the Yards," p. 615; Martin, "Certain Wise Men," p. 50; *Commonweal,* "Industrial Areas Foundation, Inc.," 20 August 1940, p. 379; *Chicago Daily News,* 16 February 1945; Heitzman, "Back of the Yards Neighborhood Council," p. 54; Back of the Yards Neighborhood Council, Minutes, 5 March 1945, 14 October 1948; Files of Back of Yards Neighborhood Council, "History of the Back of Yards Neighborhood Council," and June Blyth, "Back of the Yards Neighborhood Council," and June Blyth, "Back of the Yards Reverses Flight to Suburbia," *Commerce,* January 1956, p. 22.

20. *Back of the Yards Journal,* 4 December 1939; Back of Yards Neigh-

borhood Council, List of Projects and Minutes, 13 November 1947; and Breckenfeld, "Chicago: Back of the Yards," p. 187.

21. *Back of the Yards Journal*, 16 November, 21 November, and 30 November 1939; Back of Yards Neighborhood Council, "1941 Annual Report," p. 5; and Hoehler, "Community Action by Packinghouse Workers," p. 46.

22. *Back of the Yards Journal*, 5 July 1945, 11 July and 21 November 1946; Files of Back of Yards Neighborhood Council, List of Projects; Back of Yards Neighborhood Council, Minutes, December 1947, p. 3, and "1941 Annual Report," pp. 4–5; Files of Back of Yards Neighborhood Council, "History of Back of the Yards Neighborhood Council"; Back of Yards Neighborhood Council, "1941 Annual Report," p. 4–5; and Hoehler, "Community Action," p. 11.

23. Files of Back of Yards Neighborhood Council, List of Projects; *Back of Yards Journal*, 24 April 1945, 3 July 1946; Files of Back of Yards Neighborhood Council, "History of Back of Yards Neighborhood Council," and List of Projects; *Chicago Sun*, 20 May 1945; Zygmuntowicz, "Back of Yards Neighborhood Council," p. 57; and *Back of the Yards Journal*, 20 September and 10 May 1945.

24. *Back of the Yards Journal*, 28 February 1946; Files of Back of Yards Neighborhood Council, "History of the Back of the Yards Neighborhood Council" and "Report on Back of the Yards Community Council to the Community Fund" (1948), p. 1.

25. *Back of the Yards Journal*, 25 January 1945, 18 July 1946; Breckenfeld, "Chicago: Back of Yards," p. 188; and Back of Yards Neighborhood Council, Minutes, 14 October 1948.

26. *Back of the Yards Journal*, 28 March and 12 September 1940; *Chicago Tribune*, 15 September 1940; Back of Yards Neighborhood Council, "1941 Annual Report," p. 4; Breckenfeld, "Chicago: Back of the Yards," p. 195; *Back of the Yards Journal*, 28 July, 5 July, 12 July, and 19 July 1945, and 18 July 1946; Interview with Father Joseph Kelly; *Back of the Yards Journal*, 14 June, 21 June, 23 June, and 9 August 1945; and Interview with Evelyn Ostrowski.

27. *Back of the Yards Journal*, 6 January 1945; *Chicago Herald-American*, 3 January 1944; Back of Yards Neighborhood Council, Minutes, 5 January 1944, p. 1; *Back of the Yards Journal*, 6 January 1944; *Chicago Herald-American*, 3 January 1944; and *Chicago Sun*, 25 February 1944.

28. Interviews with Evelyn Ostrowski and Msgr. Edward Plawinski.

29. *Chicago Sun*, 19 January 1944; Interview with Joseph Meegan; *Back of the Yards Journal*, 2 March 1944; *Chicago Daily News*, 29 February, 25 February, 3 March, and 29 March 1944; and *Chicago Daily Times*, 25 February and 28 February 1944.

30. *Chicago Herald-American*, 3 January 1944; *Chicago Times*, 4 January 1944; *Chicago Sun*, 5 January 1944; *Back of the Yards Journal*, 6 January 1944; *Chicago Sun*, 7 January, 16 January, and 3 January 1944; and *Chicago Herald-Examiner*, 6 January 1944.

31. *Back of the Yards Journal*, 6 January and 20 January 1944; *Chicago Tribune*, 5 January and 8 January 1944; *Chicago Daily News*, 4 January 1944; *Chicago Sun*, 8 January 1944; and Back of Yards Neighborhood Council, Minutes, 19 January 1944, p. 1.

32. Back of Yards Neighborhood Council, Minutes, 19 January 1944, p. 1; *Chicago Sun*, 17 January 1944; *Chicago Daily News*, 17 January 1944; *Back of the Yards Journal*, 20 January 1944; *Chicago Tribune*, 24 February 1944; *Chicago Sun*, 15 February 1944; *Chicago Daily News*, 27 February and 24 February 1944; *Chicago Sun*, 23 February 1944; *Chicago Daily News*, 32 February 1944; *Chicago Herald-Examiner*, 23 February 1944; and *Back of the Yards Journal*, 16 March 1944.

33. *Back of the Yards Journal*, 9 March 1944; *Chicago Sun*, 6 March and 9 January 1944; *Chicago Daily Times*. 20 February and 25 February 1944; *Chicago Daily News*, 20 February, 1944; *Chicago Sun*, 26 February 1944; and Interview with Msgr. Edward Plawinski.

34. *Chicago Sun*, 10 March and 11 March 1944; *Back of the Yards Journal*, 16 March 1944; and *Chicago Tribune*, 10 March 1944.

35. *Chicago Sun*, 10 March, 11 March, and 12 March, 1944; *Chicago Daily News*, 10 March 1944; *Chicago Herald-American*. 11 March and 12 March 1944; *Back of the Yards Journal*, 16 March 1944; and Hoehler, "Community Action," p. 49.

36. Interview with Herbert March; Back of Yards Neighborhood Council, Minutes, 7 November and 5 December 1945, p. 1; *Back of the Yards Journal*, 15 November 1945, 3 January 1946; Back of Yards Neighborhood Council, Minutes, 5 December 1945, p. 1; Interviews with Evelyn Ostrowski, Leslie Orear, Msgr. Edward Plawinski, Herbert March, and Sigmund Wlodarczyk; and *Back of the Yards Journal*, 17 January 1946.

37. *Back of the Yards Journal*, 20 December 1944; 10 January, 17 January, and 24 January 1946; Back of Yards Neighborhood Council, Minutes, 6 February 1946; p. 1; *New York Times* article, n.d., in Files of Back of Yard Neighborhood Council; *Chicago Sun*, 25 November 1945 and 17 January 1946; Martin, "Certain Wise Men," p. 50; Interview with Herbert March; *Back of the Yards Journal*, 21 February 1946; Zygmuntowicz, "Back of Yards Neighborhood Council," p. 52; and Hoehler, "Community Action," pp. 49–51.

38. *Back of the Yards Journal*, 14 March 1946; Theodore Purcell, *Worker Speaks His Mind*, p. 60; and Files of Back of Yards Neighborhood Council, Letter from Stanley Piontek to Joseph Meegan (6 February 1946).

39. *Chicago Tribune*, 15 June 1948; *Chicago Herald-American*, 17 June 1948; and Interview with Evelyn Ostrowski.

Conclusion

1. William Gleason, "Beating Back Blight," p. 3, in Files of Back of Yards Neighborhood Council; Back of Yards Neighborhood Council, "The Future of the Back of the Yards," 1953, pp. 5–7, and "The Story of Why Rent Control Ended and What Can Be Done about It," both in Files of Back

of Yards Neighborhood Council; Meegan, "First 106 Days," p. 4; and Back
of Yards Neighborhood Council, "Annual Report, 1952," p. 12, in Files of
Back of Yards Neighborhood Council.

2. Back of the Yards Neighborhood Council, "Future," pp. 1–13;
Gleason, "Beating Back Blight," pp. 2–4, 5–6; National Association of Real
Estate Boards, *Blueprint for Community Conservation*, p. 27, in Files of
Back of Yard Neighborhood Council; Blyth, "Back of Yards Reverses
Flight," p. 25; Meegan, "First 106 Days," pp. 6–7; Breckenfeld, "Chicago:
Back of the Yards," p. 202; *Back of the Yards Journal*, 8 February 1961;
and Robert Bradner, "Urban Renewal, Rehabilitation," *Savings and Loan
News*, July 1962, p. 7.

3. Gleason, "Beating Back Blight," p. 7, 9; Back of Yards Neigh-
borhood Council, "Operation Destiny," pp. 7–8, 9–10, in Files of Back of
Yards Neighborhood Council; National Association of Real Estate Boards,
Blueprint, p. 28; Msgr. Thomas Meehan, "Conservation in Back of the
Yards," pp. 2, 9, in Files of Back of Yards Neighborhood Council; Back of
Yards Neighborhood Council, "Seventeenth Annual Report, 1956," pp. 11–
13, in Files of Back of Yards Neighborhood Council; Schaeffer, "Back of the
Yards"; *Chicago Daily News*, 21 June 1974; Blyth, "Back of Yards Re-
verses Flight," pp. 20–21, 24; Breckenfeld, "Chicago: Back of Yards," pp.
202, 204; Back of Yards Neighborhood Council, "Fifteenth Annual Report,
1954," in Files of Back of Yards Neighborhood Council; *Back of the Yards
Journal*, 20 May 1959, 19 April 1961; Back of Yards Neighborhood Council,
"Twentieth Annual Report, 1959," pp. 5–7, in Files of Back of Yards
Neighborhood Council; Meegan, "First 106 Days," p. 9; Meehan, "Conservation in Back of Yards," p. 2; *Back of the Yards Journal*, 1 April 1964; and
Back of Yards Neighborhood Council, "Future," p. 1.

4. Letter from Adlai Stevenson to Joseph Meegan (23 April 1951) and
Back of Yards Neighborhood Council, "Twelfth Annual Report, 1951," both
in Files of Back of Yards Neighborhood Council.

Index